The Nature and Limits of Human Understanding

The Nature and Limits of Human Understanding

The 2001 Gifford Lectures at the University of Glasgow

Edited by Anthony Sanford

Contributors:
Philip Johnson-Laird
George Lakoff
Michael Ruse
Lynne Rudder Baker
Brian Hebblethwaite

T&T CLARK
A Continuum imprint
LONDON • NEW YORK

T&T CLARK LTD
A Continuum imprint

The Tower Building
11 York Road
London SE1 7NX

370 Lexington Avenue
New York 10017–6503
USA

www.continuumbooks.com

First published 2003

ISBN 0–5670–8946–0 (hardback)
0–5670–8947–9 (paperback)

British Library Cataloguing-in-Publication Data
A catalogue record for this book is available from the British Library

Typeset by Fakenham Photosetting Limited, Fakenham, Norfolk
Printed and bound in Great Britain by Biddles Ltd, Guildford and Kings Lynn

Contents

Contributors

Lynne Rudder Baker, Professor of Philosophy and Graduate Program Director, University of Massachusetts at Amherst, is the author of 3 books: *Saving Belief: A Critique of Physicalism* (Princeton University Press, 1987), *Explaining Attitudes: A Practical Approach to the Mind* (Cambridge University Press, 1995), and *Persons and Bodies: A Constitution View* (Cambridge University Press, 2000). She has written dozens of articles in philosophy journals such as *Journal of Philosophy, Philosophical Review, Philosophical Studies, Noûs, Philosophy and Phenomenological Research, American Philosophical Quarterly, Faith and Philosophy, Philosophical Explorations, Philosophy of Science,* and others. In 2001, Anthonie Meijers edited a volume of critical essays on her work, *Explaining Beliefs: Lynne Rudder Baker and her Critics* (Stanford: CSLI Publications). Baker has presented papers all over the world. Her interests focus on metaphysics, philosophy of mind, action theory, and philosophical theology.

Brian Leslie Hebblethwaite is a Life Fellow of Queens' College, Cambridge. Before retirement he was Lecturer in the Philosophy of Religion in the Faculty of Divinity at Cambridge and Dean of Chapel at Queens' College. He is Editor for Ethics for the *Theologische Realenzyklopädie.* Hebblethwaite is the author of nine books, including *Evil, Suffering and Religion* (1976, revised edition 2000), *The Problems of Theology* (1980), *The Adequacy of Christian Ethics* (1981), *The Christian Hope* (1984), *The Incarnation* (1987), *The Ocean of Truth* (1988), *The Essence of Christianity* (1996) and *Ethics and Religion in a Pluralistic Age* (1997).

George Lakoff is Professor of Linguistics and a member of the Cognitive Science faculty at the University of California at Berkeley. He has taught at Harvard University and the University of Michigan, and been a fellow at the Center for Advanced Study in the Behavioral Sciences at Stanford. He has served as President of the International Cognitive Linguistics Association, on the Governing Board of the Cognitive Science Society, and is on the

Science Board of the Santa Fe Institute. His major books include *Metaphors We Live By* (with Mark Johnson, 1980), *Women, Fire, and Dangerous Things* (1987), *More than Cool Reason* (with Mark Turner, 1989), *Moral Politics* (1996), *Philosophy in the Flesh* (with Mark Johnson, 1999) and *Where Mathematics Comes From* (with Rafael Núñez, 2000). He is now at work with Jerome Feldman on a new book, *From Molecules to Metaphors: The Neural Theory of Language.* Throughout Lakoff's career, he has studied the nature of thought and how it is expressed in language. He has also been active in applying the knowledge gained from scientific enterprises to philosophy, literary studies, mathematics, politics and religion.

Phil Johnson-Laird was born in Yorkshire, England. He left school early and spent ten years in a variety of occupations, including autodidact, quantity surveyor (five boring years), selling newspapers (one interesting day), jazz musician (occasional gigs as a semi-pro), and music critic (on the BBC). As an alternative to military service, he worked as a porter in Guy's Hospital in London (following in Wittgenstein's footsteps). He married Maureen Sullivan in 1959, and they have two children. In 1961, Phil went to University College, London, to read psychology. He later gained his PhD under the supervision of Peter Wason; and in 1972 they published *The Psychology of Reasoning.* In 1971, he was a visiting member of the Institute of Advanced Study, Princeton, where he began a collaboration with George A. Miller that led to their book *Language and Perception* (1976). Subsequently, he held positions at the University of Sussex and at the Medical Research Council's Applied Psychology Unit in Cambridge, where he was also a Fellow of Darwin College. Ruth Byrne and he collaborated on a study of reasoning, which they described in their book, *Deduction* (1991). He returned to Princeton in 1989 to join the psychology faculty at the University. He has published over 200 papers and ten books, including *Mental Models* (1983), *The Computer and The Mind* (1988), and *Human and Machine Thinking* (1993).

Michael Ruse is Lucyle T. Werkmeister Professor of Philosophy at Florida State University. He has written many books on Darwinian themes, including *The Darwinian Revolution: Science Red in Tooth and Claw* (University of Chicago Press, 1979); *Monad to Man: The Concept of Progress in Evolutionary Biology* (Harvard University Press,

1996); and *Can a Darwinian be a Christian? The Relationship between Science and Religion* (Cambridge University Press, 2001). He is a Fellow of the Royal Society of Canada, and of the American Association for the Advancement of Science. Michael Ruse's deeply committed Quaker headmaster is revolving in his grave at the thought that Ruse gave some of the Gifford Lectures.

Tony Sanford is a Professor of Psychology at the University of Glasgow. Since the late 1970s he has been carrying out research into how human beings understand language, using techniques of experimental psychology. Amongst his books are *Understanding Written Language* (with S. C. Garrod, Wiley, 1981) and *Communicating Quantities* (with L. M. Moxey, Erlbaum, 1993). In 1983 he delivered a short series of Gifford Lectures on The Cognitive Psychology of Understanding, published as *The Mind of Man* (Harvester Press, 1987), and has been interested in the nature of understanding in general ever since. Amongst his present research interests is the issue of how partial knowledge is reconciled with individuals believing that they are inherently consistent.

Preface

This collection of Gifford Lectures in Natural Theology was presented during the summer of 2001, at the time of the 550th anniversary of the founding of the University of Glasgow. The Gifford Lectures, founded through the bequest of Adam Gifford, 1820–70, Lord of Session, are an important part of the University calendar. For more than 100 years, they have provided a forum for presenting to both academics and the public important ideas about the nature of the universe. Because natural theology is not based on revelation, it easily leads towards matters of science, logic and philosophical reasoning. Many eminent scientists have given Gifford Lectures at the Scottish universities, including the physicist Eddington (1928), the physiologist Sherrington (1940), as well as eminent theologians, such as Karl Barth (1937–8) and Gabriel Marcel (1949–50). The series embodied in this volume is multidisciplinary, covering contributions from cognitive science, biology, philosophy and psychology

Although the norm for Gifford Lectures is to have a single lecturer present a series, in the present case, the decision was taken to invite five lecturers to present two lectures each, and to stimulate audience participation by having a round-table discussion halfway through the series. In this volume we present each lecture as a chapter, grouping the pairs of lectures as separate Parts.

The topic is The Nature and Limits of Human Understanding. How we understand, and how our understanding is limited, is a multifaceted and very important problem. Are there any generalizations that can be made about the way we normally understand things? Are there any limits *in principle* on what we can understand? Humans differ in intellectual and intuitive capacities: are there things in principle that one person could understand and another simply could not? Can we conceive of what it means for another person or another species to be able to understand less than we do ourselves? How can we characterize understanding so that we might be able to characterize alien intelligence in general, and could this include other cultures, other times in history, beings from other worlds, if there are any, and understanding in advanced robots? Our understanding of the process of understanding itself must inform the way we judge and interact with others, and hence have an impact on our moral and ethical behaviour.

I have been interested in the general question of the nature of understanding since I was invited to deliver a set of Gifford Lectures in Glasgow, on the psychology of understanding, in 1983 (Sanford 1987). At that time, and since, I have become more and more aware of the scale of the issues, and the number of perspectives that could be taken. Since then I became interested in the possibility of hosting a lecture series in which experts from a variety of disciplines would come together to present their own takes on the nature of human understanding. I was lucky enough to have my idea taken up by the University of Glasgow Gifford Lectureship Committee, who suggested it go ahead for the 550th anniversary, and allowed me a very free rein in terms of the composition of the lectures. The lecturers themselves were given free rein to interpret the theme in the way they best saw fit.

The idea was that the series as a whole should provide some insights into how much we know about our own understanding, its limits and its place in the scheme of things. As hoped for, the views portrayed by such a diverse set of lecturers as these are very varied and have rather different foci. The different slants taken on the issues also manifest in the quite distinct styles of presentation and argument. Such excellent variety is preserved in this volume by our decision to make only very slight adaptation for print, thus maintaining the stylistic individuality and unique 'voice' of each of the contributors.

In this Preface, my intention is simply to indicate a little about the perspectives and content of what is to come, and certainly not to offer any critique or synthesis, both of which would be beyond my brief as editor, and presumptuous in the extreme. Rather, in bringing out the orientations taken, I have provided a little background to some of them.

Recent advances in psychology, and in cognition in particular, have led to some rather general views about how human nature might be analysed. In cognitive psychology, we have seen the growth of a mechanistic view in which the mind has been likened to an information-processing system. Although on first thinking of this, many people believe that reducing human understanding to a mechanistic system is dehumanizing, the importance of considering such an approach is difficult to overemphasize. Simply to understand how we can do things like add up a set of numbers, let alone play chess, is a fairly recent achievement. Drawing analogies between humans and automata is not new (McCorduck 1979). Furthermore, theoretical developments in understanding the nature of computation during the first quarter of the twentieth century gave rise in the second half of the same century to the science of artificial intelligence, or AI. AI sees both natural and artificial intelligence (or cognition) as having a common basis. Within a computational framework, it is possible to analyse the effects of different types of constraints within the system itself. Cognitive psychology has followed a parallel course, in that various constraints on processing have been suggested, which themselves have been taken as responsible for our limits in information processing. These range from the earliest notions of limited capacity, based on channel bandwidth (Broadbent 1958), through to a limited capacity working memory (Hitch & Baddely 1976).

A second important concept to emerge during the second half of the twentieth century was the idea of a mental model (Craik 1943). The idea was that we represent aspects of the world (real or hypothetical) that we are thinking about by setting up a mental model of the thing we are thinking about. To the extent that the model corresponds to some aspect of reality, it will serve to give us accurate (if incomplete) under-standing. But if the model does not correspond well, then we will reach false conclusions. It is possible to join together the idea of mental models with ideas of limited capacity to create possible explanations for some of our errors in reasoning, and this is the line taken by psychologist Philip Johnson-Laird in Part I. Johnson-Laird also discusses the question of how under-standing superior to our own might arise, and he does it in terms of information processing concepts.

Internal constraints on processing represent one viable source of restrictions on what we may or may not be able to understand, and such constraints raise a lot of interesting questions. For instance, if we use a limited capacity working memory to set up representations of states of affairs in the world, does this mean there are some systems, or functions, that are just too complex for us to understand, simply because we cannot represent them internally? Complex economic systems come to mind. Indeed, the late Herbert Simon (1969) has claimed that we cannot under-stand complex interactions *per se*, but have to break them down into what he calls 'partial decompositions': subsystems that maintain their properties and are not changed when they are combined with other systems. With the development of powerful artefacts, such as computers, it is possible to simulate complex systems and use the simulations to study system behaviour. This is equivalent to dividing understanding between person and artefact, and is a type of understanding that goes beyond the boundaries of one individual. It is interesting to speculate here about whether an ant community as a whole 'understands' its environment, even though an individual ant might not. The normal use of understanding is in terms of the individual, of course, but at least some thinkers have speculated that the individual human mind is made up of many sub-components, each one of which is incapable of doing what the aggregate of them all can do (see, e.g., Minsky 1987).

Constraints on understanding are not just structural (a property of the way the brain is wired up), there are also content-based constraints. Every one of us has had an understanding of something that others have disagreed with, the others claiming that one is seeing just a single viewpoint. Understanding undoubtedly depends upon acts of interpretation. For interpretation to take place, a state of affairs has to be mapped onto the framework that is being used for interpretation. In Part II, linguist George Lakoff explores this idea to the full. He argues two principles: understanding is embodied, and embodiment leads to a complex metaphorical system that underlies our ways of talking and thinking about things. For instance, using containers is a major skill that we learn at a very early age, and our representation of containers-in-use may be used as ways of representing all manner of things, from how we talk about anger ('Keep a lid on it') to set theory in mathematics. Lakoff's contribution constitutes a synthesis of much material from cognitive science into a view that in principle may be applied to our conceptions of just about anything, including God, mathematics and philosophical thinking, as he shows in Chapter 4. For Lakoff, metaphors represent real constraints on how we understand in practice, while the embodied primitives on which metaphors rest represent limits on how we might understand at all. The notion of embodiment is particularly important, since it entails that understanding depends upon the bodies we have and how we interact with the world. Understanding is not abstract at all: indeed the burden for those who would support the embodiment notion is to show how abstractions such as mathematics and logic themselves rest on embodied conceptualizations. This is precisely what Lakoff attempts.

Biologist and philosopher Michael Ruse examines the implications of evolutionary theory for the nature and limits of understanding. His treatment includes a historical tour of many of the milestones in the development of evolutionary theorizing. Starting from the position that humans evolved along with the other life forms, past and present, that inhabited the earth, he argues that even the 'highest' of our tools for understanding, such as mathematics and logic, are effectively behaviours that have until now supported our survival. He addresses the question of whether science as a means of understanding the world is essentially part of our biology, or whether in some sense human understanding transcends the animal, humans being civilized through our culture and religion. The line taken is that culture and biology are inseparable, and may be understood in terms of evolutionary theory. Although Ruse comes from a very different background, there is some convergence here with Lakoff's position on embodied understanding, and also on the importance of metaphor in science.

In Chapter 6, Ruse explicitly addresses the question of how Darwinism may offer a basis for our understanding of ethics and ethical behaviour. He traces the history of Social Darwinism, and how in various incarnations it has been used to suggest how we should behave, and to some extent explain why we should behave in the ways suggested. He introduces his own views about how evolutionary principles may lead to ethical principles, hinging his arguments on the innate disposition of humans to interact in a collaborative way. It is interesting that developments in cognitive science are also beginning to unravel possible mechanisms by which collaboration, and recognition of the state of mind of others, might be possible.

Ruse's arguments work at two levels. First, the group level, where our personal understanding of how to act ethically, or appropriately, lies rooted in our human natures, which at base demand collaboration with other humans. Secondly, at the level of biological theorizing, they provide a general explanation for why we have the ethical outlooks that we do. Because the principles underlying interaction are not guaranteed to work (i.e., they are not algorithmic, but are, rather, heuristic), there are many situations where there is no clear black-and-white set of rules that seem to apply, which is a problem for those who would search for a set of ethical and moral absolutes outside of evolved human experience.

The two chapters by philosopher Lynne Rudder Baker in Part IV move us away from science-based considerations, and into more clearly philosophical territory. They also concern the means by which we might know things, in principle. Because the commonplace view is that science provides the means of our understanding, and that limits in scientific understanding represent the true limits of human understanding, this is what she concentrates on. She evaluates the idea that science as we know it might provide our means of understanding things, terming this approach 'scientism'. In Chapter 7, she argues that as human individuals, we have access to one very special type of knowledge – first-person knowledge. That is, it is very different for me to know that I had muesli for breakfast than to know that someone called Tony Sanford had muesli for breakfast. While we might be able to understand how first-person perspectives arise, using science as it is, it is not obvious how we might capture the experience within that framework.

In Chapter 8 Baker argues that reductionism underlies scientism, and yet that our own third-person understanding is not really reductionist in nature. Her view is that we make sense of (understand) the world in terms of what she calls 'the commonsense conception'. In this conception, the world consists of physical objects (streams, hills) and intentional objects (a driver's licence, a driving record). These and their like are the objects of everyday understanding, and they have a different status from the subatomic particles of which hills are made. Her argument, roughly, is that the reality of a physical object is not exhausted by the sum of the physical parts of which it is made. Rather, reality requires something extra. So a chair is more than the sum of its parts. Indeed, to some extent, these arguments are arguments for objects in the world for humans being defined in terms of how humans actually interact with the world. A chair is a special thing because it affords sitting, and that is the level at which we understand the notion of *chair*. Baker's discussion leads her to use third-person understanding as a way of showing the limitations of reductionist scientism as a system for understanding everything. This does seem to be related to the functionalist views that appear in Parts I–III. For instance, mental models represent the way the world divides up for humans; they cannot be simply arbitrary in nature. Nowhere, in my opinion, is this clearer than in Lakoff's message about embodiment.

If we seek to capture all our understanding within a single framework, such as the framework of science, particularly the reductionist interpretation, then, to use Brian Hebblethwaite's term, there must be no 'residue'. Brian Hebblethwaite argues that there is and probably always will be ample residue after scientific explanations have taken place (Baker argues the same to the extent that they have the same conception of scientific explanation). In a search for ultimate understanding, empirical science is very much taken to be the standard. Hebblethwaite explores the contributions of metaphysical thinking and theological thinking to the picture of human understanding, since they exemplify two main ways of thinking about the 'residue'. At the centre of Hebblethwaite's concerns is the need to make sense of consciousness, mind, morality, art, the beautiful and the good. Why do such things exist; why are they part of our lives, as they most certainly are? Hebblethwaite surveys a number of metaphysical systems-approaches to these problems. In Chapter 10, he explores what theological understanding might add. He defines theology as metaphysics plus revelation, and argues that theological understanding enriches our conceptions by dealing with phenomena where science appears unable.

I hope that readers enjoy these lectures as much as did the full audiences at the University of Glasgow in the summer of 2001. I would like to extend my thanks to the Gifford Committees for supporting this project, both financially and intellectually, and extend especial thanks to Professor Neil Spurway, who encouraged me greatly throughout, and to his successor as Chairman of the Gifford Committee, Professor Alexander Broadie, who gave his excellent advice freely. My biggest debt of gratitude is to the speakers themselves, who gave their time and minds unstintingly, and made the whole thing possible.

Anthony J. Sanford
Glasgow, September 2002

REFERENCES

Barth, K. 'The Knowledge of God and the Service of God' (Delivered in Aberdeen, 1937–8).

Broadbent, D. E. (1958) *Perception and Communication*. London: Pergamon Press.

Craik, K. (1943) *The Nature of Explanation*. Cambridge: Cambridge University Press.

Eddington, A. (1928) *The Nature of the Physical World*. Cambridge: Cambridge University Press.

Hitch, G. J., and Baddeley, A. D. (1976) 'Verbal reasoning and working memory', *Quarterly – Journal of Experimental Psychology*, 28: 603–21.

McCorduck, P. (1979) *Machines Who Think*. San Francisco: Freeman.

Marcel, G. 'The Mystery of Being' (Delivered in Aberdeen, 1949–50).

Minsky, M. (1987) *The Society of Mind*. New York: Simon & Schuster.

Sanford, A. J. (1987) *The Mind of Man: Models of Human Understanding*. Brighton, Sussex: Harvester Press.

Sherrington, C. S. (1940) *Man on His Nature*. Cambridge: Cambridge University Press.

Simon, H. A. (1969) *The Sciences of the Artificial*. Cambridge, MA: MIT Press.

Part I
The Psychology of Understanding

P. N. Johnson-Laird

1
Illusions of
Understanding*

P. N. Johnson-Laird

The philosopher Ludwig Wittgenstein famously remarked: 'the limits of my language are the limits of my world' (Wittgenstein 1922: 5.6). This view has something to recommend it, because knowledge has to be expressed in language. Yet, for a psychologist such as the present author, it is odd. Language is not a fixed enterprise. It develops and changes from day to day both in individuals and in society. And individuals can understand more than they can say. When they do so, they may struggle to adapt the language to express their meaning. They coin neologisms, and they strain against the grammar and usage of their language. Yet their understanding may still run ahead of what it is possible for them to say. Moreover, Wittgenstein's thesis presupposes that if there is anything that we understand, then it is our own native tongue. The title of the series of lectures from which this book

*   The research reported in these two chapters is a result of many collaborations, and the author thanks the following colleagues for their help: Tony Anderson, Malcolm Bauer, Ruth Byrne, Paolo Cherubini, Vittorio Girotto, Eugenia Goldvarg, Paolo Legrenzi, Maria Sonino Legrenzi, Bonnie Meyer, Tom Ormerod, Fabien Savary, Walter Schaeken, and Yingrui Yang. He is also grateful to Tony Sanford and Simon Garrod for their hospitality in Glasgow: his visit was coals to Newcastle, because they are real experts on the nature of human understanding. Some of the research reported here was supported by a grant from the National Science Foundation (Grant 0076287) to study strategies in reasoning.

derives was The Nature and Limits of Human Understanding, and this chapter, which is based on the first lecture, argues that one limit of human understanding is a systematic inability to understand language.

This inability may strike you as paradoxical. How can you fail to understand your own language? You acquired it at your mother's knee; it is yours inalienably. You know it intimately, so securely that with a few trivial exceptions – rare words, prolix constructions – you must understand it. But, as this chapter will show, there are many symptoms of the human inability to understand language.

One symptom is the strange way in which you think you understand something when a moment's reflection should convince you otherwise. Suppose I tell you:

> During the Renaissance, Ghiberti and Donatello cast bronze doors for the baptistery of the cathedral in Florence.

You understand me. But, what is 'bronze'? And what is a 'baptistery'? Indeed, what exactly is a 'cathedral'? Paul Valéry, the French symbolist poet (and, one is tempted to say, psychologist – for he spent hours introspecting each day before breakfast), likened the process of comprehension to a man crossing an abyss on a rickety plank. If he rushes confidently across, then all will be well. But, if he pauses to think about the meaning of a word, then the bridge will collapse beneath him (Valéry 1958 [1939]).

A second symptom of the human inability to understand language is the existence of deep philosophical riddles about the meanings of simple words. A good example is a two-letter word in common use. It has already occurred in this chapter three times. There are probably more books about the meaning of this word than any other in the language. The word is: 'if'. Children start to use it quite early in their linguistic development, and adults have the utmost confidence that they know what it means and that their listeners understand it too. But, what does 'if' mean? There is no consensus amongst modern philosophers or linguists about the meaning of conditionals, that is, about the meaning of assertions of the form: 'If A then B'. So a paradox exists. All of us blithely use conditionals in daily life; we seem to communicate successfully; but when we stop in mid-bridge and ask 'what do they mean?', we don't know.

If (*sic*) we don't understand 'if', then it follows that there are other words that we don't understand either. The most important of them is 'cause'. When we assert that one event caused another, we can paraphrase the claim, as Hume (1988 [1748]) pointed out, by saying: 'If the first event hadn't have happened then the second wouldn't have happened'. Conditionals are close to causation. Once again, we all make causal claims on a daily basis. The concept is built into our lexicon:

To anger someone is to *cause* them to become angry.
To lift something is to *cause* it to move upwards.
To reveal something is to *cause* it to be visible.

But, as will not be news to you, no one knows for sure the meaning of 'cause'. Like Valéry's man on the tottering bridge, we make our causal claims and rush on without pausing to analyse what they mean.

Something mysterious is going on. And my two chapters in this book aim to solve the mystery. They will try to explain three things: how we understand language; how we succumb to systematic misunderstandings; and how these 'illusions' in understanding lead us to make errors in reasoning. My first chapter concerns the comprehension of sentences and our illusions in understanding them. My second chapter concerns our limited ability to detect inconsistencies, and our tendency to resolve them with causal explanations even though we seem unable to analyse the concept of causation itself. In short, the two chapters aim to illustrate the nature and limits of the human understanding of language.

On Understanding

What happens when you understand an assertion in your native tongue? Introspection tells you almost nothing about the process. Most of understanding is profoundly unconscious. People take the word 'unconscious' to refer to something Freudian: impulses that you are not aware of pertaining to sex and violence. Freud argued that free association on a psychoanalyst's couch could lead you to become aware of your unconscious impulses, and his therapeutic maxim was 'where Id was, let Ego be'. Psychology, however, has another usage of 'unconscious' going back at least to the nineteenth-century polymath, Hermann von Helmholtz. He argued that unconscious inferences underlie visual perception. He also argued that human beings make judgements that cannot be expressed in language, and that are accordingly not communicable, for example, discriminations in colour (Helmholtz 1962). No amount of free association on an analyst's couch, or anyone else's for that matter, enables you to become aware of these unconscious processes. They make consciousness possible. You can no more gain introspective access to them than you can feel your own nerve impulses.

So, what are the unconscious processes that underlie the comprehension of language? Consider a sentence used to make an assertion, such as: 'The boy stood on the burning deck.' Once you have recognized the words in the sentence – no mean feat – there are three main steps in grasping the significance of its utterance. Figure 1 outlines them. The first step is to compose the meaning of the sentence out of the meanings of its words according to the grammatical relations amongst them. The second step is to use general knowledge to modulate this composition, for example, to determine who is referred to by 'the boy' in the preceding example. And the third step is to use this interpretation to construct a mental representation of the

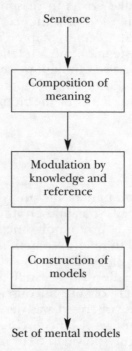

Figure 1: The main steps in understanding a sentence in natural language

situation described in the assertion. Each of these processes operates concurrently, not on sentences as a whole, but almost word by word. That is, you normally grasp the full significance of what is said word by word, and you are only occasionally led up the garden path and have to go back to an earlier point in a sentence to reinterpret it. In what follows, each of the three steps will be described in more detail.

The Composition of Meanings

Natural language has what logicians refer to as a 'compositional semantics'. That is to say, you have a mental system for parsing sentences in your language, which uses your unconscious knowledge of its grammar. But, as it parses, it does more than merely assign a grammatical structure to a sentence. It combines the *meanings* of the words in the sentence according to the grammatical relations amongst them. Your representations of the meanings of words are the ingredients; the grammatical relations amongst them are the recipe. Thus, the two sentences:

The man bit the dog.

and:

The dog bit the man.

have the same ingredients, but different recipes. That is, you swap round the role of the ingredients. In one case, as it were, you fry parsley and add it to the breadcrumbs; in the other case you fry the breadcrumbs and add them to the parsley.

The great advantage of a compositional semantics is that it explains how it is possible for you to understand a potentially infinite number of distinct sentences. You have only finite means at your disposal – a finite lexicon, a grammar with a finite number of rules, and a finite number of semantic principles. These principles are likely to be linked one-to-one with the rules in the grammar. So, for example, the mental parser recognizes that:

the burning deck

makes up a noun phrase, because a rule in the grammar specifies that the sequence *definite article participle noun* constitutes a well-formed English noun phrase. (Of course, no one knows the actual labels that the mental parser assigns to the parts of speech.) And, linked to this rule for noun phrases is a semantic principle that specifies how to interpret their meaning, that is, how to assemble the meanings of the article, participle, and noun, to compose the meaning of the noun phrase. The definite article ('the') presupposes the existence of an entity in the situation under discussion; the participle ('burning') refers to a property; and the noun ('deck') refers to an entity. The semantic recipe assigns the property to the entity, and represents the presupposition of its existence. This result has an unconscious mental representation.

Not everyone accepts the idea of a compositional semantics (cf. Langacker 1987). Yet, the issue is hardly open to an empirical test until some theorist lays down constraints on what the principles that combine meanings can, and can't, do. The author is tempted to say that at present these semantic principles are so powerful that they can do anything – they could, if necessary, call for someone to look up a telephone number in the Glasgow telephone directory. What is clear, however, is that the human compositional system has limits on its performance. Consider the following passage:

> A teacher punished a child of another teacher. The brother of the teacher whose child was punished, who was also a teacher, proceeded to assault the teacher who punished the child of the teacher he was the brother of. The teacher who was the brother of the teacher whose child was punished was arrested on the complaint of the teacher who was assaulted by the brother of the teacher whose child the teacher who was assaulted had punished.

It becomes progressively harder to understand the passage. The relative clauses grow ever longer until your mental parser is unable to cope with assembling their meanings. In fact, the meaning of the passage is simple:

> One teacher punished the child of another teacher whose brother, another teacher, assaulted the first teacher but was arrested when he complained.

The model for this passage was a late nineteenth-century newspaper, the *Sunday Strand,* which had stories of this style. Back in those days, they paid their journalists by the word, and evidently had nothing left to pay an editor.

A compositional semantics calls for a grammar, a mental lexicon containing words and their meanings, and a set of semantic principles for assembling meanings according to each rule in the grammar. Theorists understand the principles of grammar, thanks to the work of linguists such as Chomsky (e.g. 1995). They understand compositional principles, thanks to the work of logicians and computer scientists. It is child's play to write a computer program that implements a compositional semantics for a fragment of language. The present author has even written such programs himself.

Knowledge, Modulation, and Reference

Knowledge modulates the composition of meanings in several ways. It can have a crucial effect on comprehension. The following assertion seems commonplace:

The pilot put his plane into a stall just before landing it on the runway.

But every noun and verb in it is ambiguous. According to the *American Heritage Dictionary*, the words have the following numbers of meanings:

Pilot, noun,   4
Plane, noun,   7
Land, verb,   7
Put, verb,   14
Stall, noun,   8
Runway, noun,   7

If we multiply out the numbers of ambiguities, then the sentence has over 150,000 possible meanings. You may feel that the lexicographers have too refined a conception of the different meanings of these words, but even if each word is restricted to two meanings, there are still 64 potential meanings of the sentence to sort through. Cognitive scientists have been struggling with the problem of disambiguation for some years (see, e.g., Miller 1996). The best computer systems are over 90 per cent correct in their interpretations, which seems very good until you recollect that this percentage implies that the systems fail with most sentences. Humans do a better job on disambiguation, and they rely on knowledge of the language and the world.

Knowledge of the world can overrule the compositional process. Consider the following passage:

> Apart from her husband, a hairdresser, she was the only woman among 52 men on the tour. As a costumier, she filled a much-needed gap, because when a company of actors is putting on a play in a different town each night, no damage to the costumes is too trivial not to be mended.

Did you notice anything unusual about this passage? Naive listeners tend to report after some thought: it's odd that her husband was a woman. Few individuals notice that 'a much-needed gap' means, not that *she* was much needed, but rather that her absence was much needed. And hardly anyone notices that the final sentence contains a supererogatory negation. It ought to read: No damage is too trivial to be mended.

Knowledge is also essential for determining the referents of pronouns, noun phrases, and other expressions (see, e.g., Garrod & Sanford 1994; Garnham 2001). Given the earlier assertion:

> The boy stood on the burning deck.

compositional semantics cannot tell you which boy or which deck it refers to. You have to infer such referents from the context, that is, from previous utterances or from a knowledge of the situation under discussion, or both.

Mental Models and Their Construction

The result of the first two steps – compositional semantics and modulation by knowledge – must be an expression in an unconscious mental language. The third and final step in comprehension is to use this expression, like a line of code in a computer programming language, to construct a *mental model* of the situation. The idea of mental models goes back to the work of the Scottish psychologist, Kenneth Craik. In his book, *The Nature of Explanation* (1943), he wrote:

> If the organism carries a 'small-scale model' of external reality and of its own possible actions within its head, it is able to try out various alternatives, conclude which is the best of them, react to future situations before they arise, utilize the knowledge of past events in dealing with the present and the future, and in every way react in a much fuller, safer, and more competent matter to the emergencies which face it.

This hypothesis was prescient but programmatic. The present author and his colleagues have developed a theory in which mental models are the end result of understanding natural language, and we have implemented the theory in a computer program (e.g. Johnson-Laird 1983; Johnson-Laird & Byrne 1991). But, what, you may wonder, *is* a mental model?

Our theory adopts three main principles that pin down mental models and that distinguish them from the other sorts of proposed representations in psychological theories. The first principle is of *iconicity*:

> A mental model has a structure that corresponds to the known structure of what it represents.

Like an architect's model of a building, the parts of a mental model correspond to the parts of what it represents. This principle is hardly novel. One precursor is Wittgenstein's (1922) 'picture' theory of language, but he in turn was anticipated, most notably by the great nineteenth-century American philosopher and logician, Charles Sanders Peirce (see, e.g., Peirce 1992 [1898]). Iconicity was central to his theory of signs, and he used the term 'icon' to refer to a sign with a structure resembling the structure of what it represents. Hence, visual images are iconic. But, many mental models cannot be visualized. Consider the assertion that President Bush owns three cars. Figure 2 represents a model of this assertion. The individual, the entities, and the relation between them, are represented by corresponding parts

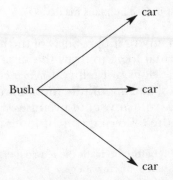

Figure 2: The structure of a mental model of the assertion: 'President Bush owns three cars.' The arrows denote the relation of *ownership*.

in the model. Perhaps you can visualize President Bush and the cars. But you cannot visualize the relation of ownership *per se*. Hence, visual images are a special case of mental models, and many mental models do not yield visual images.

One advantage of the iconic nature of mental models – an advantage that Peirce appreciated and exploited in his own diagrammatic system for logic, his so-called 'logic graphs' – is that you can use some assertions to build a model and then use the model to draw a conclusion that does not correspond to any of the original assertions. Here is an example (see Schaeken, Johnson-Laird & d'Ydewalle 1996). Someone tells you:

Pete listens to the radio before he reads the newspaper.
He reads the newspaper before he does his washing.
He eats his breakfast while he listens to the radio.
He plans his day while he does his washing.

You can envisage a mental model with the following structure:

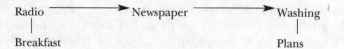

Where 'radio' denotes a model of Pete listening to the radio, and so on, time is the left-to-right axis, and the vertical axis allows for different events to be contemporaneous. Granted that each event takes roughly the same amount of time, you can draw a conclusion from this model:

Pete eats his breakfast before he plans his day.

The conclusion is an emergent property of the model. In contrast, it is tricky to use formal logic to draw the same conclusion. One difficulty is that logic does not tell you *which* conclusion to draw from a set of premises, and an infinite number of different conclusions follow logically from any set of premises. From the premises above, for instance, the following conclusion is a valid deduction:

Pete listens to the radio before he reads the newspaper, *and* Pete listens to the radio before he reads the newspaper.

Only lunatics and logicians are likely to draw this conclusion. It does not tell you anything new. Yet, it is logically valid.

The second principle of the model theory is as follows:

Each mental model represents a possibility.

Possibilities are central to the theory. Suppose, for example, that someone makes the following assertion about some playing cards:

There's a king on the table, or there's an ace, or both.

The assertion is consistent with three possibilities, and you can construct a separate mental model of each of them, as shown here on three separate lines:

King
       Ace
King   Ace

When we have asked people to list the possibilities consistent with the assertion, the majority of them indeed list these three possibilities (Johnson-Laird & Savary 1996).

The theory makes a straightforward prediction: the more models of possibilities that individuals have to hold in mind, the harder it should be for them to cope. The prediction appears to be true. Here is an example to try for yourself. Consider the problem:

George is in Glasgow or else Edith is in Edinburgh, but not both.
Edith is in Edinburgh or else Anne is in Aberdeen, but not both.
What follows?

The problem is quite hard (see Bauer & Johnson-Laird 1993). You can envisage the two possibilities compatible with the first assertion:

George in Glasgow
               Edith in Edinburgh

But, it is difficult to incorporate those from the second assertion. In fact, the solution is as follows:

George in Glasgow   Anne in Aberdeen
               Edith in Edinburgh

Hence, there are only two possibilities, and an emergent conclusion is:

> Either George is in Glasgow and Anne is in Aberdeen or else Edith is in Edinburgh.

Given a big enough increase in complexity, the human model-building system collapses under the load. The following problem defeats many people:

> George is in Glasgow or Edith is in Edinburgh, or both.
> Edith is in Edinburgh or Anne is in Aberdeen, or both.
> What follows?

The first assertion is consistent with three possibilities:

George in Glasgow	
	Edith in Edinburgh
George in Glasgow	Edith in Edinburgh

The task of adding the three possibilities compatible with the second assertion is hard. The correct answer is:

George in Glasgow		Anne in Aberdeen
	Edith in Edinburgh	
	Edith in Edinburgh	Anne in Aberdeen
George in Glasgow	Edith in Edinburgh	
George in Glasgow	Edith in Edinburgh	Anne in Aberdeen

An emergent conclusion from these five possibilities is:

> George is in Glasgow and Anne is in Aberdeen, or Edith is in Edinburgh.

Such problems begin to run up against a limitation in human understanding. Human beings cannot hold in mind many different possibilities. If you have ever wondered about the mental ability of a super-intelligent being, then such a being would grasp at once that the two preceding assertions yield five possibilities.

Another limitation on human understanding is illustrated by a different sort of example. Imagine a world in which there are four persons: Ann, Bill, Cath, and Dave, and suppose that the following two assertions are true about this world:

Everybody loves anyone who loves someone.
Ann loves Bill.
Does it follow that that Cath loves Dave?

Most people say, 'No' (as shown in unpublished experiments that Paolo Cherubini and the present author have carried out). The problem, however, has pushed up against another barrier to understanding. Let us see what does follow from the two assertions. Our understanding of the initial situation is shown in the following model, where the arrow denotes the relation of *loving*:

Ann   ⟶   Bill   Cath   Dave

Since everybody loves anyone who loves someone, the model can be updated accordingly:

It follows that everybody loves Ann, and indeed most reasoners can draw this conclusion. But, this new model can be updated once more according to the assertion that everybody loves anyone who loves someone. The result is the following model (which ignores the fact that, strictly speaking, all four persons love themselves too):

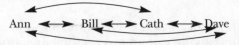

Here, the double-headed arrows denote that the two individuals love each other. As you will see, everyone loves everyone. And, of course, Cath loves Dave. The conclusion does follow from the premises. We can all understand the validity of this inference as it is slowly stepped out for us with the use of diagrams. Few of us, however, can spontaneously see at once that the conclusion follows. A super-intelligent individual would grasp the inference immediately. As the super-intelligent Sherlock Holmes remarked:

> it is not really difficult to construct a series of inferences, each dependent on its predecessor and each simple in itself. If, after doing so, one simply knocks out all the central inferences and presents one's audience with the starting-point and the conclusion, one may produce a startling, though possibly meretricious, effect. (Conan Doyle 1930: 511)

The difficulty in the example is not that there are too many possibilities for you to hold in mind, but rather that you need to grasp that a series of inferences can be made, and you need to keep track of their expanding consequences in the model.

The third principle in the theory of mental models is the subtlest and has the most surprising consequences. It is dignified with a name: the principle of truth. What it postulates seems obvious, at first:

> The *principle of truth*: mental models represent only what is true, and not what is false.

The principle seems transparent. But, do not be fooled. It yields unexpected consequences, which the author discovered only from his computer program implementing the theory. The first consequence of the principle, however, *is* obvious. When you understand an assertion, you represent only the possibilities compatible with its truth. For example, given the earlier assertion:

> There's a king on the table, or there's an ace, or both.

you represent only the true possibilities:

King
       Ace
King   Ace

You do not normally think about what the assertion rules out as false, namely, there is neither a king nor an ace on the table. But, another consequence of the principle of truth is that each clause in an assertion is itself represented in a possibility only when it is true in that possibility. Consider again the three preceding mental models. The first mental model represents a possibility in which there is a king on the table. In this possibility, it is false that there is an ace on the table, but the model does not represent this information explicitly. Similarly, the second mental model represents a possibility in which there is an ace on the table, but it does not represent explicitly that in this possibility it is false that there is a king on the table. Individuals appear to work according to the principle that what isn't there in a mental model isn't there in the world. But, they are not always consistent, because sometimes absence from a mental model merely represents ignorance about what is or isn't there in the world.

The way in which the theory captures the principle of truth is as follows: individuals make a mental footnote about what is false in each possibility, but these footnotes are fleeting. They are soon forgotten in normal circumstances. But, if individuals do retain the footnotes, then they can use them to transform their *mental* models into *fully explicit* models. A fully explicit model represents each clause in an assertion in each possibility. Hence, a fully explicit set of models for the assertion, 'There's a king on the table, or there's an ace, or both', is as follows:

King	¬ Ace
¬ King	Ace
King	Ace

The symbol ¬ represents negation, and so the first of these models represents a possibility in which there is a king but not an ace.

The representation of conditionals is more problematical. Consider, for example, the conditional:

If there is a king on the table then there is an ace.

This assertion makes salient one possibility, namely, the one in which there is a king and an ace on the table. Individuals construct a mental model of this possibility. But, of course, there may not be a king on the table. The conditional is compatible with this possibility in which its 'if' clause – its so-called 'antecedent' – is false. Individuals represent this possibility in an implicit mental model, one that serves as a place-holder with no explicit content. They make a mental footnote that the implicit model represents the possibility, or possibilities, in which it is false that there is a king on the table. They therefore construct two mental models of the conditional:

King	Ace
. . .	

where the ellipsis denotes the implicit model of the possibilities in which it is false that there is a king. These possibilities distinguish the meaning of the conditional from that of the conjunction:

There is a king on the table and there is an ace.

The conjunction is compatible with just one possibility, the one corresponding to the model of the conditional in which there is a king and an ace.

If individuals retain the footnotes on mental models then they can convert them into fully explicit models. Hence, given the conditional: 'If there is a king on the table then there is an ace', what are the possibilities in the case that there isn't a king on the table? Could it be that there is an ace on the table? Most people say: yes. Could it be that there isn't an ace on the table? Again most people say: yes. In other words, there are no constraints on the possibilities when there isn't a king on the table. And so the fully explicit models of the conditional are as follows:

> King Ace
> ¬ King Ace
> ¬ King ¬ Ace

There is good evidence to support this account of conditionals. My colleagues and I have collected some of it from psychological experiments. But, the French psychologist Pierre Barrouillet and his colleagues have discovered perhaps the most striking phenomenon (e.g. Barrouillet & Lecas 1999). They asked young children to list the possibilities compatible with a conditional. Given a conditional similar to the one about the cards, nine-year-olds tend to list just one possibility:

> King Ace

They construct only the explicit mental model of the conditional and they overlook the implicit model in which it is false that there is a king. Slightly older children list two possibilities:

> King Ace
> ¬ King ¬ Ace

These models correspond to a so-called 'biconditional' interpretation:

> If there is a king, and only if there is a king, on the table then there is an ace.

They can start to enumerate the possibilities corresponding to the fully explicit models, but they have a limited ability to hold information in mind. Only teenagers are able to enumerate all three possibilities:

King	Ace
¬ King	Ace
¬ King	¬ Ace

The ability to hold information in mind depends on what psychologists refer to as 'working memory' (Baddeley 1986). It is the sort of memory that you use to remember a telephone number that you've just looked up in the directory, as you walk back across the room to pick up the telephone. Working memory is crucial to thinking and reasoning. Barrouillet and his colleague Jean-François Lecas have shown that a measure of its capacity correlates with the number of models that their experimental participants list as compatible with a conditional. Working memory is thus roughly analogous to your computer's central processor. The imaginary super-intelligent being will need to have a very large working memory.

Illusions in Understanding and Reasoning

Mental models can represent spatial relations, events and processes, and the operations of complex systems. They can yield both inductive and deductive inferences. But, as we have seen, they normally represent only what is true. This focus on truth may be a sensible adaptation to the limited human ability to hold information in mind, or, as psychologists say, to the limited processing capacity of working memory. There just isn't enough processing capacity left over to worry about what is false. The claim is plausible. But, all of us pay a price for our inability to think about both what is true and what is false. We do not fully understand our own language. We think we understand an assertion when in fact we do not. Moreover, we don't understand that we don't understand it. And that is a recipe for trouble.

Here is a problem for you to try:

Only one of the following assertions is true about a particular hand of cards:
There is a king in the hand or there is an ace, or both.
There is a queen in the hand or there is an ace, or both.
There is a jack in the hand or there is a ten, or both.
Is it possible that there is an ace in the hand?

Nearly everyone says yes. When the author's former student Eugenia Goldvarg gave this problem to some Princeton students, 99 per cent of them said 'Yes', and Princeton students are very good reasoners (Goldvarg & Johnson-Laird 2000). They appeared to be thinking in the following way:

> The first assertion allows three possibilities, and an ace occurs in two of them. And so an ace is indeed possible. Similarly, the second assertion is compatible with the same conclusion. So, an ace is possible.

The inference is very tempting. But it is an illusion. One way to disabuse yourself of its conclusion is to consider how many of the three assertions in the problem would be true if there were an ace in the hand. The first assertion would be true, and the second assertion would also be true. But, that is contrary to the problem's rubric, which asserts that only *one* of the three assertions is true.

To reach the correct answer, you have to think about both the truth of an assertion and the concurrent falsity of the other two assertions. If the first assertion is true, then the second and third assertions are false. The second assertion is:

> There is a queen in the hand or there is an ace, or both.

In what circumstances is this assertion false? We already know the answer. It is false when there is neither a queen *nor an ace*. So, if the first assertion is true, then there cannot be an ace. An analogous argument applies when the second assertion is true: the first assertion is false, and so there is neither a king *nor an ace*. Finally, if the third assertion is true, then both the first and the second assertions are false, and there is still no ace. There are accordingly five possibilities compatible with the information in the problem:

King	¬ Queen	¬ Ace	¬ Jack	¬ Ten	(Premise 1 true)
¬ King	Queen	¬ Ace	¬ Jack	¬ Ten	(Premise 2 true)
¬ King	¬ Queen	¬ Ace	Jack	¬ Ten	(Premise 3 true)
¬ King	¬ Queen	¬ Ace	¬ Jack	Ten	(Premise 3 true)
¬ King	¬ Queen	¬ Ace	Jack	Ten	(Premise 3 true)

As you can see, there is not an ace in the hand in any of these possibilities.

It is easy to construct illusions of impossibility too. That is, problems to which nearly everyone responds, 'No, that's impossible', but where the response is an illusion. Yet, when the same premises as those above were stated with the following question:

Is it possible that there is a jack?

the participants nearly all responded, 'Yes', again. They considered the third assertion, and its mental models showed that there was a jack. But, this time they were correct, as the fully explicit models show. So the focus on truth does not invariably lead to error. In fact, as the computer program implementing the theory shows, the inferences that give rise to illusions are sparse in the set of all possible inferences.

The principle of truth limits your understanding, but it does so without your realizing it. The participants in our experiments rated how confident they were in their responses. They were highly confident, and they were no less confident when they succumbed to an illusion than when they made a correct response to a control problem.

You seldom encounter problems like the preceding ones in daily life. And so you may want to comfort yourself with the thought that these problems are curios – items to be displayed in the glass cases of the psychologist's laboratory – and that they have little bearing on thinking in daily life. But, what follows should disabuse you of this false comfort. As a first step in the direction of more realistic problems, let us look at a highly potent illusion:

If there is a king in the hand then there is an ace or else if there isn't a king in the hand then there is an ace.
There is a king in the hand.
What follows?

Over two thousand individuals have tackled this problem (see Johnson-Laird & Savary 1999). Nearly all of them have responded:

There is an ace.

The response is so seductive that when the author's computer program told him that this response was wrong, he spent half a day looking for the 'bug' in the program. There was none. The program was right; the author was wrong. This epiphany led to the discovery of the illusions.

With the preceding problem, most people say to themselves that if the first conditional is true then one possibility is that there is a king and an ace, and that if the second conditional is true then the other possibility is that there is not a king but there is an ace. There are just the two possibilities:

>   King   Ace
> ¬ King   Ace

So, either way there is an ace. The premise that there is a king eliminates the second of the two possibilities. Hence, there is bound to be an ace. The trouble with this line of thinking is that it neglects what is false. In particular, the force of 'or else' conveys that one of the conditionals may be false. A so-called 'exclusive' interpretation means that one of them must be false. So, suppose that the first conditional is false. What would that mean? Certainly, it would mean that there could be a king in the hand without an ace. Hence, even though the second premise asserts that there *is* a king in the hand, the potential falsity of the conditional shows that an ace may not be in the hand. The inference that there is an ace in the hand is illusory.

Assertions akin to those in this second illusion do occur in daily life. But, now, you may comfort yourself with the thought that perhaps the illusions are not so deep-seated after all. And that with a little practice, or a little explanation, individuals will begin to see through them, and the illusions will go away. Unfortunately, our evidence suggests that the illusions are entrenched, and that it is not easy to get rid of them. In one study, the experimenter, Bonnie Meyer, warned some participants that the problems were very difficult, and that they needed to think carefully to reach the right answer. She also asked these participants to think aloud as they were working on the problems. Here is what a typical participant said as she tackled the preceding illusion:

> If there is a king there is an ace or else if there is not a king there is an ace. So there's always an ace. There is a king ... If there is a king then there is an ace or if there is not a king then there is an ace. So, either way you have an ace, and you have a king. So, you have a king and an ace – I guess. If there is a king there is an ace ... or if there is not a king then there is an ace. Yes. So regardless you have an ace. I think ... So there has to be something else because that just seems way too easy. And something is wrong somewhere – I don't know what it is.

This participant falls straight into the trap, and never succeeds in climbing out of it. Meyer also tested a group of participants who were not warned about the difficulty of the problems. And here is a typical protocol from one such participant:

> If there is a king there is an ace or else if there is not a king there is an ace. There is a king. So there is an ace.

The participant merely states the premises and then the erroneous conclusion.

Illusory inferences occur in all sorts of reasoning, including reasoning about causal relations, possibilities and probabilities, and reasoning based on quantifiers such as 'all' and 'some'. In many of our studies, we have also tried out various ways to eliminate illusions. We have been able to reduce the difference in accuracy between illusions and matching control problems that the participants get right. But, it is not easy. My former colleague Yingrui Yang carried out a study in which he taught the participants to think explicitly about what is true and what is false. Such thinking is time consuming. The difference between illusions and control problems vanished. But, performance on the control problems fell from almost 100 per cent correct to around 75 per cent correct (Yang & Johnson-Laird 2000). So far, we have been unable to discover any simple antidote to the illusions.

A fellow Gifford lecturer George Lakoff (in discussion after the lecture on which this chapter is based) suggested that perhaps a theory of how people use language – a so-called 'pragmatic' theory – might explain the illusions. He sketched an account of one such illusion. The difficulty is, however, to explain both the excellent performance on the control problems and the variety of different illusions. There are many other sorts than those in this chapter. Here is one from real life. A professor of chemistry warned his students on the web page for his course:

> either a grade of zero will be recorded if your absence [from class] is not excused, or else if your absence is excused other work you do in the course will count ...

He had in mind two possibilities: absent from class without excuse and you get a grade of zero; absent from class with an excuse and you get a grade based on other work. His students probably interpreted him in this way too. Knowledge of the ways of the world helps one to make this interpretation. But, if 'either A or else B' conveys two alternative propositions, then what the statement really says is that if the first proposition is true then the second proposition is false, and vice versa. The first proposition is:

A grade of zero will be recorded if your absence is not excused.

and its falsity is compatible with the possibility of your having no excuse but *not* getting a grade of zero:

¬ excused   ¬ zero   (first proposition false)

The second proposition is:

If your absence is excused other work you do will count.

and its falsity allows the possibility of your having an excuse but other work *not* counting:

excused   ¬ other work counts (second proposition false)

A student who was absent without excuse could point out to the professor that according to the rule he should not necessarily get a grade of zero. The student would be right, though he might not want to count on the professor seeing reason. The illusions are second nature for most of us. Hence, whenever you are tempted to write 'or else' in a sentence, it is a good idea try out 'and' or 'but' in its place. The professor would have been unimpeachable had he written the following prescription:

A grade of zero will be recorded if your absence is not excused, *but* if your absence is excused other work you do in the course will count ...

The principle of truth is a sensible adaptation of natural language to the all-too-human limitations of working memory. People cannot hold very much in mind at any one moment. The consequence is that they speak a language that they do not always understand. This limitation on understanding is not constrained to the curios of the psychological laboratory, though it is those arcane studies that first revealed the phenomenon. In daily life, speakers are likely to make assertions that they think that their listeners understand, and that their listeners think that they understand too. Both parties can be wrong. And, yet, as probably happened with the professor and his students, communication succeeds.

Sometimes discourse challenges all the limitations on human understanding – the limitations on compositionality, the limitations on holding possibilities in mind, and the limitations on thinking about what is false. Language then overwhelms you. One example comes from a UK Government leaflet explaining the death grant (a grant to help to defray the cost of a spouse's burial):

> Death grant is payable where either of the following conditions is satisfied by the person on whose [National Health] contributions the grant is claimed:
> - The contributor must have paid or been credited with at least 25 contributions of any class at any time between 5 July 1948 or the date of entry into insurance, if later, and 5 April 1985, or the date on which he reached 65 (60 for a woman), or died under that age, whichever is the earliest; or
> - Since 6 April 1985 the contributor must have actually paid contributions in any one tax year before the relevant year, on earnings of at least 25 times the lower earning limit for that year. The relevant year is usually the income tax year in which the death occurred, but if immediately before the date of death, the person on whose contributions the grant is claimed was himself dead or over 65 (60 for a woman), it is either the year in which he reached that age, or the year in which he died, whichever is earlier.

My former colleague Sheila Jones once challenged the then Minister of Health, the late Richard Crossman, with the question: 'Why can't Government leaflets be sensible?' To our astonishment, he thought the idea was silly. People would then get what they were entitled to, and that would cost the Government too much money. The limitations on human understanding can be exploited by anyone, even philosopher-kings.

2
Models, Causation, and Explanation

P. N. Johnson-Laird

Life is full of surprises. Not long ago, for instance, the author was sitting with some friends drinking an espresso after lunch in a pleasant piazza in an Umbrian town. We were waiting for Paolo, who had gone to fetch the car to pick us up. We knew that if he had gone to get the car then he would be back in five minutes (because we had walked from the car park to the restaurant). We also knew that he had gone to get the car. Five minutes went by. Then another; and another. After 20 minutes with no sign of Paolo we began to wonder what had happened to him. We were in a common everyday situation. Something had happened – or in this case *not* happened – that was surprising. It was not what we had expected. We believed:

If Paolo has gone to get the car, then he will be back in five minutes.

and:

Paolo has gone to get the car.

So, we inferred validly:

He will be back in five minutes.

But, the world did not conform to our expectations. So, what do you do in such a situation?

The first thing is to think. When a surprise occurs, by definition, the world is not consistent with your beliefs and their consequences. Something has to 'give'. The previous example is typical of daily life, but, if you are a scientist, you also encounter phenomena that are inconsistent with your hypotheses. You have to try to reason your way to consistency. A variety of terms refer to this sort of thinking: *diagnostic* thinking, *trouble-shooting*, *non-monotonic* reasoning, *defeasible* reasoning, *explanatory* reasoning, *abduction*. The plethora of jargon shows that the topic is under investigation in a variety of disciplines, including philosophy, artificial intelligence, and psychology. And it suggests – perhaps correctly – that no one really understands this sort of thinking. The author and his colleagues refer to it with yet another piece of jargon: 'reasoning to consistency'. We have proposed that it depends on two main steps: you detect an inconsistency, and then you infer a *causal* explanation to resolve it (Girotto *et al.* 2000). The sort of causal diagnoses that you are liable to create in the case of Paolo are, for example:

Possibly, he couldn't find the car.
Possibly, it was towed.
Possibly, it was stolen.
Possibly, the town's one-way streets forced him to make a detour (the correct answer).

Of course, there are limitations on your ability to create causal explanations. Sometimes, what happens is the '*Marie Celeste*' effect. The eponymous example is a true historical case. You believe that if a ship is at sea, it will have a crew. You board the *Marie Celeste*. You discover that no crew is aboard. But you are unable to infer what has happened to them.

Reasoning to consistency sets the scene for this chapter. Its aim is to examine two further barriers to human understanding: our limited ability to detect inconsistencies, and our limited comprehension of the concept of cause.

The Detection of Inconsistency

The detection of inconsistency seems straightforward. Yet, it reveals fundamental limitations on human understanding, and indeed on any other system for understanding, including the mind of a super-intelligent being. When there is a direct inconsistency between two simple assertions, its detection is trivial. I assert:

> Evelyn is a man.

You assert:

> Evelyn is not a man, but a woman.

We know that no one can be both a man and not a man, and so we infer that the two assertions cannot both be true.

Unfortunately, not all inconsistencies are of this sort. A *set* of assertions can be inconsistent, but have the interesting property that if any assertion is dropped from the set, the remaining assertions are consistent. Here is an example:

> If Jean loves Vivien then Vivien loves Pat.
> If Vivien loves Pat then Pat loves Evelyn.
> Jean loves Vivien and Pat doesn't love Evelyn.

Since Jean loves Vivien it follows from the first assertion that Vivien loves Pat, and therefore from the second assertion that Pat loves Evelyn. But, the third assertion states that Pat doesn't love Evelyn. There is an inconsistency: the three assertions cannot all be true. But, remove any one assertion, and the remaining pair of assertions can both be true. Of course, we can construct an inconsistent set with many more assertions in it:

> If A then B.
> If B then C.
> If C then D.

and so on indefinitely until we arrive at:

> If Y then Z

and then:

> A and not Z.

There an inconsistency, but it depends on every conditional in the chain. Remove one conditional link, or the final assertion, and all is well.

There is a general recipe for checking the consistency of a set of assertions. You search for a possibility in which all the assertions are true. That is, you take all the *clauses* in the assertions: A, B, C, ..., and you search for a way to assign truth or falsity to each of them so that all the assertions come out true. The search is feasible for a set of beliefs based on a handful of clauses, such as A, B, and C, for example:

A or B, or both.
Not-B or C, or both,
A and not-C.

Each clause can be either true or false, and so the three clauses call for you to examine eight possible assignments of truth values. For example, if A is true, B is true, and C is true, then the assertions are not consistent, because the first two are true, but the third is false. But, if A is true, B is false, and C is false, all three of the assertions are true. Hence, they are consistent.

In general, with a set of beliefs based on n clauses, you have to examine 2^n possibilities. As n increases, this number grows so rapidly that it soon ceases to be feasible to examine all the possibilities. For example, if a set of beliefs is based on a hundred clauses, then you need to check 2^{100} possibilities. That works out to 1,267,650,600,228,229,401,496,703,205,376 possibilities. If you could check each possibility in a millionth of a second, then it would still take you 40 thousand million million years to examine all of them. Of course, you might not have to examine all of them to find a consistent interpretation. Nevertheless, the worst case happens when the assertions are inconsistent: you have to check all possible interpretations. Each of us has beliefs based on many more than a hundred clauses, and so we cannot examine their consistency in this way. Such a search is what computer scientists refer to as 'computationally intractable'. It means that no computer – not even one as big as the universe running at the speed of light for the lifetime of the universe – can cope with such problems as the number of clauses grows larger. The so-called 'quantum' computer, which is based on quantum events in fundamental particles, may offer some help. We will have to wait and see.

A still severer problem exists in checking for consistency. If the assertions contain quantifiers, such as 'all' or 'some', then no procedure can be guaranteed to determine whether a set of assertions is consistent. The search may never end. In effect, any procedure may get lost in the 'space' of possibilities, and so no procedure – not even one in a quantum computer – can be guaranteed to discover that an inference is invalid.

These limitations are, as far as one can tell, irremovable obstacles to human understanding. So, how have humans coped with them? On the one hand, Romantics are inclined not to care about consistency. Walt Whitman in his *Leaves of Grass* proclaimed on their behalf: 'Do I contradict myself? Very well then I contradict myself, (I am large, I contain multitudes)'. On the other hand, most of us tend to keep our beliefs in segregated models. We know, or we think we know, that this belief has no bearing on that belief. The belief, say, that Mrs Thatcher won her first general election in 1979 is, we suppose, independent of the belief that bronze is an alloy. We build mental models of beliefs in separate domains, and the fact that we can build a mental model is prima facie evidence that the relevant set of beliefs is consistent.

One consequence of this account is that the way that we check consistency is to see whether or not we can build a mental model of the relevant set of beliefs. My colleagues have tested this hypothesis, and it appears to be true. The best evidence is from the 'litmus' test of illusory inferences (see my first chapter). Here is one example (from Johnson-Laird *et al.* 2000). Is it possible that both of the following assertions could be true about the same table at the same time:

There is a pin and/or a bolt on the table, or else a bolt and a nail on the table.
There is a bolt and a nail on the table.

If you have read the first chapter, you can probably guess that nearly everyone said, 'yes', but that the response is an illusion. We tested 128 Italian students, and all but three of them responded 'yes'. The second assertion matches the second clause of the first assertion, and so the two assertions seem consistent. Yet, suppose that the second assertion is true. It follows that both clauses of the first assertion are true. But, that is impossible, because the force of 'or else', as expressed in Italian, makes clear that when one clause is true, then the other clause is false. So, the two assertions cannot both be true: they are mutually inconsistent. We replicated the experiment using the following sort of problem:

Only one of the following assertions is true:
    The tray is heavy or elegant, or both.
    The tray is elegant and portable.
The following assertion is definitely true:
    The tray is elegant and portable.

The logic is the same, but the content is different. The participants still succumbed to the illusion. They thought that the
description of the tray was perfectly consistent, and that it was
indeed elegant and portable. Of course, if that were really true,
then both of the initial assertions would be true too, contrary to
the rubric that only one of them is true.

Knowledge often overrides compositionality (see my first
chapter), and so – as in the earlier passage about the costumier
(see p. 10) – you may fail to detect inconsistencies. Your
oversights in reading such passages are matched by the oversights
of authors. Daniel Defoe in his novel *Robinson Crusoe* has his hero
swim out naked to the wreck of his ship, and then in no time he
is stuffing his pockets with biscuits. Lady Bertram's pug in Jane
Austen's *Mansfield Park* undergoes an authorial sex change. The
literary critic John Sutherland (e.g. 1996) has compiled several
books of such inconsistencies, to which these examples are due.
It is not quite an inconsistency but, why, Sutherland asks, did
Victor Frankenstein in Mary Shelley's novel have to *construct* a
body? His aim was to reanimate the dead.

Causal Explanations

Once you have noticed an inconsistency between the consequences
of your beliefs and the way the world is, your task is to understand
what may have gone wrong. Almost always, if you succeed, you will
create a *causal* explanation. As Hume (1988 [1748]) remarked, 'All
reasonings concerning matter of fact seem to be founded on the
relation of *Cause and Effect*.' Indeed, in our everyday reasoning
causation is crucial. As an example, consider the following problem:

Tom's enemy Jerry was stabbed to death in a cinema during the
afternoon. Tom was on a train to Edinburgh when the murder
took place.
What follows?

When my former colleague Tony Anderson gave this problem to
people, they all responded: 'Tom is innocent'. Anderson said

to one group of participants: 'No, that's not so, can you think of any other possibility?' And he made the same remark to every subsequent explanation that these participants created. They created slightly more explanations than a group who was merely told: 'Yes, that's possible, can you think of any other possibilities?' Figure 3 summarizes the main explanations that people produce. They tend to start with spatial manipulations of the situation before they consider action at a distance. In general, the orders in which individuals generate their explanations are correlated. But, few people create the more ingenious cases of a robot or of a post-hypnotic suggestion for the victim to stab himself. As Figure 3 shows, the explanations were almost always causal. They explained how it was possible for Tom to have *caused* Jerry's death.

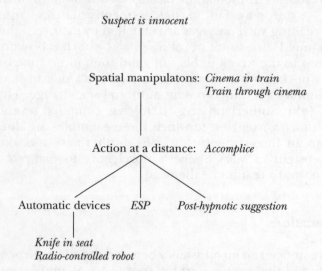

Figure 3. A summary of the explanations for the cause of the murder in the cinema.

Here is another problem for you to think about:

If a pilot falls from a plane without a parachute, the pilot dies.
This pilot did not die, however.
Why not?

Most people give causal explanations, for example, the plane was on the ground, or the pilot fell into a deep snowdrift. Only a few give a 'logical' response, pointing out that a premise is missing:

This pilot did not fall from a plane without a parachute.

People seem to prefer causal explanations over logical explanations.

Yet, there is a puzzle. When you stop to analyse 'cause', you discover – like the man on Valéry's tottering bridge (in my first chapter) – that you are not certain what it means. One consequence is a state of confusion in those domains where causal analysis matters. A prime example is causation in the law. In daily life, you blame people that cause harm; and in the law, they may be culpable either in civil or criminal actions. Two contrasting examples from case law illustrate the sort of legal confusions that are commonplace.

In the first case, nine manufacturers of guns negligently oversupplied shops in US states that have weak gun laws. Criminals came into possession of the guns and they murdered relatives of the plaintiffs. The court found that some of the gun manufacturers were the 'proximate' cause of the homicides. The expression 'proximate' cause is used in common law, but what it means is unclear. It seems not to refer to proximity in space or time, or to the most immediate cause in a chain of causes, though legal theorists have made these interpretations (see Hart & Honoré 1985: 86).

In a contrasting case, a building contractor negligently left open an unguarded lift shaft, and a young lad knowing that the lift was not there impersonated a lift attendant and invited the plaintiff to step into it. He was injured and sued the contractors. The court in this case took a traditional view: the contractors were not liable, because the causal connection was blocked by the free action of a third party, the young lad who exploited the situation created by the contractors. You may wonder why the free action of the criminals in the first case did not also block the causal connection between the gun manufacturers and the murders.

An important point lurks beneath both these cases. Neither the gun manufacturers nor the building contractor caused the unfortunate events. They merely enabled them to occur. The law of tort, however, fails to distinguish between negligence that *causes* harm and negligence that *enables* harm to occur (Johnson-Laird 1999). The result is confusion.

Why does the law neglect the difference between causing and enabling? The short answer is because of the limitations in human understanding. The long answer lies in an old argument from philosophy, which has infected both jurisprudence and psychology. The argument can be illustrated by an example about a forest fire. Together, lightning and dry timber caused the fire. It would not have happened in the absence of either. Both are individually necessary and jointly sufficient to cause the fire. Yet, people tend to speak of the lightning as the *cause* of the fire, and dry timber as the *enabling* condition that allowed the fire to occur. John Stuart Mill (1874 [1843]) therefore argued that there is no difference in meaning or logic between causes and enabling conditions. He thought that what one chooses to treat as the cause is often capricious, but he did suggest that the cause is the most recent or precipitating event.

Hart and Honoré (1985) in their magisterial review of causation and the law followed Mill. They assumed that causes and enabling conditions do not differ in meaning. They argued that the cause is the unusual factor – the lightning rather than the dry timber, or else a voluntary human action. Indeed, Girotto, Legrenzi, and Rizzo (1991) have independently discovered that voluntary human actions are the main events that reasoners seek to undo in thinking about the causes of unfortunate events. Psychologists have also followed Mill, and they too have argued that causes and enabling conditions do not differ in meaning. What distinguishes them are other factors: the cause is what is inconstant rather than constant (Cheng & Novick 1991), or what violates a norm rather than conforms to it (Kahneman & Tversky 1982; Kahneman & Miller 1986; Einhorn & Hogarth 1986), or what is conversationally relevant rather than irrelevant in explanations (Mackie 1980; Turnbull & Slugoski 1988; Hilton & Erb 1996).

All these hypotheses could be true: they are not mutually exclusive. But, they all rest on a false foundation. There *is* a difference in both meaning and logic between causes and enabling conditions (Goldvarg & Johnson-Laird 2001). When a cause *causes* an effect, one can say: 'if the cause happens the effect is bound to happen'. The claim is accordingly compatible with three possibilities:

Cause	Effect
¬ Cause	Effect
¬ Cause	¬ Effect

where there is a temporal constraint that causes do not precede their effects. Some effects have unique causes, for example scurvy is caused only by a lack of vitamin C. Other effects have

alternative causes, for example forest fires. The preceding possibilities allow that the effect may have alternative causes. Where a
cause is unique, however, there are only two possibilities:

> Cause   Effect
> ¬ Cause   ¬ Effect

When an enabling event, or 'enabler' for short, *allows* an effect
to occur, one can say: 'if the enabler happens then the effect may
happen depending on whether a cause also occurs'. The claim is
accordingly compatible with all four possibilities:

> Enabler   Effect
> Enabler   ¬ Effect
> ¬ Enabler   Effect
> ¬ Enabler   ¬ Effect

This set is tautological, that is, it is compatible with all possible
contingencies. Nevertheless, it is useful to know that the presence
of the enabler allows the effect to occur. If you do not know that
the presence of pure oxygen allows fires to burn, then an
assertion to that effect is informative. Some enablers are unique,
for example, you can only read your email online if you are
logged on to an email system. With a unique enabler, the
assertion: 'if the enabler occurs then the effect may happen', is
compatible with only three possibilities:

> Enabler   Effect
> Enabler   ¬ Effect
> ¬ Enabler   ¬ Effect

On this analysis, the assertions 'A causes C' and 'A allows C' (in
the sense of enable) differ in meaning and therefore in logic. But,
as we have seen, it can be hard to hold in mind three or more
possibilities. Individuals are much more likely to consider *mental
models* of causal relations, that is, those possibilities in which both
the antecedent A and consequent C occur:

> A   C
>   . . .

These mental models do not distinguish between causing an
event and enabling it to occur.

This account of causality is controversial. On the one hand, some theories imply that it is too strong and that causation is a probabilistic notion (see, e.g., Reichenbach 1956; Suppes 1970; Cheng 1997). Yet, the following assertion:

Lack of vitamin C *often* causes scurvy.

differs in meaning from:

Lack of vitamin C causes scurvy.

If causation were intrinsically probabilistic, however, then the two assertions would be synonymous. On the other hand, some theories imply that the present account is too weak and that causation calls for more than temporally ordered possibilities (e.g., Carnap 1966; Hart & Honoré 1985; Harré & Madden 1975; Cheng, 1997). These additional factors may be a background generalization governing specific causal claims, a causal power of some sort, or a causal mechanism. Yet, if such factors were intrinsic to the meaning of causation, then the following assertion would be a self-contradiction:

Your psychokinesis will cause the knife to stab the victim, though how it has such an effect is in principle inexplicable and does not depend on any mechanism.

This assertion may be false, but, if so, it is false as a matter of fact, not as a self-contradiction.

Eugenia Goldvarg and the present author asked individuals to list what was possible and what was impossible for a set of 25 different causal assertions (Johnson-Laird & Goldvarg 2001). The assertions included both those of the form:

A causes C

and those of the form:

A allows C.

The contents concerned matters about which the participants had no strong views, for example, 'Running the new application causes the computer to crash', and we rotated the contents over the different sorts of causal relation. Table 1 presents the percentages of responses to the two preceding sorts of assertion. As the Table shows, the participants' responses corroborated the theory. For assertions of the form, 'A allows C', they tended to list all four possibilities, or to make the unique enabling interpretation. They also showed some confusion between this assertion and a causal one – a phenomenon that is understandable if individuals focus on mental models of causal relations. For assertions of the form, 'A causes C', they listed the possibilities for the weaker or the unique causal relation. These results are contrary to claims that causes and enabling effects do not differ in meaning. They are also contrary to a probabilistic account of causation, because no event should be listed as 'impossible' given such an interpretation of 'A causes C'.

A further study showed that individuals can distinguish causes from enabling conditions when they occur in the same scenario (Goldvarg & Johnson-Laird 2001). Consider the following scenario, for example, and ask yourself which is the cause and which is the enabling condition:

Given that there is good sunlight, if a certain new fertilizer is used on poor flowers, then they grow remarkably well. However, if there is not good sunlight, poor flowers do not grow well even if the fertilizer is used on them.

	Percentages of Responses			
Listed as possible	a c a ¬c ¬a c ¬a ¬c	a c a ¬c ¬a ¬c	a c ¬a c ¬a ¬c	a c ¬a ¬c
Listed as impossible	—	¬a c	a ¬c	a ¬c ¬a c
A allows C:	55	20	25	—
A causes C:	—	—	75	10

Table 1: The percentages of responses in an experiment in which the participants listed what was possible, and what was impossible, given various sorts of causal assertion (Johnson & Goldvarg 2001). The balance of responses was idiosyncratic.

Most people judge that the fertilizer is the cause and that the sunlight is the enabling condition. Now, consider the contrasting scenario:

> Given the use of a certain new fertilizer on poor flowers, if there is good sunlight then the flowers grow remarkably well. However, if the new fertilizer is not used on poor flowers, they do not grow well even if there is good sunlight.

In this case, most people consider that the fertilizer is the enabling condition, and that the sunshine is the cause. They make these judgements even when the order of the clauses is changed so that the first entity referred to is the cause instead of the enabling condition.

The first scenario, according to a computer program implementing the theory, has the following fully explicit models:

Sunlight	Fertilizer	Grow
Sunlight	¬ Fertilizer	Grow
Sunlight	¬ Fertilizer	¬ Grow
¬ Sunlight	Fertilizer	¬ Grow
¬ Sunlight	¬ Fertilizer	¬ Grow

Hence, the sunlight and the fertilizer do not have equivalent roles. The sunlight is indeed an enabling condition that allows the fertilizer to cause the flowers' growth.

The second scenario has the following fully explicit models:

Sunlight	Fertilizer	Grow
¬ Sunlight	Fertilizer	Grow
¬ Sunlight	Fertilizer	¬ Grow
Sunlight	¬ Fertilizer	¬ Grow
¬ Sunlight	¬ Fertilizer	¬ Grow

The causal roles have been swapped around: the fertilizer is the enabling condition that allows the sunlight to cause the flowers' growth. In these scenarios, cause and enabling condition differ in meaning, and naive individuals are able to identify them reliably. This phenomenon corroborates the model theory, but it counts against the need for a mechanism in assigning causal roles in a scenario. Most individuals do not know the mechanism underlying the growth of plants. And whatever it is, it can hardly underlie the interpretations of *both* scenarios.

Are models of temporally ordered possibilities all that underlie causal relations? Consider an example suggested to us by Jonathan Evans:

> If this train goes to Paris then the next train goes to Brussels.

It refers to a temporal order between two possibilities, but does it make a causal claim? It all depends. The assertion can be clarified so that it does *not* make a causal claim:

> If this train goes to Paris then the next train goes to Brussels, but it just so happens: the one event does not cause the other.

But, it can also be clarified in another way so that it does assert a causal relation:

> If this train goes to Paris then the next train goes to Brussels, since the Paris train passes over the points and switches them.

This assertion describes a mechanism that acts as a cue to a causal interpretation. But, such a mechanism is not part of the meaning of causation. It cannot be, because it embodies further causal relations, for example, the weight of train *causes* a relay to close, which *causes* current to flow, which *causes* a motor to turn, which *causes* the points to move.

If the existence of a mechanism is not part of the meaning of a causal claim, then what does distinguish a mere correlation from a causal relation? For Hume (1988 [1748]), of course, there was no difference: constant conjunction amounted to a causal relation. For naive individuals, however, the answer appears to be *necessity*. When a conditional expresses a correlation, it is a contingent matter and one can easily envisage that it is possible for the antecedent to occur without the consequent. If the relation between the two trains just so happens, then it could equally well just not so happen. But, if the relation is causal then the occurrence of the antecedent renders the consequent necessary.

One reason that it is so difficult for all of us to analyse causal relations is that we normally rely on mental models of them. They make explicit only the cases in which the antecedent (the cause or the enabler) and the effect both occur. We realize that the cause or enabler need not occur, but we tend not to build explicit models of these possibilities. Hence, when we reason, we easily fall into fallacies. Here are two examples (from Goldvarg & Johnson-Laird 2001). Given a problem of the form:

A causes B.
B prevents C.
What follows?

most people draw the valid conclusion:

A prevents C.

They construct the following mental models of the premises:

a   b   ¬ c
             . . .

where the ellipsis denotes the possibilities in which A does not
occur. The fully explicit models of the premises show that the
conclusion is correct. Given a problem of the form:

A prevents B.
B causes C.
What follows?

most people also infer

A prevents C.

This conclusion is supported by the mental models of the
premises:

a   ¬ b
             b   c
             . . .

But, these mental models are misleading. C could have other
causes than B, and so A need not prevent C. The fully explicit
models of the premises, as constructed by the computer program,
are too much for human reasoners to hold in mind:

       a   ¬ b   c
       a   ¬ b   ¬ c
     ¬ a   b   c
     ¬ a   ¬ b   c
     ¬ a   ¬ b   ¬ c

They show, however, that in the first possibility both A and C do occur.

Not all philosophers agree with Mill that there is no difference in meaning between causes and enabling conditions. A fellow Gifford lecturer Canon Brian Hebblethwaite pointed out to the author that Thomas Aquinas distinguished their meaning. It is important for Aquinas to distinguish between what God causes and what God allows.

Conclusions

Language may limit our worlds (Wittgenstein 1922). But, all of us are also limited by an inability to understand language. My first chapter showed that one limitation follows from the principle of truth: we think about what is true when we envisage a possibility, but we have great difficulty in holding in mind what is false in that possibility. This second chapter has shown that Valéry's dictum about the understanding of words is true. We think we understand a word, such as 'cause', and as long as we keep going all is well. If we stop to analyse it, however, all is lost. In daily life, this odd phenomenon may not matter, but there are occasions in which it is important to know what we mean. The law presents many such occasions. It makes no clear-cut distinction between causes and enabling conditions. One consequence is the occurrence of inconsistent judgments in legal cases.

My two chapters have focused on human limitations in understanding natural language. Analogous problems, however, apply to human perception. The single biggest limitation on human understanding is the inability to construct correct models of causal relations. When a complex system goes wrong, its human operators are often unable to build a model of the cause, and so they are also unable to infer a cure. For example, an engine fell off an early DC-10 airliner as a result of faulty maintenance (see Perrow 1984: 137). The plane is designed to fly on the remaining two engines, but when the engine fell off it severed the cables controlling the leading edge slats, which are extended on take off to provide more lift. The slats on the wing therefore retracted. Even in this situation, it is still possible to fly the plane provided that the crew realizes what has happened. Unfortunately, the lines transmitting the warning signal on slat position were also severed. Again, if the crew had known that the warning signal was not working, they might still have been able to fly the plane. But, as Perrow notes, warning signals do not warn us that they can no longer warn us. It was impossible for the crew to construct the correct model of the situation, and so the plane stalled and crashed with the death of 273 victims.

Another failure in understanding occurs when individuals construct the *wrong* model of the situation, and stick with it despite all the evidence to the contrary. The operators at Chernobyl, for example, were convinced that the reactor was still intact after the explosion, and their difficulty in envisaging its destruction led to a delay in evacuating personnel and thus ultimately to many deaths from radiation sickness (Medvedev 1990). In an ambiguous situation, the danger is that we build the wrong model, interpret new information in the light of this model, and continue in this way until our private reality conflicts horribly with the true situation.

Yet another limitation on understanding occurs when there are too many possible models for individuals to determine which is the correct one. In less than a minute after the turbine tripped at Three Mile Island on 28 March 1979, there were more than a hundred alarm signals, many instruments had gone off their scales, and the computer printer was lagging far behind the messages waiting to be printed. It was not until two hours later that the operators were able to determine the correct model of what had happened – a pressure-operated relief valve was stuck open. The death grant leaflet described in my first chapter (see p. 25) creates the same problem: there are too many possibilities for us to hold in mind.

The basic thesis of the two chapters is that human understanding depends on the construction of mental models from perception, from imagination, and from the comprehension of language. The limits on human understanding arise from limits in these processes and from limits in 'working memory' – those components of the brain that enable individuals to hold in mind information whilst they think about it. One consequence is the principle of truth, which limits their focus to what is true, and which normally excludes what is false. The aim in comprehending discourse is to envisage the situation that it describes rather than to take to pieces the meanings of words. Hence, when such analysis is needed, it calls for a skill that humans do not naturally possess. They have therefore been confused for centuries by such concepts as causation, because their system for understanding language is not designed to reveal its meaning. The cognitive sciences, however, are beginning to help us to understand these unconscious matters. To conclude with a pertinent illusory inference, one of the following assertions is true and one of them is false:

If you had difficulty in understanding this chapter, then its basic thesis is false.
If you had no difficulty in understanding this chapter, then its basic thesis is false.

What follows?

References

Baddeley, A. (1986) *Working Memory*. Oxford: Oxford University Press.

Barrouillet, P., and Lecas, J.-F. (1999) 'Mental models in conditional reasoning and working memory', *Thinking & Reasoning*, 5: 289–302.

Bauer, M. I., and Johnson-Laird, P. N. (1993) 'How diagrams can improve reasoning', *Psychological Science*, 4: 372–8.

Carnap, R. (1966) *Philosophical Foundations of Physics*. New York: Basic Books.

Cheng, P. W. (1997) 'From covariation to causation: A causal power theory', *Psychological Review*, 104, 367–405.

Cheng, P. W., and Novick, L. R. (1991) 'Causes versus enabling conditions', *Cognition*, 40: 83–120.

Chomsky, N. (1995) *The Minimalist Program*. Cambridge, MA: MIT Press.

Conan Doyle, A. (1930) *The Complete Sherlock Holmes*, Vol. II. New York: Doubleday.

Craik, K. (1943) *The Nature of Explanation*. Cambridge: Cambridge University Press.

Einhorn, H. J., and Hogarth, R. M. (1986) 'Judging probable cause', *Psychological Bulletin*, 99: 3–19.

Garnham, A. (2001) *Mental Models and the Interpretation of Anaphora*. Hove, East Sussex: Psychology Press.

Garrod, S. C., and Sanford, A. J. (1994) 'Resolving sentences in a discourse context: How discourse representation affects language understanding', in Gernsbacher, M. A. (ed.), *Handbook of Psycholinguistics*. San Diego, CA: Academic Press: 675–98.

Girotto, V., Johnson-Laird, P. N., Legrenzi, P., and Sonino, M. (2000) 'Reasoning to consistency: How people resolve logical inconsistencies', in Garcia-Madruga, J., Carriedo, M., and Gonzalez-Labra, M. J. (eds), *Mental Models in Reasoning*. Madrid: *Universidad Nacional de Educación a Distancia*, 83–97.

Girotto, V., Legrenzi, P., and Rizzo, A. (1991) 'Event controllability in counterfactual thinking', *Acta Psychologica*, 78: 111–33.

Goldvarg, E., and Johnson-Laird, P. N. (2000) 'Illusions in modal reasoning', *Memory & Cognition*, 28, 282–94.

Goldvarg, E., and Johnson-Laird, P. N. (2001) 'Naive causality: A mental model theory of causal meaning and reasoning', *Cognitive Science*, 25: 565–610.

Harré, R., and Madden, E. H. (1975) *Causal Powers*. Oxford: Blackwell.

Hart, H. L. A., and Honoré, A. M. (1985) *Causation in the Law*. 2nd edn. Oxford: Clarendon Press. [1959]

Helmholtz, H. von (1962) 'The recent progress of the theory of vision' (trans. P. H. Pye-Smith) in Kline, M. (ed.), *Popular Scientific Lectures*. New York: Dover: 93–115.

Hilton, D. J., and Erb, H.-P. (1996) 'Mental models and causal explanation: Judgements of probable cause and explanatory relevance', *Thinking & Reasoning*, 2: 273–308.

Hume, D. (1988) *An Enquiry Concerning Human Understanding*. Ed. A. Flew; La Salle, IL: Open Court. [1748]

Johnson-Laird, P. N. (1983) *Mental Models: Towards a Cognitive Science of Language, Inference and Consciousness*. Cambridge: Cambridge University Press; Cambridge, MA: Harvard University Press.

Johnson-Laird, P. N. (1999) 'Causation, mental models, and the law', *Brooklyn Law Review*, 65: 67–103.

Johnson-Laird, P. N., and Byrne, R. M. J. (1991) *Deduction*. Hillsdale, NJ: Lawrence Erlbaum Associates.

Johnson-Laird, P. N., and Goldvarg, E. (2001) 'Models of cause and effect', Paper presented at a workshop on mental models, Brussels, 23–4 March 2001.

Johnson-Laird, P. N., Legrenzi, P., Girotto, P., and Legrenzi, M. S. (2000) 'Illusions in reasoning about consistency', *Science*, 288: 531–2.

Johnson-Laird, P. N., and Savary, F. (1996) 'Illusory inferences about probabilities', *Acta Psychologica*, 93: 69–90.

Johnson-Laird, P. N., and Savary, F. (1999) 'Illusory inferences: A novel class of erroneous deductions', *Cognition*, 71: 191–229.

Kahneman, D., and Miller, D. T. (1986) 'Norm theory:

Comparing reality to its alternative', *Psychological Review*, 93: 75–88.

Kahneman, D., and Tversky, A. (1982) 'The simulation heuristic', in Kahneman, D., Slovic, P., and Tversky, A. (eds), *Judgment under Uncertainty: Heuristics and Biases*. Cambridge: Cambridge University Press: 201–8.

Langacker, R. (1987) *Foundations of Cognitive Grammar*. Stanford, CA: Stanford University Press.

Mackie, J. L. (1980) *The Cement of the Universe: A Study in Causation*. 2nd edn. Oxford: Oxford University Press.

Medvedev, Z. A. (1990) *The Legacy of Chernobyl*. New York: W. W. Norton.

Mill, J. S. (1874) *A System of Logic, Ratiocinative and Inductive: Being a Connected View of the Principles of Evidence and the Methods of Scientific Evidence*. 8th edn. New York: Harper. [1843]

Miller, G. A. (1996) 'Contextuality', in Oakhill, J., and Garnham, A. (eds), *Mental Models in Cognitive Science*. Hove, East Sussex: Psychology Press: 1–18.

Peirce, C. S. (1992) *Reasoning and the Logic of Things: The Cambridge Conferences Lectures of 1898*. Ed. K. L. Ketner, Cambridge, MA: Harvard University Press.

Perrow, C. (1984) *Normal Accidents: Living with High-risk Technologies*. New York: Basic Books.

Reichenbach, H. (1956) *The Direction of Time*. Berkeley: University of California Press.

Schaeken, W. S., Johnson-Laird, P. N., d'Ydewalle, G. (1996) 'Mental models and temporal reasoning', *Cognition*, 60: 205–34.

Suppes, P. (1970) *A Probabilistic Theory of Causality*. Amsterdam: North-Holland.

Sutherland, J. (1996) *Is Heathcliff a Murderer? Great Puzzles in Nineteenth Century Literature*. Oxford: Oxford University Press.

Turnbull, W., and Slugoski, B. R. (1988) 'Conversational and linguistic processes in causal attribution', in Hilton, D. (ed.), *Contemporary Science and Natural Explanation: Commonsense Conceptions of Causality*. Brighton, Sussex: Harvester Press: 66–93.

Valéry, P. (1958) 'Poetry and abstract thought', in *The Collected Works of Paul Valéry*. Vol. 7. *The Art of Poetry*. Princeton: Princeton University Press. [1939]

Whitman, W. (1993) *Leaves of Grass*. New York: Modern Library. [1855]

Wittgenstein, L. (1922) *Tractatus Logico-Philosophicus.* London: Routledge & Kegan Paul.

Yang, Y., and Johnson-Laird, P. N. (2000) 'How to eliminate illusions in quantified reasoning', *Memory & Cognition*, 28: 1050–9.

Part II
The Embodied Mind, and How to Live with One

George Lakoff

3

How the Body Shapes Thought: Thinking with an All-Too-Human Brain

George Lakoff

Why It Matters

The mind isn't what we thought it was. Philosophy wasn't even close in its speculations.

For over two thousand years, philosophers have mostly viewed the mind as disembodied. The disembodied mind was not an empirical discovery, but rather a philosophical creation – an a priori philosophical doctrine that has shaped our understanding of ourselves and our world. Even the early development of cognitive science from formal logic, artificial intelligence, and generative linguistics was itself shaped by those a priori philosophical views. First-generation cognitive science was more philosophical than empirical.

But over the past two decades, something truly remarkable has happened. With the help of neuroscience and a truly empirical cognitive linguistics, cognitive science has transcended its own a priori philosophical beginnings. A new understanding of the mind has emerged, empirically based and freed from age-old philosophical baggage. The new view of mind changes everything – massively, in an almost shocking way.

The magic lamp of science has been rubbed and the genie has exchanged the old view of mind inherited from the philosophers for a new one: in the new view, thought is *largely unconscious, embodied, and metaphorical.*

Where in the old view, mind was symbolic, modelled by the algorithmic manipulation of abstract symbols, as in a digital computer or a logical deduction, thought in the new view is biological and neural, not a matter of symbols.

Where, in the old view, thought was disembodied and abstract, thought in the new view is embodied – physical in nature, with concepts precisely and exquisitely sculpted by neural circuitry that evolved to run a body: neural circuitry for vision, for bodily movement, for emotion, for empathic connection, and for functioning with a clunky physical body in a physical environment rife with peculiarities. The peculiar structures of our concepts reflect the peculiarities of our bodies, our brains, our interpersonal life, and our experiences.

Where mind was seen only as conscious in the old view, in the new view it is mostly – my guess is 95 per cent or more – *unconscious*, that is, not directly accessible to conscious introspection. We do not, and cannot, directly know our own minds. Descartes was in error. Phenomenology, which depends on conscious introspection, has real utility as a guide to mind, but it is limited to the conscious tip of the iceberg of the cognitive unconscious.

Where the old view saw thought as literal and consistent – a proper topic for logic – in the new view, thought is literal only in part. So-called 'abstract thought' is largely metaphorical, making use of the same sensory-motor system that runs the body.

The genie is out of the bottle and it's not going back in. The change from a mind that is disembodied, literal, and conscious to one that is unconscious, metaphorical, and shaped by the body is staggering and all-pervasive. Once you recognize the truth and import of these discoveries, you can't go back to believing what you used to believe.

The central philosophical ideas – Time, Events, Causation, Morality, the Self, and even Being, Truth, and Knowledge, are not what they were thought to be, namely, literal and univocal. Each is a mostly metaphorical concept, drawing on the body for its logic; and each is multivocal, defined by many, mutually inconsistent metaphors.

Causation, for example, is not just a simple, literal, univocal aspect of nature. Causation is a human concept, not an objective feature of the world. There is not one causation, but nearly two dozen, each with its own logic – and each metaphorical in a very different way. There are, of course, phenomena in the world that we can reasonably call 'causal'. But they are not all of a piece; they work by different logics; we reason about them via different metaphor systems; and it is our minds, not the external world, that make them all forms of one thing: 'causation'.

Central philosophical distinctions, like metaphysics versus epistemology, go out the window – as do other classical dichotomies: objective versus subjective, realism versus idealism, rationalism versus empiricism, Anglo-American analytic philosophy versus Continental philosophy, structuralism versus post-structuralism. In each dichotomy, both poles dissolve before the new conception of mind; each dichotomy was a mistake. The result: philosophy becomes more interesting, more challenging, and much more worthy of public attention. A new philosophy is urgently needed to keep up with the science. We have called such a philosophy 'embodied realism'.

Was Wittgenstein right that philosophy is just figuring out language games and dissolving puzzles? Or is the correspondence theory of truth right, with the consequence that there are real philosophical problems because the world has an objective structure? The answer is, 'Neither!' From the perspective of the embodied mind and embodied realism, both views make empirically incorrect assumptions. Yes, embodied realism has real philosophical insights, dealing with real philosophical problems. But the insights are new and the problems are not the old ones. Philosophy benefits, because it is taken out of old, pointless entanglements that were based on an inadequate view of mind.

Even mathematics and the philosophy of mathematics benefit from the spread of cognitive science and neuroscience throughout our intellectual life. The old romantic mythology of mathematics went like this:

> Mathematics is abstract, disembodied, and transcends the human mind, yet it is real. It has an objective, literal existence independent of any beings with minds. Indeed, mathematics structures the universe, and characterizes the very nature of rationality via mathematical logic, as well as the very nature of intelligent thought, via artificial intelligence.

It was a nice myth while it lasted, but it's not true. When we understand mathematical ideas via cognitive science, every part of the old romance goes up in smoke. Poof! Mathematics is embodied – even the idea of infinity as we shall see. Mathematics does not transcend real, embodied minds, and it is not purely literal – it is metaphorical, grounded in embodied experience. What does mathematics become? Not the measure of the universe, or of rationality, but something even *more* interesting, *more* beautiful, *more* challenging – and much *more* accessible and understandable.

A similar story holds for morality. Moral concepts too are embodied and metaphorical, and to understand this in full detail is to give up forever on the idea that there is a transcendent morality based on transcendent universal reason. After all, no part of our conceptual system is transcendent and *there is no transcendent universal reason.* There is more than one moral system that people use, and there are about two dozen fundamental metaphors for characterizing morality, metaphors that are commonplace around the world, but not consistent with each other.

For example, morality can be seen as a matter of empathy, care, and responsibilty. Or it can be see as obedience to a moral authority.

Morality can be seen as a matter of accounting, of balancing the moral books – in one of a number of ways. Suppose someone harms you. You may find it moral to balance the books by seeking restitution, having him do something good to make up for the harm. Or one can find it moral to insist on retribution (harming him back), or revenge (taking something good away from him). Or one may find it moral to forgive the moral 'debt' – to wipe it from the account books.

For some, morality is toeing the line, staying on a moral path defined by rules and not deviating from them. For others, morality is a matter of balance and fairness, of finding a middle way. Still others find morality in community, in maintaining community norms.

It is common for some to find morality in the avoidance of immorality, with immorality seen as akin to a disease, a contagion that can be contracted through contact with immoral people. The moral solution is quarantining immoral people – imprisoning them, ghettoizing them, or stigmatizing them. Or one may find morality in purity, in avoiding all taints of the immoral and in regularly purifying oneself.

Others see evil as a tangible force in the world that cannot be avoided, and find morality in discipline, in being morally strong so as to stand up to evil.

For many people, certain of these metaphors *define* what morality is. And they define morality in different, often inconsistent, ways.

Does that mean that we give up on morality as a guide for our lives? Not at all! The cognitive science of moral ideas requires us, as we shall see, to become *more* morally sensitive, *more* insightful about the nature of morality, and *more* morally responsible. Understanding the embodied metaphorical nature of moral concepts makes moral understanding that much more urgent and far more possible.

The same can – and will in the next lecture – be said of both science and religion. *The central theoretical concepts of science are not literal, disembodied, and objective.* They too are embodied and largely metaphorical. Naive scientific realism cannot work. But embodied scientific realism can, as we shall discuss. Scientific laws are not *in* the world, nor do they objectively 'fit' the world. But that does not make science one bit the less valid when we understand embodied realism. To come to grips with the embodied metaphorical nature of scientific concepts is to give a new dimension to scientific theorizing, to understand science better and to understand the world more realistically.

Finally, religion. Every conceptualization of God is metaphorical. There are three basic classes of metaphors for God and they are very different from one another. When one understands just how *all* the various conceptions of God are inescapably metaphorical, then the question 'Does God exist?' becomes a strange question: God under which metaphor? To recognize that the question is inherently metaphorical is to know that no answer can be literal. That is what makes the question strange.

Is there a 'soul' that lives on after death? Obviously, cognitive science can't say for sure, but it can say more for sure than any a priori philosophy has. Cognitive science and neuroscience can tell us what properties are embodied and therefore what properties a disembodied soul *cannot* have. When we are done with our list in Chapter 4 of what a soul cannot be, our understanding of a 'soul' will be utterly and irrevocably changed.

Is spiritual life dismissed by such understandings? No. But it is a very different conception of spiritual life than one finds in anything like the most common versions of Western religions. Spiritual life is physical, utterly of the body, of this world not any other. This is an understanding of spiritual life that is inconsistent with most traditional interpretations of Christianity, Islam, and so on, yet it is focused as much – or *more* – on spiritual and moral practice.

That is where these lectures are going, towards embodied realism as a scientific, philosophical, moral, and spiritual undertaking all of a piece, undifferentiated, characterizing a way of life.

The Story in Brief: How the Body Shapes Concepts

The science behind these lectures is well known and well documented, backed up by an extensive and profound literature in cognitive linguistics, neuroscience, cognitive anthropology, and cognitive and developmental psychology. I have done my best to survey that literature, make it accessible, and contribute to it with the help of distinguished colleagues in such works as *Philosophy in the Flesh* (with Mark Johnson; 1999), *Metaphors We Live By* (with Mark Johnson; 1980), *Where Mathematics Comes From* (with Rafael Núñez; 2000), *More Than Cool Reason* (with Mark Turner; 1989), *From Molecules to Metaphor: The Neural Theory of Language* (with Jerome Feldman; forthcoming) as well as my own books, *Women, Fire, and Dangerous Things* (1987) and *Moral Politics* (1996, 2000). For the sake of these short chapters, I will review some relevant details as briefly as I can.

Brevity is best, because the details are somewhat dull in themselves, one by one. It is only when the details are put together in a larger picture that their truly radical consequences appear.

A World Without Colour

I used to believe in the correspondence theory of truth and other verities of Anglo-American analytic philosophy. I was *raised* to believe in it. It was what my teachers told me back in the early 1960s and what all the latest books said back then. According to this theory, a sentence like 'The chair is red' is supposed to be true just in case the entity designated by 'the chair' is in the set of red things in the world.

The idea behind this theory of truth was, in its basic outlines, as follows. We start with a metaphysics: the world, at any time, is made up of objects, with properties, and with relations holding between them. Sentences of a natural language have 'referring expressions' that can designate objects, and other expressions that can designate properties and relations. Hence the expressions of a language can 'fit' the world as inherently structured.

In formal logic, the world as seen in this metaphysics is replaced by set-theoretical models. The entities in the world are modelled by the 'abstract objects' in the model; the properties of the entities in the world are modelled by sets of abstract objects in the model; and the relations between entities in the world are modelled by sets of *n*-tuples in the model. This allows one to characterize a world-state. Intensional logics then go on to talk about relations between world-states, either complete or partial.

In my own early work on generative semantics, I assumed all this. I further assumed an early cognitive theory in the early 1970s, namely, that all mental models were partial world-state models. The idea was that language, via generative semantics, could fit the mental models and that the mental models could fit the world. It was an attempt at a correspondence theory of truth with the intervening step of partial mental models taken from logic.

When I found out that this whole picture was false, I almost fell off my chair. It was the summer of 1975. I was listening to a lecture by Paul Kay on how the neurophysiology of colour vision explained the Berlin & Kay (1969) results about the meanings of colour terms. The result was this: Each language has *basic* colour terms – single morphemes that exclusively designate colour, rather than say blood or grass. The number of such terms differs from language to language, from as few as two to as many as eleven. The portion of the colour field covered by such terms may differ considerably from language to language. *But the best examples of the terms are always the same focal colours, for example, focal red or green.*

This fact was explained by research on the neurophysiology of colour vision at Berkeley by De Valois and his colleagues (De Valois & Jacobs 1968; De Valois & De Valois 1975) Colour is a function of the following factors:

1 the reflective properties of objects;
2 lighting in the given area;
3 three kinds of colour cones in the retina, responding to high, medium, and low frequencies;
4 neural circuitry connected to the cones, with neurons in the brain responding maximally to certain wavelengths as filtered by the cones.

Though there are only three kinds of colour cones, the complex neural circuitry connecting them gives rise to *four* primary colours: red, green, blue, and yellow.

Focal colours (e.g., red or blue) correspond to neural activation peaks over the circuits. Basic colours that are not primary (e.g., orange) are produced when two or more circuits are simultaneously active and when each is maximally firing given the firing of the other (or others).

This explains the universality of focal colours, regardless of the number of basic colour terms. It also explains much of the internal structure of colour categories – what counts as 'light red' or 'deep red' or 'pink'.

What we learn from all this is that colour is not out in the world. Colour arises from the interaction of two factors in the world external to us – reflected wavelengths of light and nearby lighting – and two bodily factors, namely, colour cones and the neural circuitry connected to them. Rather, colour is embodied and interactional – what Locke called 'secondary'.

One cannot merely identify colour with wavelengths. Any colour can be produced by combining three different wavelengths of light – and this can be done with different combinations of three wavelengths. What the three wavelengths can do is to activate the colour cones to different degrees. The complex neural circuitry then produces an experience of a colour.

When I learned this, it became clear that the correspondence theory of truth is false. The sentence 'The chair is red' could not be true just in case the entity designated by 'the chair' is in the set of red things in the world – because *there is no set of red things in the world* independent of our bodies and brains and perceptual systems. To me this was a shock. What I had been taught and what was generally believed in the field of semantics was not true.

Other philosophical positions were disconfirmed by this fact as well. Plato's idealist view of abstract essences cannot work for colour, since colour is embodied, tied to colour cones and neural circuitry. The embodiment of colour also ruled out certain common Continental views, for example, that meaning is subjective or arbitrary, a matter of how disembodied signs were fitted to the world. The commonalities of normal human bodies – the *same* colour cones and circuitry – ruled out the view of meaning as purely subjective. Colour is neither purely objective (out there independent of us) nor purely subjective, in the sense of being just a matter of individual experience.

Next, we learn something deep about subjective experience. Our understanding of how colour is tied to neural activation tells us nothing about the subjective experience of colour, the colour *qualia*. Knowing which circuitry produces the experience of red does not explain – or even describe – the experience of red in itself. The quality of subjective experience cannot be explained by our theories of neural activation alone. On the other hand, the quality of our subjective experience of colour *is* tied to neural activation – colour doesn't occur without neural activation and it changes systematically as the neural activation changes. In short, the quality of our subjective experience is not disembodied, not floating in air. The quality of experience is tied to neural functioning. Descartes was wrong. There is no mind–body separation.

Moreover, the meaning of colour terms is not a matter of free-floating symbols to be fitted to an external reality. Fodor is wrong as well. Functionalism – Putnam's early idea that one can study everything about the mind including concepts via abstract computation using abstract symbols – is also falsified. The meaning of colour terms is not in abstract symbols manipulated by algorithm. It requires embodiment – in the very neural circuitry linked to the colour cones. The first generation of cognitive science itself, which arose from a priori philosophy, was disproved by neuroscience. Indeed, the science suggested a new philosophy, as we shall see.

Most philosophers consider colour an exceptional case. It isn't. It is the typical case. Any concept at all must be neurally embodied. The reason is simple: we think with our physical brains. For any given concept, the question is not *whether* it is neurally embodied, but *how*.

Basic-Level Categories

Colour was just the beginning of my disillusionment with the philosophy I had been taught. In that same summer of 1975, I heard Eleanor Rosch give one of her first lectures on basic-level categories, which are mid-level categories such as *chair*, as opposed to the superordinate *furniture* or subordinate *rocking chair* – or *car* as opposed to *vehicle* or *sports car*. Rosch had demonstrated that basic-level categories have different cognitive properties than superordinate categories. They are defined by our capacities for gestalt perception, motor movement, and mental imagery. Compare *chair* and *furniture*. You can get a mental image of a chair, but not of a general piece of furniture (as opposed to a chair, bed, table or couch). You have motor schemas for interacting with chairs, but none for interacting with general pieces of furniture. In short, the basic level is the highest level at which mental imagery, motor schemas, and gestalt perception characterize the entire category and the basic level is the optimal level at which people interact with objects.

Brent Berlin has shown that, in a jungle culture where people can name over 800 plants, they are almost entirely accurate with respect to biological taxonomies at the basic level (around the 90 to 95 per cent level), but their accuracy falls by half at the next lowest level. The basic level appears to be the level at which we have evolved to function optimally in the physical environment given our sensory-motor systems. It is also the level at which we learn earlier, remember best, and know most.

The basic level, which is a reality about human conceptual systems, is not a mere reflection of external reality, but a matter of our interaction with our environments. Like colour, it is embodied and interactional. Our concept of a chair has to do, after all, with our ability to sit, which has everything to do with our bodies. It is a fundamentally embodied concept.

Image Schemas

As concepts, spatial relations present vexing problems for any serious student of the mind. Back when I was still trying to make formal logic work for natural language semantics, I was stumped by spatial relations. In English, we have concepts corresponding to prepositions like 'in', 'on', 'through', 'around', 'behind', 'in front of', 'above' and so on. Each language has a different set, with a different range of meanings. Yet in each language, such concepts have a perceptual dimension. *They link what we see with what we know.* Given a scene with one object located with respect to another, we know which spatial relations term to use, whether more than one would work, how well they work if they don't fit perfectly and what regions of space they cover. At the same time, we *reason* with spatial relations concepts, for example, we know that:

If A is in B and B is in C, then A is in C.

Moreover, we can use spatial relations to form mental images, and we can reason in terms of those images.

The dual perceptual and conceptual nature of spatial relations concepts raises the following questions:

How do you link what you see with what you know?
How can a 'concept' be 'perceptual' in nature?
How are such concepts learned, given that every language has a different set?

The first major insight came from Len Talmy, again in the summer of 1975. Talmy, looking at a wide variety of languages, made a major discovery. Spatial relations terms can be broken down into primitive spatial relations, where each language uses the same primitives, but puts them together in different ways. The central sense of English 'on', for example, uses the primitives Above, Contact, and Support. Not all languages have a complex concept corresponding to 'on', but they all have ways of expressing Above, Contact, and Support. Or take English 'into', which combines *in* and *to* in the following way: 'In' is defined relative to a Bounded Region schema; it locates an object at the interior of a bounded region. 'To' is defined relative to a dynamic Source–Path–Goal schema, and locates an entity on a path with a goal. 'Into' combines both the Bounded Region and Source–Path–Goal schemas, so that the goal is in the interior of the bounded region and the source is outside the bounded region.

Talmy also noticed that primitive image schemas fall into three types:

1 *Topological* (where relative nearness is preserved under deformations); Bounded Region is one example and a Path is another. Change their size and twist them around, and they remain bounded regions and paths.
2 *Orientational* (defined relative to bodily orientations); 'in front of' is an example.
3 *Force-dynamic* (making use of some kind of force); 'against' is an example.

In addition, each primary image schema comes with a 'trajector' and a 'landmark'. For example, in 'The car is in the garage', the garage is the landmark, relative to which the car (the trajector) is located. Further detailed research on this topic has been done by Langacker (1986, 1990, 1991), Herskovitz (1986), Brugman (1981), and others.

What is important for our purposes is that all of these are embodied, with orientations like 'in front of' defined relative to beings with fronts, and force-dynamic schemas defined relative to how muscles operate.

Talmy's insights led to decompositions of spatial relations into primitive image schemas with topological, orientation, and force-dynamic properties (see Talmy 2000). But Talmy and other cognitive linguists stopped short of explaining *how* image schemas could serve both a perceptual and conceptual function, and failed as well to answer the question: Just what *is* an image schema anyway?

Those questions were answered by Terry Regier in his celebrated book *The Human Semantic Potential* (1996). Regier realized that certain well-known neural structures and mechanisms in the visual cortex have the right structure to 'compute' image schemas with visual properties. He reasoned, for example, that topographic maps of the visual field could compute topological image schemas (e.g., Bounded Regions and Paths) and that orientation-sensitive cell-assemblies could compute orientational image schemas (e.g., 'above' and 'in front of'). Using techniques of computational neural modelling, Regier constructed a program that learns the spatial relation terms of a language and correctly names spatial relations projected on a computational model of the retina. In short, Regier came up with the only plausible hypothesis to date as to how image schemas are neurally embodied.

Regier's model shows us how it is possible for very specialized neural structures in the visual system to 'compute' primitive spatial relations that are simultaneously *per*ceptual and *con*ceptual. The model explains how it is possible for all human beings to have the same primitive image schemas, which can be combined differently in different languages. It shows us how portions of the brain that evolved earlier can be adapted to characterize concepts. Finally it shows us just how dependent our concepts are on our peculiar neuroanatomy, which we inherited through evolution. Concepts did not just arise *de novo* with human beings. Human concepts require the use of the products of nonhuman evolution, adapting aspects of the sensory motor system to a new conceptual use. In order to think using spatial relations concepts, you have to have the right kind of visual system!

Action Concepts and Verbs

Regier had shown for the first time just how it is possible for a physical system – networks of neurons in the brain – to characterize *concepts*. It was the first step in answering the question: How can a brain, which works by neurochemistry, have *ideas*? Regier's discovery began research in earnest on a neural theory of thought and language, both at Berkeley and at the University of Chicago, where Regier took up a professorship. At Berkeley, the next dramatic advance was made by David Bailey.

Bailey asked how it was possible to learn words for embodied concepts. He limited his study to verbs of hand motion. Each language has such verbs – English, for example, has 'push', 'pull', 'grasp', 'hold', 'drop', and so on. The verbs in each language cover a different range of actions. But the range depends on what the hands can do. Movement, however, is complicated. Simple movements, like opening and closing the hand or pointing the index finger, are the products of motor synergies, complex circuits that are governed by small clusters of neurons in the motor cortex. Complicated movements are orchestrations of simple motor synergies performed by the prefrontal cortex, with neural connections called 'bindings' to the synergies in the motor cortex. When you move, a prefrontal circuit fires in sequence, coordinating the simple motor synergies dynamically and with feedback. How do you learn to connect verbs to such complex circuitry in just the right way?

The crucial insight came from an unlikely place – studies of how cats move. Cats have three gaits – a strut, a trot, and a gallop. Each is governed by very different neural circuitry. But, remarkably enough, the activation of these circuits is governed by a single neural cluster. If it is firing slowly, the cat struts, if it is firing at a moderate rate, the cat trots, and if at a high rate, the cat gallops. This is called a single neural *parameter* with three values.

For his research, Bailey needed to find a body – an online virtual body. He found one on the University of Pennsylvania website. Its name was Jack. It had every virtual bone, muscle, and motor synergy. All it needed to 'move' were the complex motor schemas with bindings to the motor synergies. Bailey needed to construct computational neural models of the motor schemas and bindings, and to model neural parameterizations, that is, minimal information structures, that could control the schemas. Then he designed a neural learning model that could learn to pair the right verbs with the right parameters and parameter values and to generalize correctly. When completed, Bailey's model had learned both to provide the right verb given an action and the right action given a verb.

It was a remarkable accomplishment, but with an important theoretical bonus. We know from studies of mental imagery and of dreaming that when you imagine or dream that you are moving your body or seeing something, the same part of the brain involved in real moving and real seeing is activated. The difference is that, with dreams of movement, neural connections to the body are inhibited, and with visual imagination, inputs to the visual system come from the brain, not through the retina. Understanding what it means to move and see is thus a matter of imagination, the creation of *a neural enactment* using the same parts of the brain used to actually move and perceive.

The distinction between parameters and actual neural enactments has allowed for a Neural Theory of Language. In the theory now under development, word meaning and meaningful grammatical constructions are characterized via the pairing of neural parameters for embodied concepts with neural parameters for phonetics, linear order, and other aspects of linguistic form. The result is an embodied theory of language understanding.

But what about intentionality – the link between concepts and the world? What about abstract thought – about concepts like justice, love, morality, and causation? What about inference? What could it mean for inference to be embodied? And how is abstract reasoning embodied? What could it even mean for *abstract* concepts and reasoning to be *embodied*? To answer these questions, we need first to return to the late 1970s.

Conceptual Metaphor

Perhaps the most radical discovery that changed the theory of mind was made by Michael Reddy in 1977 and independently by me in 1978. Reddy, in his classic paper on the Conduit Metaphor (1979), showed that the very concept of communication is metaphorical. Not metaphorical according to Aristotle's theory of metaphor, which most of us learned in school. It turns out Aristotle was mistaken. What most of us learned in school as a 'definition' of metaphor is in fact a false theory.

Metaphor is not a mere matter of words, not based on similarity, not just a feature of poetic or rhetorical language, and not deviant. Rather, metaphor is conceptual, not merely linguistic. A metaphor is a systematic conceptual mapping from one conceptual domain (the source) onto another (the target). It may introduce conceptual structure. And metaphor functions primarily to allow sensory-motor reasoning to apply to subjective judgements. No concept is wholly metaphorical; there is usually some minimal conceptual skeleton in the target domain – though not enough to do much reasoning with. Most of the abstract inferences – and much of the lexicography – for abstract concepts come via metaphor.

Reddy's original example of the Conduit Metaphor is a good example. The mapping looks like this:

Ideas Are Objects.
Words Are Containers (for idea-objects).
Communication Is Sending (idea-objects in word-containers).

In the metaphor, a communicator puts idea-objects into word-containers and attempts to 'get the idea across' to her interlocutor. Communication is successful if her interlocutor 'gets' what she says. The metaphor has further details. Idea-objects don't fit into any old word-containers; there are right and wrong words for ideas, and it is up to the speaker to put her ideas in the right words. In most cases, 'the meaning is in the words'. But when a speaker is insincere, her words may be 'hollow' or 'empty'. A speaker who is trying *not* to communicate directly may 'hide her meaning' in 'dense' paragraphs. Reddy lists more than 140 such common, everyday metaphorical expressions for this one conceptual metaphor.

Eve Sweetser (1990) and Alan Schwartz (unpublished) have observed that the Conduit Metaphor is a special case of a much more general and elaborate metaphor system – The Mind As Body system (see Lakoff & Johnson 1999: ch. 12). The general mapping is as follows:

The Mind Is A Body.
Thinking Is Physical Functioning.
Ideas Are Entities (relative to which the body functions).

This general metaphor has four special cases of physical functioning: Manipulating objects, Perceiving, Moving, and Eating.

The Conduit Metaphor is a special case of Thinking As Manipulating Objects. This metaphor includes the conception of Understanding As Grasping, Teaching As Providing Students With Ideas, and includes such expressions as 'tossing ideas around', 'playing with ideas', and 'shaping a theory'.

In the special case where Thinking Is Perceiving, there are the following metaphors: Knowing Is Seeing, Coming To Know Is Observing, Understanding Is Seeing Clearly, Communicating Is Showing, and so on. This metaphor is used in expressions like: 'shedding light on the subject', 'being enlightened', 'pointing out a fact', 'a clear presentation', a murky paragraph', and so on.

Another special case is Thinking Is Moving, in which one can 'lead someone step by step through an argument', 'follow an argument' or 'get lost', 'talk in circles', 'go directly to the point', 'reach conclusions', 'skip steps in an argument', or 'zoom through a lecture'.

My favourite is Thinking Is Eating, where Ideas Are Food, Communicating Is Feeding, Accepting Is Swallowing, Understanding Is Digesting, and so on. This metaphor gives rise to such expressions as 'spoon-feeding your students', 'regurgitating information in the exam', 'letting ideas simmer for a while', and so on. French, as you might expect, has a very elaborate version of this metaphor. My favourite expression is 'aux petits oignons' (stewed with spring onions), which means a particularly exquisite idea.

These examples are clearly metaphorical. They are systematic. They involve applying the reasoning of the physical source domains to the abstract target domain. Moreover, they define a huge proportion of our modes of understanding what ideas, thought, understanding, and communication are. Try having a conversation about thinking, communicating, and understanding for ten minutes without using any of these metaphors or any of the reasoning that arises from their use. I bet you can't. Note that even when you speak of communicating an idea *to* someone, the *to* is coming from the directional path of the Conduit Metaphor, where Communication Is Sending an idea *to* someone.

Three other important metaphors for ideas are these:

- Thought Is Language, with examples like 'Do I have to spell it out for you?', 'Let me make a mental note of that', 'She's an open book to me', 'I can read her mind', 'The argument is abbreviated', 'He's reading between the lines', 'That's Greek to me', and so on.
- Thought Is Mathematical Calculation, with expressions like 'It doesn't add up', 'What does it all add up to?', 'What's the bottom line?', 'Give me an accounting of what went on', and 'We won't count that'. And finally:
- The Mind Is A Machine, including such expressions as 'I'm feeling a little rusty today', 'The wheels are really turning now', 'He's cranking out ideas', and 'He had a breakdown'.

Each of these metaphors for mind conceptualizes ideas in a somewhat different way, with different inferences. Yet they define the normal way we think of ideas and of the mind. One of the most interesting developments to come out of the theory of conceptual metaphor is the discovery of the mechanism of conceptual blending, by Gilles Fauconnier and Mark Turner (2002). In a blend, distinct conceptual structures, including metaphors, can be bound together in well-specified ways. A particularly important blend is the complex metaphor for mind that binds together the metaphors for thought as step-by-step movement, as the product of a machine, as mathematical calculation, as language, and as object manipulation. The result is the central metaphor of Artificial Intelligence, namely, that The Mind Is A Computer, a machine that thinks by doing mathematical calculation via manipulating symbols in a 'language' step-by-step. Because each of the component metaphors is a commonplace part of our conceptual system, it is easy to think of the mind as a computer. This metaphor was also the basis of first-generation cognitive science back in the 1960s and 1970s, and it is still used today.

This use of these metaphors is actually part of a more general blend – one that characterizes a major philosophical movement: Anglo-American analytic philosophy. There are many variants of Anglo-American analytic philosophy, for the most part they include certain basic tenets:

- Thought can be represented adequately without reference to the body.
- It can be modelled as the manipulation of symbols that are meaningless in themselves.
- Truth is correspondence between symbols (either words or representations of concepts) and the world.
- Meaning is literal and based on truth. Meaning is public, and shared.
- Concepts are defined as a set of necessary and sufficient conditions expressed symbolically.
- Philosophy consists in conceptual analysis.

These tenets are entailments of the set of everyday metaphors for mind that we have just described.

We can see this by looking at a collection of 17 entailments of the metaphors in this system. Entailment (1) is part of the blend because in each case ideas are mapped onto external objects in the world that exist independent of the speaker: physical objects, locations, food, linguistic symbols, numbers, and products of machines.

The Mind As Body System

(1)   Ideas have a public, objective existence independent of any thinker.

(2)   Ideas correspond to things in the world.

Thought As Motion

(3)   Rational thought is direct, deliberate, and step-by-step.

Thought As Object Manipulation

(4)   Thinking is object manipulation.

(5)   Ideas are objective. Hence, they are the same for everyone, that is, they are universal.

(6)   Communicating is sending.

(7)   The structure of an idea is the structure of an object.

(8)   Analysing ideas is taking apart objects.

Thought As Language

(9)   Thought has the properties of language.

(10) Thought is external and public.

(11) The structure of thought is accurately representable as a linear sequence of written symbols of the sort that constitute a written language.

(12) Every idea is expressible in language.

Thought As Mathematical Calculation

(13) Just as numbers can be accurately represented by sequences of written symbols, so thoughts can be adequately represented by sequences of written symbols.

(14) Just as mathematical calculation is mechanical (that is, algorithmic), so thought is.

(15) Just as there are systematic universal principles of mathematical calculation that work step-by-step, so there are systematic universal principles of reason that work step-by-step.

(16) Just as numbers and mathematics are universal, so thoughts and reason are universal.

The Mind As Machine

(17) Each complex thought has a structure imposed by mechanically putting together simple thoughts in a regular, describable, step-by-step fashion.

These 17 entailments of our everyday metaphor system for the mind characterize the central tenets of Anglo-American analytic philosophy, as Johnson and I discuss in great detail in *Philosophy in the Flesh* (1999: chs 12 and 21). That we already have these metaphors makes such a philosophy seem natural to many English speakers (though certainly not to all!).

One of the ironies about this is that Anglo-American analytic philosophy, even though it is defined by this combination of metaphorical entailments, does not – and cannot – recognize the very existence of conceptual metaphor. The reason is that concepts, in that philosophical theory, have to correspond to things in the world that exist independent of any thinker. This is a version of the correspondence theory of truth. Obviously, conceptual metaphors are aspects of human cognition. The correspondence theory of truth cannot hold for them. The idea that concepts are concepts *of* things in the world – to be defined by necessary and sufficient conditions on external reality – cannot hold for conceptual metaphors. Thus, there is a contradiction between the existence of conceptual metaphors and Anglo-American philosophy. It is no wonder then that conceptual metaphor has not found a place within Anglo-American analytic philosophy. This is especially true of formal semantics, where meanings of concepts are seen as mapping onto set-theoretical models, taken as models of an external reality assumed to consist of objects with properties and relations. Conceptual metaphors just don't fit that philosophically driven theory of semantics.

And yet, the irony is that the central tenets of the philosophy arise from our most commonplace conceptual metaphors about the mind and ideas!

Inference, Embodiment, and Intentionality

Our trip back into the 1970s gave us a glimpse into how abstract concepts and abstract reason could be embodied, namely, via conceptual metaphors with sensory-motor source domains! That's a bit oversimplified as we shall see, but it's a good approximation for now.

Our story now resumes in Berkeley in the mid-1990s. As David Bailey was modelling the learning of verbs of hand motion, he recruited the help of the student in the office next door, Srini Narayanan. Narayanan created a precise computational means of modelling all the relevant neural information needed for Bailey's task. What he did was take Petri nets, a common off-the-shelf form of AI, and extend them in important ways to do appropriately restricted neural modelling.

Narayanan then took 40 or 50 of Bailey's motor schemas and represented them in his model. As he did so, he made a remarkable discovery: *They all had the same structure!* Recall that motor schemas come in three parts: the simple motor synergies controlled by the motor cortex; the complex motor schemas in the prefrontal cortex; and bindings between the two. When the synergies and the bindings were factored out because they occurred elsewhere, what remained for prefrontal motor control were neural schemas of the same basic structure – with various options and alternatives.

That structure is simple:

1   getting into a state of readiness;
2   the initial state;
3   the starting process;
4   the main process (either instantaneous or prolonged);
5   an option to stop;
6   an option to resume;
7   an option to iterate or continue the main process;
8   a check to see if a goal has been met;
9   the finishing process;
10 the final state.

This should come as no surprise. Any high-level motor activity you undertake, from scratching your head to turning on a light switch to sipping a cup of tea, will have this structure. There are variations and complications, of course. One of these structures can be embedded in another. The structure may be encapsulated as a single simple element. There are options: purpose or no purpose, iteration or no iteration, an instantaneous or extended process, encapsulation or no encapsulation, and so on.

Narayanan presented his results at the research group run by Jerome Feldman and myself at the International Computer Science Institute. I immediately recognized that structure, as any linguist would. It is the structure of aspect in the languages of the world, the structure that linguistic systems impose to structure events. Verbs have inherent aspects: the verb 'tap' is inherently iterative and imperfective. Inherently 'tap' does not have a final state built in, while 'open' does – the state in which the object opened has become accessible, the 'open' state. Every language also has a collection of grammatical and/or morphological means to change the inherent aspect of the verb. 'Is opening' picks out the central process, 'has opened' designates a final state, and 'is about to open' designates the state of readiness.

But aspect applies to any event at all, not just bodily movements. If aspect has the same structure as all motor control, that means that we understand the structure of any event at all (no matter how 'abstract') in terms of what our bodies can do. Not only is this not strange, but there is a well-known conceptual metaphor, Events Are Actions, by which any event can be conceptualized as an action by an agent with a body. An example is 'The wind blew open the door', where the wind is conceptualized metaphorically as a living being, blowing on the door.

Importantly, aspect has a logic that is difficult to characterize and which had been worked on extensively but never fully worked out. Narayanan then asked a fateful question. Could the same neural system that could move your body also perform abstract inferences about events? Could it reason that, after France fell into a recession, it was *in* a recession, that the fall was not intentional, and so on? In other words, could the general neural motor control schema that he had found also do abstract reasoning? Could the system that controls bodily movements also reason about abstract domains that are metaphorically conceptualized in terms of bodily movements?

To test this, Narayanan turned to the theory of conceptual metaphor, where a mass of results has indicated that abstract reasoning is done in terms of sensory-motor reasoning. Narayanan took as his abstract domain the field of international economics. He then did an Internet search of the *Wall Street Journal,* the *Economist,* and the *New York Times* Business Section looking for examples of verbs expressing physical actions, for which he had a model of the neural control structure for the action. He came up with thousands of examples and chose 30 for his dissertation. These were cases such as 'France fell into a recession; pulled out by Germany', 'India stumbles in liberalization plan'.

Narayanan then constructed a neural theory of metaphor, in which conceptual metaphors *are* neural circuits linking source and target domains. His model contained three fundamental parts:

1 *Simple circuitry* characterizing the literal logical relations holding among economic concepts. These of course could not provide the right inferences for understanding the metaphorical sentences in his news stories.

2 *Motor control circuitry* for performing the bodily actions in the source domains.
3 *Metaphorical mapping circuitry*, so that the motor inferences could be mapped onto abstract economic concepts. These mappings allowed the motor inferences to combine, via metaphor, to achieve abstract reasoning that could be combined with the purely abstract economic inferences.

The model worked. It successfully characterized the inferences from the new stories. The same neural circuitry that could run a body could do abstract inference!

That doesn't mean that the brain actually works this way, but it is suggestive. The brain tends to use structure already developed and adapt it to other tasks. If it has structures that are being used for complex motor control, and if it has a neural mechanism for conceptual metaphor, linking the motor system to higher cortex, it would make sense if the motor control system together with the existing metaphorical connections actually performed the abstract reasoning rather than have essentially the same circuitry copied in a very different part of the brain.

In fact, one should be able to test this hypothesis using fMRI technology. The testing has already begun. Tim Rohrer (2001) at the UCSD cognitive science department, working with Martin Sereno and Marta Kutas, has reported a positive result in initial studies. Touching the hand activates a well-known region of motor cortex. Literal language for the hand – e.g. 'grasp', 'manipulate' – activates a subpart of the hand region of the motor cortex. And so does metaphorical language about the hand, for example: 'Can you grasp what I'm saying?' 'Don't try to manipulate me into accepting your ideas'. The first results indeed point in the direction of confirming Narayanan's hypothesis: The same neural circuitry that can move your body can do abstract inference via conceptual metaphor.

Incidentally, this evidence is the tenth type of evidence to be used to substantiate the existence of conceptual metaphor. A survey of experimental evidence from cognitive psychology appears in *The Poetics of Mind* by Raymond Gibbs (1994). Impressive recent experiments have been performed by Lera Boroditsky of the MIT cognitive and brain sciences department (2000). A survey of other evidence types is given in Lakoff and Johnson (1999: ch. 6). At this point, there can be little doubt that conceptual metaphor is cognitively real.

Primary Metaphor and the Neural Theory

In *Metaphors We Live By* (1980), Mark Johnson and I hypothesized that certain very basic conceptual metaphors arose from correlations in everyday experience. The example we gave was More Is Up, with expressions like 'The temperature is rising', 'Stock prices hit bottom', 'Thefts have soared in London', and so on. We suggested that the regular correlation of quantity with verticality, as when one creates piles or pours liquid into a glass, would result in such a metaphor.

In 1997, this hypothesis was confirmed in child language acquisition research by Christopher Johnson. In a study of the acquisition of the Knowing Is Seeing metaphor, Johnson found that children first learn literal 'see' as in 'See doggie' and 'See Daddy'. Then they learn cases which he referred to as 'conflations', where the domains of seeing and knowing are co-active, that is, where both are at issue, as in sentences like: 'See Daddy come in. See what I spilled'. Finally, children learn pure metaphorical cases such as 'See what I mean'. Johnson has argued that metaphor arises from such conflation, or neural co-activation, in everyday experience of the source and target domains of the metaphor. The cases he looked at occurred before the age of three.

Naryanan's neural model of metaphorical mappings comes with a learning theory, called 'recruitment learning', which explains Johnson's results. In recruitment learning, when neural clusters are regularly co-active, neural connections of a certain type are learned between them. As the slogan goes, 'Neurons that fire together wire together'. Narayanan's theory predicts that large numbers of simple conceptual metaphors arising from conflations should be learned in childhood, beginning before the age of three and extending after that.

Joseph Grady, also in 1997, argued on independent grounds that such was indeed the case. He has found persuasive linguistic evidence that complex metaphors of the sort described by Johnson and myself should actually be described as conceptual blends of simple metaphors that arise by conflation, what he calls 'primary metaphors'. These are well-known cases like States Are Locations, Purposes Are Destinations, Causes Are Forces, Anger Is Heat, and so on. Grady, in his 1997 dissertation, examines a wide range of such cases, pointing out that such primary metaphors appear to be widespread around the world, since most human beings experiences such conflations regularly. For example, if you want to achieve a *purpose*, it is common to have to go to a particular *destination* to do it.

Grady's research gave substance to Johnson's conflation research and Narayanan's neural recruitment model, since it showed that apparent counterexamples (apparently ungrounded complex metaphors) were actually blends and extensions of primary metaphors.

Taken together, the research by Narayanan, C. Johnson, and Grady jointly provides a neural theory of the acquisition of conceptual metaphors. The prediction is that in early childhood, say by the age of four, we should have learned hundreds of conceptual metaphors (not all of them linguistically instantiated). These should guide the formation of new abstract concepts and forms of abstract reason based on sensory-motor inference.

Mirror Neurons

The last part of our story is perhaps the most interesting. We shift scenes from Berkeley to Parma, Italy, where a group of neuroscientists led by Giovanni Rizzolatti and Vittorio Gallese made a remarkable discovery (Rizzolatti *et al.* 1996; Rizzolatti & Arbib 1998; Gallese *et al.* 1996; Fadiga *et al.* 1995). They discovered, in a study of macaque monkeys, that the same neurons in the prefrontal cortex that fire during complex motor actions also fire when the animal sees a person or another monkey doing the *same* motor action. In short, the neurons in this part of the prefrontal cortex are linked both to visual perception and motor action, *for the same motor actions.* These are called 'mirror neurons'. In a region adjacent to the mirror neurons, they found what they called 'canonical neurons'. These fire either when a complex motor action is performed *or when the animal sees an object of the kind that the action is normally performed on.* The same canonical neurons that fire when the monkey eats a banana fire when the monkey sees the banana. The mirror neurons, by contrast, fire when either the monkey eats the banana or sees another monkey eating a banana, but not just when the monkey sees a banana. This research has since been extended to human beings (Iacoboni *et al.* 1999).

Think back now to the Bailey and Narayanan research pairing verbs with neural parameters governing actions. Action verbs apply not only to one's own actions, but to the actions of others as well. But Narayanan's models were originally created only for one's own action, not actions by others. At that point, it was a problem to relate first-person experience with third-person actions. The discovery of mirror neurons linked first-person experience to third-person descriptions, since the same neural executing schema (or 'X-schema') over mirror neurons could characterize both.

Here is how this idea was seen as working technically: The neural X-schemas that Narayanan was modelling have a neural structure that can be characterized independently of its bindings to the motor synergies. Such a structure can also have bindings to schemas for visual perception as well. In short, Narayanan's models are just what would be appropriate for modelling structures over the mirror neurons and canonical neurons in human beings. With metaphorical connections added, such embodied structures can characterize abstract reasoning.

Up to now we have characterized a theory of understanding in terms of neural enactments of sensory-motor actions and perceptions, together with any metaphorical neural mappings to abstract concepts. This account left out intentionality. Mirror neurons allow us to include it. The mirror and canonical neurons connect our brains to the world we function in with our bodies. They allow us to characterize a neural theory of mind that includes intentionality – the connection of actions to objects via canonical neurons.

As we shall see in Chapter 4, mirror neurons do even more than that. The region of the brain where they occur is connected to the brain's emotional centres. It appears that such circuitry governs empathy. We know from Paul Eckman's research that configurations of facial muscles express certain emotions. Presumably, our mirror neurons fire when we see the same configurations of facial muscles on someone else that our facial muscles would make. And *that* firing can activate our own emotional centres. In short, that allows us to empathize – to feel someone else's pain or joy. We will see in Chapter 4 how this relates to an embodied moral theory. The mirror neurons and canonical neurons allow our brains to go outside ourselves. Chapter 4 will also focus on what that has to do with an embodied account of religion and spiritual experience.

Grammar from a Neural Perspective

I am a linguist, and so it should not be surprising that I am concerned with grammar. From the perspective of the Neural Theory of Language, as it is being developed at Berkeley, grammar turns out to be a system of learned neural connections between the neural parameters of our conceptual system (which is grounded in the sensory-motor system) and the neural parameters of our phonological system (also grounded in that part of the sensory-motor system concerned with phonetics or signed languages). In short, grammar consists of learned neural connections between the independently grounded conceptual and phonological systems. Grammatical constructions are thus not innate. Grammar is inherently cross-modal, rather than modular. And grammatical universals follow from (1) shared aspects of embodied conceptual systems, (2) the fact that grammar lies in conceptual–phonological links, (3) the properties of neural systems carrying out those linkages, and (4) in the way in which grammar is used in communication. This is the very opposite of what Chomsky had proposed back in the 1950s on an a priori philosophical basis.

Conclusion

The embodied metaphorical mind is a new account of mind. It comes out of research in neuroscience, cognitive linguistics, and other branches of cognitive science. It contradicts earlier philosophically based cognitive theories. It happens to share certain features with the ideas of philosophers like Merleau-Ponty and Dewey, but goes well beyond what they had envisioned. It contradicts the basic tenets of Anglo-American analytic philosophy and most of twentieth-century Continental philosophy as well.

The new view of mind calls for a new philosophy, what Mark Johnson and I have called, from the perspective of issues like truth and meaning, 'embodied realism', and what we have called 'experientialism' from the perspective of issues like morality, aesthetics, spiritual experience, and all issues pertaining to how to live one's life. Those are the issues I will take up in the next chapter, beginning with questions of consciousness, causation, and the nature of mathematics.

4
How to Live With an Embodied Mind: When Causation, Mathematics, Morality, the Soul, and God Are Essentially Metaphorical Ideas

George Lakoff

How we understand the nature of mind is all-important for a wide range of very general human concerns. Given the account of the embodied mind in Chapter 3, we are in a position to see just how important it is to understand the nature of the mind. The issues I discuss below are consciousness, the soul (if there is one), causation, the nature of mathematics and mathematical truth, why mathematics works in science, and finally morality and religion. Since I have discussed many of these matters elsewhere, I will be stressing the overall relationship among these topics within an experientialist philosophy, rather than the details of each.

The Problem of Consciousness

What has been called 'the problem of consciousness' has many dimensions. In Chapter 3, I discussed only one of those dimensions, the Neural Language Problem: How the physical brain gives rise to ideas and language – how detailed brain structures and mechanisms result in the detailed conceptual and linguistic structures that we use in drawing inferences and communicating.

What has been called 'consciousness' is not a single thing, but the confluence of many distinct phenomena. It is made up of at least the following aspects, which may well have distinct characteristics and different origins.

1 *Neural language:* The neural computational aspects of thought and language. Though unconscious in themselves, these underlie and make possible whatever conscious thought and language use occurs.
2 *Attention:* The capacity to focus on one aspect of experience rather than another.
3 *Memory:* Not only the ability to remember events, but also the capacity to use previously developed sensory-motor patterns in perception and action, what Edelman (1992) refers to as 'the remembered present'.
4 *Self-monitoring:* The ability to monitor what one is doing and thinking.
5 *First-person perspective:* The perspective of an experiencer or actor.
6 *Unity:* We know our brains compute, say, colour and shape in different places, yet we experience the colour and shape of objects in a unified way. The problem of the unity of consciousness is the problem of how the many parts of our brains produce a unified sense of experience.
7 *Mental causality:* The ability to decide to perform some action and consciously carry it out, monitoring it as one does it.
8 *Self-awareness:* The fact of sentience, of sensing what is happening.
9 *Qualitative experience, or qualia:* The way things look, sound and feel – why red looks red, not green; how a cello sounds; how a rose petal feels.

All of these aspects of consciousness are under intense study, and extraordinarily interesting research is being done on many of them. (See, especially, Crick 1994; Damasio 1999; and Edelman & Tononi 2001.)

It is an open question to what extent these phenomena are amenable to scientific study via the methods of neural computation. Francis Crick, for example, has argued plausibly that attention can be studied by such means (Crick 1994). I believe that all but two of the dimensions of consciousness can ultimately find an explanation in neural computational models. Those two, which stand outside of neural computation, are *awareness* and *qualitative experience, or qualia.* I can imagine no way in which these two aspects of consciousness could be characterized in terms of current neural computation.

Although I believe that there can be no complete neural computational theory of consciousness, there are *correlations* between aspects of consciousness and the neural underpinnings of reasoning and language use. For example, our brains create colour on the basis of neural impulses transmitted by colour cones in the retina. A great deal is known about the neural circuitry involved in colour perception. But the computational properties of those circuits do not, and cannot, account for the way that red looks and how it differs from the way that green looks. Nonetheless, there is a *correlation* between the levels of firing of certain neurons and our qualitative experience of colour. But we know that *correlation* is not *causation.* There is no causal model of how the firing of certain neurons results in our qualitative experience of red, while the firing of other neurons results in our qualitative experience of green.

I mention this for an important reason. Most people think that their thought processes are conscious, while research in cognitive science has shown that the mechanisms of thought, like the mechanisms of language, are mostly *un*conscious. Indeed, the theory we will be presenting here is a theory of unconscious conceptual and linguistic structures and processes. Our claim is that the mechanisms of thought and language are neural computational mechanisms, of which we are unaware – that is, mechanisms we are not capable of being conscious of. But if thought is unconscious, why do we have the feeling that it is conscious?

The answer, I believe, lies in the correlations between certain kinds of neural activity and corresponding qualitative experience. Take, for example, the qualitative experience of hearing sounds. A considerable amount is known about the neural activity in the auditory cortex. This neural activity correlates with something we do not understand – the qualitative experience of hearing sounds, such as speech sounds. The kind of neural computational theory given here could, in principle, give an account of the kinds of neural computations going on in the auditory cortex when we hear speech sounds. Somehow or other, in ways we do *not* understand, there is a correlation between neural activity and the qualitative – conscious – experience of hearing.

Now consider the experience of 'hearing yourself think' when no sound is actually being produced. How can you 'hear' when there is no sound? Yet we all do.

Hearing involves the activation of neurons in the auditory cortex – usually by neural connections coming from the ear. But neural activation in the auditory cortex need not originate in the ears. The activation could originate elsewhere in the brain. Imagine hearing someone mention your name. You can 'hear' your name being said, even though there is no sound. This is a product of auditory imagination. The same is true of dreaming. You can 'hear' sounds in your dreams, even though no physical sound was ever made. Auditory imagination is, of course, considerably degraded; it doesn't sound like the real thing. Yet it is clearly recognizable as an instance of the real thing.

The auditory cortex takes input not only from the ears, but also from other areas of the brain. When you speak, you are thinking using concepts expressible in language. The neural circuitry constituting the grammar of your language links the areas of the brain concerned with thought with those areas devoted to phonetics. The activation in the regions of thought flows via those grammatical circuits to the phonetic areas (speech and hearing). If we speak, we move our mouths and produce sounds. But we can also imagine speaking. Imagine saying the sentence, 'How are you?' When you do, you can 'hear' what you are imagining yourself saying. The reason appears to be that, as with the visual cortex, your auditory cortex is getting input from other areas of your brain. You are 'hearing yourself think' – that is, 'hearing' the words expressing your thoughts.

There is a qualitative experience in hearing yourself think. You can 'hear' differences in vowel quality: in your mind, say 'ah' to yourself and then say 'eeh'. You can 'hear' the qualitative differences among speech sounds – even though there is no sound. The reason is that the some of the same parts of the auditory cortex are being activated as when you actually hear the sounds with your ears. When you hear yourself think, the conscious qualitative experience of 'hearing' correlates with activation of the auditory cortex. The activation of the cortex can be modelled by neural computation; the conscious qualitative experience, which is a very different kind of thing, cannot.

I believe that the feeling we have that thought is conscious comes in large part from the conscious qualitative experience of 'hearing' activations in the auditory cortex produced when we think. It also comes from other types of conscious qualitative experience that is triggered by and correlates with thought, for example, mental imagery or motor imagery.

But we know from a wide variety of experimental evidence that thought itself – the activation of concepts and the performance of inferences – is largely unconscious, as is the activation of the corresponding phonological means to express thought. I believe, following central results in cognitive science, that thinking and the mapping of thought to the appropriate linguistic forms are unconscious and achieved via neural computation, as discussed in Chapter 3.

The Computation–Consciousness Correlation

The basic mechanisms of thought – conceptual structure, mental simulation, and inference – can be modelled using neural computation. What are beyond neural computation are awareness and qualitative experience, or *qualia.* I will call these, jointly, *qualitative awareness.* Qualitative awareness seems to occur only when there is corresponding neural activation, which *can* be modelled via neural computation. In short, neural activation may not be able to model qualitative awareness, but it *can* model when that awareness occurs. For example, a sequence of thought can be modelled via neural computation. The corresponding stream of *consciousness* cannot be modelled by neural computation, but the ordering of the corresponding neural activations can be. The same is true of inference. Inferences can be modelled by neural computation at the neural level. Our qualitative awareness of inference cannot be modelled by neural computation, though the ordering of the corresponding neural activations can be.

This means that neural computation is anything but irrelevant to consciousness. The *type* of qualitative awareness you have *is* a matter of neural computation, though qualitative awareness itself *is beyond* neural computation. Since neural computation can (in principle) model when and where neural activation occurs, and since neural activation is a prerequisite for qualitative awareness, it follows that neural computation is necessary but not sufficient for an account of qualitative awareness, and hence of consciousness.

The tight correlation between qualitative awareness and neural activity suggests strongly that *consciousness is embodied – neurally embodied,* even though the mechanism of consciousness is not neural computation alone.

The Soul

The soul is usually seen as the locus of consciousness. Consciousness appears to be embodied. But the soul, since it is supposed to live on after death, must be disembodied. There is a contradiction here.

Cognitive science cannot tell us whether or not souls exist – whether there is life for a soul after the body dies, or before it is born, as in theories of reincarnation. But the cognitive science of the embodied mind can tell us what kinds of experiences you need a body for. If there is a soul that lives after the body dies, then it cannot have those experiences and perform those actions. In short, cognitive science can tell us a lot about what a soul isn't, if souls exist at all. Suppose, for the sake of argument, we assume that souls do exist. Then we can ask, as a scientific question, 'What is a body required for?' And hence, 'What can a disembodied soul not do?'

The general argument has the following form:

> If certain peculiarities of thought and experience necessarily result from corresponding peculiarities of the way we are embodied, then they cannot be attributed to a soul conceived of as *dis*embodied.

For example, consider the question of whether the soul can see colour. Without a body, the soul has no colour cones and none of the requisite circuitry to compute colours. Since colours are not out there in the world, and since they require these parts of a body, it follows that the soul by itself cannot compute colours.

Well, what about vision? Can a soul see at all? Let's start with 3-D vision, which requires a pairing of neural inputs from the left and right retinas lined up in ocular dominance columns with corresponding left and right inputs next to each other. The information required for 3-D vision comes from the difference between left and right neural activity in such pairs. But without bodies, souls have no retinas and no corresponding neural circuitry, hence no 3-D vision.

You can see where this is going. Take any aspect of vision that is well understood via neuroscience, where certain sense organs and neural circuitry is required. Then a disembodied soul has no such bodily apparatus and so is incapable of that aspect of vision. Since a huge amount is known about the neuroscience of vision, it seems clear that the soul cannot see.

Hearing works the same way. For hearing you need an acoustic cortex, which consists of a frequency-intensity map getting input from sound-wave stimulation of the inner ear. With neither a cochlea nor an acoustic cortex, a soul cannot hear. Indeed, a soul cannot perceive at all.

But what about thinking? Could a soul think? As we saw, a body is necessary for human concepts and thought using those concepts. For spatial relations concepts, we need topographic maps of the visual field, orientation-sensitive cell assemblies, and much more. Souls could not have visual image schemas. Since a (left) prefrontal cortex is needed to characterize reasoning about events and actions, disembodied souls could not reason about events and actions. And if abstract thought mostly uses conceptual metaphors with source domains in the sensory-motor system, it follows that metaphorical thought is beyond souls. In short, reasoning as we know it using ordinary human concepts cannot be done by disembodied souls.

Could a soul empathize? As we saw in Chapter 3, empathy appears to require the mirror neurons and connections to the emotional centres of the brain. To recognize the feelings someone else has, you need to be able to see what their facial muscles are doing, sense via the mirror neurons what it would be like for your facial muscles to do that, and know, via connections to the emotional centres, what you would feel like if your face were doing that. The soul could not empathize without a body.

Could a soul be conscious? Would it have qualitative awareness, that is, awareness and qualitative experience? As we have just seen, qualitative awareness depends on, and correlates with, neural activity. With no neural activity, there is no qualitative awareness. In short, the soul, being disembodied, not only could not perceive or think, but it would have no consciousness at all.

Traditionally, it is believed that your soul, not your body, makes you who you are. Your soul characterizes your essence – your basic personality and character. However, in recent years, cases have been found of a disease called FTD, or frontotemporal disorder, where patients lose function in the right frontal and/or temporal lobes of their brains. Here are descriptions of what happens: Patients with asymmetric *right frontal* dysfunction exhibit marked behavioural alterations which include: verbal disinhibition, antisocial behaviour, loss of concern for others, and changes in previously established patterns of dress and political ideology. Those with selective *right temporal* dysfunction exhibit loss of empathy, intensification of political or religious ideas, verbal preoccupation, and blunting of emotional feelings.

Dr Bruce L. Miller, of the University of California at San Francisco, has described such cases as 'changes of self'. Who you are has everything to do with how you behave towards others, whether you are empathetic or thoughtful, whether you are discreet, whether you care what others think of you, how you dress, what your political and religious beliefs are, what your emotional reactions are. When all these can change radically and permanently because of brain degeneration, it's hard to say who 'you' really are: the 'you' before or after the brain change? If your personality and character can change because of a bodily change in the brain, and if your soul is unchanged when your body changes or dies, then the soul cannot be the locus of your personality and character. In other words, if there is no one thing that you essentially are independently of your body, then the soul could not be the locus of who you essentially are.

If we assume a soul exists and that it is disembodied, then it cannot have any of the properties that require a body. In short, the soul, if it exists:

- cannot see, hear, or otherwise perceive;
- cannot think using ordinary human concepts;
- cannot empathize with human beings;
- is not conscious;
- is not the locus of anyone's personality or character.

But these are exactly the properties that most people take as *definitional* of a soul that lives on after death. What's the point of having a 'soul' that lives on after death, but can't perceive, think, empathize, have conscious experience, and doesn't have your personality or character?

Causation

The idea of a disembodied soul as the seat of conscious thought is representative of a general denial of the body at the heart of Western culture, religion, and philosophy. The disembodied soul is sister to disembodied thought, disembodied knowledge, and disembodied truth. Once one understands the details of how thought, knowledge and truth are not just mediated by the body, but rather *shaped* by the body, our world view changes, not subtly, but massively. I turn next to causation, because it is central to issues of knowledge and truth, especially in the sciences.

One of the many great contributions of cognitive linguistics to cognitive sciences has been its concentration on the full range of conceptual and linguistic phenomena, phenomena often overlooked by cognitive psychology, philosophy, and studies in AI. Causation is a case in point. An important source of evidence comes from theories in the sciences and social sciences:

- *Causal paths and trees:* Change depends on other changes. An example is the QWERTY keyboard, first introduced in the days of the manual keyboard to keep typists from typing so fast that the keys would get stuck. Once millions of typists learned the keyboard, it was difficult to switch. Having started on the QWERTY path, there was no way to change.
- *The domino effect:* Once one country falls to communism, then the next will, and the next ... until force is applied to keep one from falling (from Vietnam War days).
- *Thresholds:* For a while there is a build-up with no effect, but once change starts, it becomes uncontrollable.
- *The plate tectonic theory of international relations:* When causal force is applied to something large, the effect lags after the action of the cause. This is used to explain the fall of communism long after the USA started putting 'pressure' on communist governments.

These are real examples, taken from the social sciences, of metaphorical causal models. Each has its own logic, taken from some other domain. They show that causal models, as really used, do not share one and only one logic; rather, there are many logics of causation – and they are metaphorical.

This is true even more dramatically of the causal concepts that we use in everyday life. Many studies of causal concepts by psychologists or philosophers just look at uses of a few words, such as 'cause' and maybe 'allow' and 'prevent'. The first cognitively serious study of causation to go beyond this was Leonard Talmy's classic paper, 'Force dynamics in language and thought' (1985), which first showed that causation is metaphorically based on our embodied use of force in everyday life. Causes Are Forces is a primary metaphor, learned automatically and unconsciously in early childhood. It lies at the centre of an elaborate metaphor system for causation, described in meticulous (if not excruciating) detail in Lakoff and Johnson's *Philosophy in the Flesh* (1999). Since I am a linguist, I'll start where linguists usually start, with some representative sentences exemplifying causation. The words in bold express causation – of one sort or another.

The noise **gave** me a headache.
The aspirin **took** it away.
The democrats **blocked** the balanced budget amendment in the senate.
FDR's leadership **brought** the country out of the depression.
The home run **threw** the crowd into a frenzy.
He **pulled** me out of my depression.
That experience **pushed** him over the edge.
The trial **thrust** O.J.'s attorneys into the limelight.
They **handed** me the job.
The democrats are trying to **derail** the republicans' legislative agenda.
The wind **blew** the door open.
Meteorites have **dug out** huge craters in the moon.
The alchemist wanted to **turn** lead **into** gold.
His political views were **shaped** by the depression.
The earthquake **held up** the project.
A rise in pressure **accompanies** a rise in temperature.
Smoking **leads to** cancer.
Cancer has been **linked to** smoking.
Russia **replaced** one government with another.
He **carried** the project to completion by himself.
They **closed the door on** a settlement.
He died **from** pneumonia.
Pressure goes up **with** temperature.
He **ingratiated himself into** the community.
Necessity is the **mother** of invention.
He went blind **after** his optic nerve was severed in the accident.
A settlement **emerged** from long discussions.
Difficulties began to **arise**.

The data **forced** me to change my theory.
Trees in a forest grow toward the sun **in order to** get the light they
   need.
They **made** a mountain **out of** a molehill.
They are trying **produce** a new theory of physics.
You reap what you **sow**.
John **killed** Bill.
John **caused** Bill to die.
John **caused** Bill pain.
John **caused** trouble.
John **had** Bill killed.
John **brought it about that** Bill died.
Her husband typed her thesis **because** he loves her.
Her husband must love her – **because** he typed her thesis.
The house caught fire **because** it was made of wood.
Billy broke the window and ran away **because** boys will be boys.

All of these sentences express causation – but the not the same
concept of causation. They do not all show the same inference
patterns. As we shall see shortly, there are nearly two dozen ways
to conceptualize causation, each with its own logic and vocabulary
– and most of them metaphoric. Here is an all-too-brief tour of
our mental resources for conceptualizing causation.

   The Causes Are Forces metaphor can be seen most readily in
the metaphorical view of Causation As Forced Motion, where
States Are (conceptualized as) Locations (that is, bounded
regions of space) and Change As Motion. For example, too many
'pressures' may 'drive you into a depression', and if you are lucky,
you may 'pull yourself out of the depression'. Here the cause
'pressures' are metaphorical forces, 'drive' and 'pull' are verbs of
forced motion, applied metaphorically: linguistic expressions
indicating forced-motion-to-locations can also be used to express
caused-changes-of-states.

   Consider the verbs of forced motion, such as 'bring', 'take',
'push', 'pull', 'propel', 'throw', 'send', 'carry', 'drive', and so on.
Via the metaphors, Causes Are Forces, States Are Location, and
Change Is Motion, they can all be used to express causation,
conceptualized as caused-change-to-a-new-state. But each verb has
a different logic. When you *bring* something, it accompanies you
and you are applying force and control the whole way. But when
you *throw* something, you apply force to an object initially and
then it moves on its own. These literal logics of force are used
metaphorically in causal sentences like 'FDR *brought* the USA out

of the depression'. Here 'FDR exerted force and control over the whole period, and the verb 'throw' cannot be substituted. Compare this with 'The home run *threw* the crowd into a frenzy'. Here the home run initiated the frenzy, which then went on by itself. You cannot substitute the word *bring*. But you can say 'The home run *brought* the crowd to its feet', if the crowd rose to its feet while the home run ball was in the air.

The point here is that the source domain inferential structures concerning literal force are preserved in the target domain of general causation. There are kinds of causation with different inference structures, which are preserved under the metaphors.

The Causes Are Forces metaphor can combine with other metaphors as well. Take the metaphors Properties Are Possessions (as in 'I *have* a headache') and Change Is Acquisition or Loss (as in 'I *got* a headache' and 'My headache *went away*'). The concept of physical giving involves applying force to an object so that it is transferred to another person, while taking involves applying force to an object so that it is transferred to you. Metaphorical giving and taking occur when Causes Are Forces combines with Properties Are Possession and Change Is Acquisition or Loss. Examples are 'The noise *gave* me a headache' and 'The aspirin *took* my headache away'.

Notice how different these two conceptualizations of causation are. In caused metaphorical motion, the object of change is the *patient* that the force is applied to and that moves, as in 'He put *me* into a dangerous position'. In caused metaphorical transfer, the object of change is the *recipient* of the giving, as in 'He gave a lot of pain to *his friends*'. And just as the conceptualization of causation is different, so the grammar is different. In both cases, we have caused metaphorical motion, and so the grammar of forced motion can be used: Verb+direct object+direction prepositional phrase. But only with caused transfer can the double object construction indicating a recipient be used: 'He gives his friends a lot of pain'.

Incidentally, the verb 'cause' is conceptually ambiguous. It can express causation as forced motion (as in 'I caused him to leave') or it can express causation as forced transfer (as in 'He caused great pain to all his friends' or 'He caused his friends pain'). Depending on which concept of causation it is expressing, 'cause' takes the appropriate grammatical construction.

This is only the tip of the iceberg. There well over a dozen other forms of causation, with different inferences, different lexical items, and different grammars. In Causation As Forced Motion, there is a path from an initial location to a new location, with a force moving you along the path. In the related Causal Path metaphor, just being on the appropriate path moving under your own steam will lead you to a result, with the path seen as the cause. Examples are 'You're *on the road to* ruin', 'If you keep *going the way you're going*, you'll become an addict', and 'Smoking *leads to* cancer'. Here prevention is getting someone or something off a causal path. Here the verb *derail* is appropriate, as in 'They're moving toward victory and will win unless we *derail* their campaign or they get *bogged down*'. A variant on the Causal Path metaphor is the Causal Source metaphor, as in 'He died *from* pneumonia'. Here there is an implied Causal Path from an initial location to a resulting location.

Causation can also be conceptualized in terms of accompaniment, as in 'Pressure increases *with* temperature' or 'An increase in pressure *accompanies* an increase in temperature'. This is the accompaniment that we find in the Forced Motion metaphor with the concept of bringing, and so it can be expressed with the verb 'bring', as in 'An increase in temperature *brought* an increase in pressure'. Of course, verbs like 'throw' or 'propel' cannot be used here. One mode of accompaniment is being tied or linked together. And so we get, 'A rise in cancer has been *linked* to mercury in fish, which has been *linked* to the mercury released into the air by coal-burning electric plants'. The concept of '*Linking*' is what we use for conceptualizing 'Causal Chains'.

When causation results in a change of form, we conceptualize it via Causes Are Forces, where States Are Shapes. Examples include '*reshaping* the bureaucracy', '*reforming* politics', and so on. When causation results in a new entity, we use creation concepts, such as '*forging* a new alliance', or progeneration concepts, as in 'The Internet *gave birth to* a new era of commerce'.

In the theory of essences, essences are taken to be the causal source of natural behaviour. There is a folk version of this philosophical theory, which shows up in sentences like 'He broke the window and ran away, *because boys will be boys*', or 'The house caught fire *because it was made of wood*'.

Here is how all these apparently disparate metaphors hang together. The primary metaphor Causes Are Forces is at the centre of the system. It applies to cases of forced motion, forced transfer, and forced change of shape. In the *bringing* cases of Forced Motion, the causal force correlates with accompaniment along a causal path from a source to a resulting location. These overlaps provide conceptual links from Causes Are Forces to

Causal Paths, Causal Sources, Causal Links, and Causal Accompaniment, which is a version of Causes Are Correlations. The Causal Theory of Essences is an extension of Causes are Sources, a natural state (an essence) is a location on a Causal Path, where Nature is itself a force – an overwhelming force.

Finally, there are literal cases of various kinds, in which causation is characterized as having various degrees of directness of causal connection. In 'John *killed* Bill', the cause is direct, with cause and result as part of one event. In 'John *caused* Bill to die', the cause and the result are conceptualized as different events. In 'John *had* Bill killed', John is the ultimate cause, but there is an intermediate cause who performed the murder. In 'John *brought it about* that Bill died,' the cause is very indirect and not only a separate, but a distant event. This is expressed iconically in the grammar of English: The more direct the cause, the closer the result is to the cause in the sentence.

I will stop here. Chapter 11 of *Philosophy in the Flesh* has a great deal more detail.

There are several morals to these examples.

- We do not have a single concept of causation, but many, each with a different inference structure.
- The wide range of causal concepts and their inferences arises via metaphor.
- The central metaphor is Causes Are Forces. It combines with other metaphors to yield metaphorically complex causation concepts.
- Causation is embodied, via the exertion of force in everyday experience.
- There is no disembodied concept of causation with a single collection of inferences out there in the world.
- The world has many different patterns of occurrences. We call a large class of them instances of 'causation' because of the relationships we see with the way forces work.

What makes all these different concepts with different logics all cases of one thing? There appear to be two necessary conditions that follow from the Causes Are Forces metaphor. These conditions are:

1 The result cannot precede the cause. Under Causes Are Forces, this follows from the fact that forced motion cannot precede the application of the force.

2 The result would not have occurred without the cause. Under Causes Are Forces, this follows from the fact that forced motion does not occur without a force.

These two conditions define what Johnson and I call 'a determining factor for a situation'. This is a necessary condition for causation: everything we conceptualize as a cause is a 'determining factor for a situation' in this sense.

But though this is a necessary condition, it is not sufficient. We can see this in cases like the following, which are not cases of causation.

His birth caused his death.
His marriage caused his divorce.
His taking the course caused his failure in it.

In each of these cases, there is a necessary condition that is not a cause. Birth is necessary for death but doesn't cause it, marriage is necessary for divorce but doesn't cause it. Thus, counter to the analyses of Lauri Kartunnen in terms of inference patterns and Richard Stalnaker (1968) and David Lewis (1973), in terms of model theory, these conditions do not define an abstract logical notion of causation, but only characterize necessary conditions. However, they are necessary conditions for all the concepts, including metaphorical concepts, that we understand as causal. It is these necessary but not sufficient conditions that conceptually tie together all the very different concepts that we understand as 'causal'.

In my earlier career in generative semantics and logic, I introduced a fateful notation: CAUSE in capital letters. I assumed that there was a single abstract general concept of causation with a single logic. I also assumed that causation as a single unified phenomenon, with a single inference pattern, existed in the world and fitted the causal expressions in human language.

I was mistaken. The world contains lots of patterns. There is no single one that corresponds to all the situations we conceptualize as causal. *We, because of the embodied metaphorical character of our minds, create the unified concept of causation.* It is not just out there in the world.

This is a stunning discovery: it destroys the metaphysical realism that we were brought up to cherish – the idea of causation as a single objective structure or pattern in the world. From now on, we must always ask which of the two dozen or so metaphorical concepts of causation is being used in a theory and which detailed logic of causation is inherited from embodied experience via those metaphors.

Anytime you hear the simple word 'causation' you should ask, 'Which one?' Anytime you hear a philosopher or psychologist claim to have found the one true causation, you should confront her with these examples.

Mathematics is Embodied and Metaphorical

The disembodied view of mind in Western thought has led to the idea of mathematics as disembodied. Indeed, a mythology has arisen around mathematics, a mythology that Núñez and I call The Romance of Mathematics:

The Romance
1 Mathematics is abstract and disembodied – yet it is real.
2 Mathematics has an objective existence, providing structure to this universe and any possible universe independent of, and transcending, the existence of human beings or any beings at all.
3 Human mathematics is just a subpart of abstract, transcendent mathematics.
4 **Hence, mathematical proof allows us to discover transcendent truths of the universe**.
5 Mathematics is part of the physical universe and provides rational structure to it. There are Fibonacci series *in* flowers, logarithmic spirals *in* snails, fractals *in* mountain ranges, parabolas *in* home runs, and π *in* the spherical shape of stars and planets and even bubbles.
6 Mathematics even characterizes logic, and hence structures reason itself – any form of reason by any possible being.
7 **To learn mathematics is therefore to learn the language of nature, a mode of thought that would have to be shared by any highly intelligent beings anywhere in the universe**.
8 Because mathematics is disembodied and reason is a form of mathematical logic, reason itself is disembodied. Hence, machines can, in principle, think.

Núñez and I, in *Where Mathematics Comes From* (2000) have argued in great detail that this Romance is false in every way. Instead, mathematics, like other products of the human mind, is embodied and mostly metaphorical. Along the way, we provide a cognitive theory of mathematic ideas for advanced mathematics, and show how so-called 'abstract' ideas from higher mathematics are ultimately grounded in bodily experience and extended via conceptual metaphor.

Our argument begins with baby arithmetic, the small but real arithmetic capacities of newborns:

- the ability to subitize up to 4 objects – to distinguish 1 from 2 from 3 from 4 objects;
- the ability to do implicit baby arithmetic up to 4 – the ability to tell that if one object is present and you add one object, there should be two objects, not three, and so on.

This is determined in experiments that measure sucking rates and staring by babies in what is called the 'violation-of-expectation paradigm'. There are normal sucking rates and normal scanning patterns. Suppose a baby is presented with a stage with one puppet on it. The curtain then comes down and the mother shows the baby a second puppet and puts it behind the screen. The curtain goes up. If there are two puppets, the sucking rate and scanning pattern remain normal. But if there are *three* puppets, the sucking rate goes up noticeably and the baby stares at the stage (Wynn, 1992).

In short, such limited capacities seem to be part of the brain's neural circuitry at birth. The question we asked was how such limited baby arithmetic expanded into full-blown arithmetical concepts including laws of arithmetic. The mechanism, we argue, is metaphor. There are four basic metaphors for arithmetic that arise through normal everyday functioning:

1 The Object Collection metaphor, in which addition is adding objects to a collection and subtraction is taking them away.
2 The Object Construction metaphor, in which addition is putting objects together to form larger objects.
3 The Measuring Stick metaphor, in which sticks of the same size are laid out in a line to measure length.
4 The Motion Metaphor, in which addition is taking steps in a given direction, and subtraction is taking steps in the opposite direction.

These are primary metaphors that arise via conflation. For example, as a child puts objects in a container, she performs baby arithmetic on them and subitizes them. The same for, say, taking steps in a direction. The conflation of these activities results in neural co-activation, which in turn results in the recruitment of neural connections. These neural connections are the physical mechanism by which metaphorical mapping is accomplished. When the metaphorical mappings are spelled out in detail, the Laws of Arithmetic turn out to be entailments of the mappings. For example, the law

$$a + b = b + a$$

follows from the physical fact that you get the same number of objects in a container no matter what order you put them in.

Later, symbolic mappings are learned – mappings that link concepts to symbols and rules of symbolic computation to metaphorical inferences. Since conceptual metaphors preserve inference, the algorithmic rules of computation will always work.

What comes out of all this is a cognitive theory of arithmetic: how it extends from baby arithmetic to arithmetic laws; how the laws arise; what symbolization is; and why algorithms work. Included is a cognitive account of why

$$-1 \times -1 = +1.$$

We go on to classes, sets, and logic. We show how the idea of a class is grounded in container image schemas and how the logic of classes is the logic of container schemas under the metaphor that A Class Is A Container-Schema. We then describe Boole's metaphor for the algebra of classes in detail, in which he introduced the metaphorical mapping that creates the empty set from zero and the universal set from one. And we show how prepositional logic arises from a simple basic metaphor, namely, Propositions Are Classes Of World-States.

The point of all this is to demonstrate that formal logic is a cognitive construction and to show the detailed cognitive mechanisms by which logic is put together. Along the way we show that some of the stranger parts of set theory and logic arise from Boole's metaphor. For example, via Boole's metaphor which maps zero into the empty set, the arithmetic truth

$$0 \times n = 0$$

maps onto the metaphorical statement 'the empty class is a subclass of every class', and that statement in turn maps onto the strange statement 'every proposition follows from a contradiction'. Thus, 'the empty class is a subclass of every class' and 'every proposition follows from a contradiction' are not part of the logic of the universe, but rather are strange metaphorical inferences following from Boole's metaphor.

The heart of the book is our study of infinity. There we take up the question, 'How is it possible for a human being with a finite mind to comprehend infinity?' The answer again comes via metaphor.

There are two kinds of infinity – 'potential infinity' and 'actual infinity'. Potential infinity is open-ended. You just start counting and keep on counting indefinitely. You start making a line segment longer, and you go on making it longer and longer indefinitely. You compute a number, say pi, to n decimal places, and then n+1, and then on and on indefinitely.

Actual infinity is a different matter. You don't just keep counting and counting. You *achieve* the collection of *all* natural numbers, an infinity of them. You don't just keep extending the line longer and longer. You *reach* the point at infinity where all parallel lines meet in projective geometry. You don't just keep getting more and more decimal places for pi without reaching pi. Instead, you *reach* pi by getting the infinity of decimal places, all of them. This is actual infinity. This is the concept of infinity that is interesting in mathematics and on which a huge amount of mathematics rests.

The question is, how can a finite being conceptualize and reason about actual infinity in all its forms – infinite sets, points at infinity, infinite decimals, transfinite numbers, infinitesimal numbers, limits, least upper bounds, and so on?

The answer begins with aspect in linguistics. As we saw in Chapter 3, Srini Narayanan's computational neural model of motor control characterizes the conceptual structure of aspect. Cases of potential infinity fit what, in linguistics, is called 'iterative imperfective aspect': There is an initial state, then perhaps a starting action, then a repeated central action that goes on and on indefinitely, without end. An example would be counting by ones without stopping: 1, 2, 3, ... and forming sets of numbers as you go along: {1}, {1, 2}, {1, 2, 3}, ...

Compare this with an 'iterative completive aspect': There is an initial state, then perhaps a starting action, then a repeated central action that goes on for a finite number of iterations, then stops, resulting in a final state. An example would be counting by ones forming sets as you go along and stopping at ten, with the set of the first ten integers.

Let us now construct the following metaphor:

- The target domain is an iterative imperfective action: It has an initial state, a starting action, and a central action that iterates.
- The source domain is the corresponding iterative completive action: It has the same initial state, the same starting action, the same central action that iterates, and a final state (reached after some finite number of iterations).
- The metaphor maps the initial state to the initial state, the starting action to the starting action, and the iterated central action to the iterated central action.
- In addition, the metaphor maps the source domain final state onto a corresponding final state in the target domain, *creating a target domain final state via the metaphor.*

This last step, which adds a metaphorical final state to cases of potential infinity, produces *actual* infinity – infinity as a *thing*, an *entity*. Moreover, this mapping also imposes certain source domain inferences on the target domain. In the source domain, the final state comes after all the earlier states, and it is the *first* state that comes after all the earlier states. The metaphorical mapping imposes this inferential structure on the target domain, with the result that the final state of actual infinity comes after all earlier states and is the *first* state to come after all earlier states. These inferences characterize crucial properties of actual infinity.

Núñez and I call this metaphor The Basic Metaphor of Infinity. It is fully general, and need not be about mathematics at all. It has an open-ended number of special cases, in which the initial state, the starting action, and the iterated central action can be spelled out in detail.

Note that the concept of actual infinity is *not literal.* The target domain has no literal connection between the earlier cases that go on without end and the final state of actual infinity. The connection between the open-ended cases of potential infinity and the final state of actual infinity is not made in the target domain. The connection is made in the source domain and projected via the metaphor.

Núñez and I show how this metaphor, when fleshed out with the right special cases, characterizes a wide range of the cases of infinity in various subject matters. For example, here's how we would characterize the set of all natural numbers:

Let the initial state be the empty set.
The starting action is to produce the number 1 and form a union of the set containing 1 with the empty set.
The iterated central action is add 1 to the previously produced number and form that union of the set containing that number with the previously formed sets.
The final state is the set of *all* natural numbers.

In this special case, the fact that the final state comes after all the other states has as a special case the fact that all the previously formed sets are subsets of the set at the final state, and this is the smallest such set. This is the infinite set of *all* the natural numbers.

Now take the example of the point at infinity in projective geometry:

Let the initial state be an isosceles triangle, ABC, with AC = BC.
Let the starting action be to double the length of AC and BC.
Let the iterative action be to take the previous length of AC and BC and double it.

After each iteration, the angles CAB and CBA are closer to 90° than after the previous iteration.

At the final state, we still have an isosceles triangle, ABC, with AC = BC. AC and BC are infinitely long. C is therefore a point 'at infinity'. Angles CAB and CBA are 90°. AC and BC are thus parallel lines that meet at infinity, point C. Since the distance AB and the orientation of the triangle were arbitrarily chosen, the initial state of this instance of the metaphor fits all isosceles triangles, and in the final state, *all* parallel lines meet at infinity.

In our book, we go through many other cases: inversive geometry, mathematical induction, limits, infinite sums, least upper bounds, transfinite cardinals and ordinals, and infinitesimals. The Basic Metaphor of Infinity is precisely stated, as are each of the special cases. The result is a precise cognitive account of actual infinity for a wide range of cases in mathematics. Among those cases are four different kinds of infinite numbers.

There are two morals here:

1 Actual infinity is an embodied metaphorical human concept. It has to do with human motor control and the human concept of aspect, as well as conceptual metaphor.

2 Actual infinity is not a 'thing' in the world, nor are infinite numbers, nor are other mathematical entities.

In the last four chapters of our book we work out the metaphorical structure of Euler's classic equation:

$$e^{\pi i} + 1 = 0.$$

We show what this equation means and why its truth follows from what it means, in full detail, and in the process we set out a theory of mathematical ideas. What we learn from this is that mathematical concepts are embodied, just like other concepts. So-called 'abstract' mathematics arises by conceptual metaphor and/or conceptual blends – the basic cognitive mechanisms underlying abstract concepts in general.

What we show in detail throughout the book is that the Romance of Mathematics that we started with is false in every detail. Mathematics is not objectively true. Mathematics is not out there in the world structuring the universe. There are no parabolas out there in Barry Bonds' home runs, no logarithmic spirals in snails, no Fibonacci series in flowers. Mathematical logic is not out there providing a rational structure to the universe. Mathematics – including mathematical logic – comes out of us.

Why can mathematics work in the sciences? Not because it is out there structuring the laws of nature. Instead, mathematics, via its metaphors and conceptual blends, expresses ideas, many of them ordinary everyday concepts – concepts such as change, proportion, size, inverse, change in inverse proportion to size, and so on. There is a mathematics of change, a mathematics of proportion, a mathematics of change in inverse proportion to size.

Scientists are careful observers of the world and categorize phenomena in terms of ordinary everyday concepts such as change, proportion, size, inverse, change in inverse proportion to size, and so on. Careful scientists use their concepts to categorize physical phenomena and they use the mathematics appropriate to those concepts to do their calculations.

There is nothing mysterious here. The fit between mathematics and the physical world comes in the minds of scientists.

Morality

Kant was wrong about morality – very wrong. Morality cannot follow from universal transcendent reason, because there is no universal transcendent reason. Reason is not transcendent; it comes out of our embodied experience.

To understand what is meant by morality, we must begin empirically. How do people conceptualize morality? What are the conceptual metaphors through which morality is understood? What is the cognitive structure of a moral system? These are the empirical questions. Moral questions arise only after these are answered.

The conceptual structure of morality, so far as Mark Johnson and I have been able to discern, comes in the following parts:

- A collection of primary metaphors for morality that are widespread around the world.
- Moral systems, based metaphorically on models of the family and of childrearing, that organize the primary metaphors and assign them priorities.
- Interactions with other commonplace metaphors.

Let us begin with the primary metaphors for morality.

Morality is fundamentally about well-being and human flourishing. There are certain common correlations between well-being and ordinary experiences that give rise to primary metaphors for morality. Those correlations and the primary metaphors they give rise to are as follows:

- It is better to be strong than to be weak.
- Morality Is Strength; Immorality Is Weakness.

- It is better to be healthy than to be sick.
- Morality is Health; Immorality Is Disease.

- It is better to have possessions you need than not to have them.
- Well-being Is Wealth.

- It is better if debts are paid than if they aren't.
- Morality Is Accounting (Balancing The Moral Books).

- It is better to be able to stand upright than not to be able to.
- Moral is Up; Immoral Is Down.

- It is better to function in the light than in the dark.
- Morality Is Light; Immorality Is Darkness.

- It is better to be clean than to be dirty.
- Morality Is Cleanliness; Immorality Is Filth.

- It is better to have pure food than rotten food.
- Morality is Purity; Immorality Is Rottenness.

- It is better to be cared about than not cared about.
- Morality Is Empathy; Immorality Is Not Caring.

- Beauty is better than Ugliness.
- Morality Is Beauty; Immorality Is Ugliness.

- It is better to be whole than not to be.
- Morality Is Wholeness; Immorality Is Degeneration.

- It is better to be nurtured than to be neglected.
- Morality Is Nurturance; Immorality Is Neglect.

- It is better to be accepted by a community than not to be.
- Morality Is Community Acceptance.

- Fair treatment is better than unfair treatment.
- Morality Is Fairness.

- It is better to obey your parents than not to.
- Morality Is Obedience; Immorality Is Disobedience.

- It is better to stay where people are than to stray.
- Morality Is Staying within Boundaries; Immorality Is Transgressing.
- Morality Is Staying on a Path; Immorality Is Straying From The Path.

- It is better if moral people have power than if immoral people do.
- The Moral Order: Morality Is Preserving Traditional Power Relations.

- It is better for people to be good by nature than not to be.
- Moral Essence: Morality Is Character (or Virtue).

For the most part, these should be obvious. A few need further explication.

Well-being Is Wealth combines naturally with Morality Is Accounting. If you do something good for me, then I am 'in your *debt*' and may ask 'How can I ever *repay* you?' or say 'I *owe* you one'. If you do something bad to me, then you owe me, since by metaphorical moral arithmetic, giving something bad is the equivalent to taking something good. In this case, the moral books can be balanced in various ways. (1) Restitution: You do something equally good to make up for it. (2) Retribution: I do something bad to you. (3) Revenge: I take something good from you. (4) Forgiveness: I cancel the debt. Our notion of justice is a form of moral accounting.

Moral Essence is the basis of virtue ethics: Those who are good by nature or are raised to be virtuous, will have 'character' and will act morally.

The Moral Order is a conservative metaphor: It says that traditional hierarchies of power were there for good reason and should be maintained. American conservatives have a moral hierarchy that includes: God over Man; Man over Nature; Adults over Children; America over Other Countries; Western Culture over Other Cultures – and in more extreme cases the hierarchy extends to: The Wealthy over the Poor; Men over Women; Whites over Non-whites; Straights over Gays; and Christians over Non-Christians.

These primary metaphors for morality are widespread around the world. One can find versions of them in many cultures. But each is isolated. Among the things that allow them to fit together into a moral system are, interestingly enough, models of the family. In *Moral Politics* (1996/2002), I discovered that major political ideologies in America (and perhaps elsewhere) are based on ideal models of family life, and that such family-based models commonly give structure to moral systems by giving priorities to primary metaphors for morality.

The major family models I have investigated to date are the Strict Father model, which is the basis of conservative morality and politics, and the Nurturant Parent model, which is the basis of progressive morality and politics.

The Strict Father Model

Assumptions: The world is dangerous and children are naturally bad. The father's job is to protect and support the family. He is the moral authority. He teaches his children right from wrong, which are taken to be absolute. The child's job is to obey. Punishment is required to balance the moral books. The father's moral duty is to physically punish his children when they do wrong, assuming physical discipline in childhood will develop the internal discipline adults need to be moral people and to succeed. Children are to become self-reliant through discipline and the pursuit of self-interest. When children are mature, they are on their own and parents are not to meddle in their lives.

In this model 'character' means moral strength. Moral weakness or dependency is seen as a sign of lack of discipline and the inability to lead a moral, self-reliant life. The Moral Order makes sense here, since worldly power is a reflection of the discipline needed to lead a moral life.

This family model can be applied metaphorically so that other figures can become the moral authorities. In a common model, it is the Church that becomes the moral authority. Kantian morality is based on the metaphor of Universal Reason As The Strict Father who tells you what is right and wrong and whom you are to obey. Kant thus places moral authority in each of us, while keeping an absolute right and wrong.

The major metaphors for morality that tend to accrue to this model are Morality As Strength, Obedience, Staying Within Boundaries, Retribution, Purity, Cleanliness, Uprightness, Health, Wholeness, and the Moral Order.

The Nurturant Parent Model

Assumptions: Both parents are equally responsible for running the household and raising the children. Their job is to nurture their children and raise their children to be nurturers. To be a nurturer you have to be empathetic and responsible (for oneself and others). Responsibility implies competence, education, hard work, protection, and social connectedness. Empathy requires (1) fairness, (2) open, two-way communication, (3) a happy, fulfilled life (unhappy people are less like to want others to be happy), and (4) restitution rather than retribution to balance the moral books. To promote happiness and fulfilment, aesthetics is important. In the place of specific strict rules, there is a general ethics of care that says: Help, Don't Harm. To be of good character is to be empathetic and responsible.

The major metaphors for morality that tend to accrue to this model are Morality As Empathy, Nurturance, Connection To Others, Fairness, Light, and Beauty.

Strictness and Nurturance are two fundamentally different approaches to morality. Different people may even take them as defining what morality is. Many of the most basic moral issues in Western society come down to issues of strictness versus nurturance. The gap between these approaches appears to be irreconcilable.

Strict Morality comes with four requirements on the human mind and language:

1 *Strict categorization*: Everything is either in or out of a category.
2 *Literalness*: Moral rules, and criteria for determining whether they are followed, must be literal.
3 *Perfect communication*: Moral rules are assumed to be clearly understandable.
4 *Folk behaviourism*: People normally act so as to get rewards and avoid punishment.

We know from cognitive science (especially cognitive linguistics) that all four of these are false. The mind and language just don't work that way. Strict morality is simply incompatible with what we have learned about the embodied mind.

The study of the embodied mind and metaphorical thought have a great deal to tell us about morality and ethics. First, they allow us to gain insight into what morality and ethics are taken to mean. Second, they place cognitive constraints on moral action. A view of what human beings should do that is fundamentally at odds with the nature of the human mind and language is so out of touch with reality that it must be rejected. Nurturant morality, on the other hand, is consistent with what is known about the mind and language. It is at least a candidate for a viable approach to moral action.

Religion

All religion has a moral dimension. The major religions in the West – Judaism, Islam, and Christianity – have both strict and nurturant versions. My 1996 book *Moral Politics* contains a description of both versions of Christianity. The Torah and Talmud contain both approaches, though most American Jews today tend towards the nurturant approach. Fundamentalists in all religions, of course, take the strict approach; an ideological commitment to strict morality is what makes them fundamentalists. Religious disputes in the West often centre on strictness versus nurturance. To understand any approach to religion, you need to understand the conceptual structure of its approach to morality. Cognitive science can be quite useful here.

Does God Exist?

The following story is told of the great intellectual historian, A. O. Lovejoy. He was being considered for the presidency of Johns Hopkins University. At his interview, a member of the Board of Trustees asked him if he believed in God. His response was, 'Which one?' and he reeled off a hundred conceptions of God.

It does seem sensible to understand a question before trying to answer it. Since God is presumably ineffable, God can only be approached through metaphor. All understandings of God make use of metaphor.

I have been looking at metaphorical conceptions of God, and so far I have found three major types.

1. *God As Parent, or as having parent-like qualities:* Eve Sweetser, in her study of the Yom Kippur liturgy, found that the conceptions of God explicitly given there formed a radial category with God As Father in the centre. The properties of a parent are (a) a powerful authority figure; (b) someone who loves you; (c) someone to whom you owe your existence; (d) a protector and guide; (e) someone who prescribes and judges your behaviour; (f) the source of life; and (g) someone who has chosen to bring you into the world and take care of you – a chooser. The metaphors are: God As (a) King, Lord; (b) Lover; (c) Creator, Potter, Jeweller; (d) Shepherd; (e) Lawgiver, Judge; (f) Breath (the source of life); and (g) the Chooser of the Chosen People.

2. *God As The Infinite:* The Basic Metaphor of Infinity is not just about mathematics. It has many special cases. It is commonly used to conceptualize God as infinite. Special cases include: God as (a) All-Seeing; (b) All-Knowing; (c) All-Powerful; (d) All-Good; and (e) the First Cause.

3. *God As Immanent:* The Kabbalah says: 'Do not say, "This is a stone and not God." God forbid! Rather all existence is God and the stone is a thing pervaded by divinity.' The idea that *God is all of existence* is also central to the traditions of pantheism and naturalism in Christianity. It has the consequence that empathic projection onto anything and anyone is contact with God.

My friend, Zoketsu Norman Fischer, former Abbot of the San Francisco Zen Center, has pointed out to me that there is a generalization across these three metaphors. All of them are attempts to connect with what is outside and beyond you. His point is that that is what religion and spiritual life in general are about.

Suppose, like Lovejoy, I were asked, 'Do you believe in God?' Knowing that one can only conceptualize God via metaphor, I would go through the list, metaphor by metaphor. 'God as Father, King, Jeweller, Shepherd...' I can understand the appeal of the personification metaphors, but I can't bring myself to believe those metaphors as if they were literally true. Moreover, it's hard to believe that anyone really takes them literally, really believes that God Is Daddy! It is hard to believe that anyone takes 'The Lord Is My Shepherd' as literally true; after all, that would make you a sheep – literally, with wool and eating grass. It is taken as a metaphor.

Next, God As The Infinite. Understanding the Basic Metaphor of Infinity, I fully appreciate the beauty and preciousness of actual infinity as an idea. But I cannot take actual infinity as an objectively existing thing in the world.

Finally, God As What Exists – the world as it is. Well, what exists exists. Metaphor number 3 has a lot going for it. It makes the world sacred. I do believe the world is sacred. Metaphor 3 comes with an appropriate morality: nurturant morality, which is structured around empathy and responsibility. Empathy is a neural matter, arising from the ability of mirror neurons to allow you feel what others feel, to connect you to others and to the world.

Do I have a soul separate from my body? Given that it couldn't perceive, think, be conscious, empathize, or have my personality or character, I wouldn't want to call it a 'soul' even if it did exist.

What about spiritual experience? During meditation practice, I have what I would call spiritual experience. But, as James H. Austin argues in *Zen and the Brain* (1999), spiritual experience is a form of physical experience. There is nothing unscientific about it. It is quite bodily. And it has to be that way, because it is only through your neural system that you can experience anything at all.

Is there a metaphor for God that I – as a scientist, a cognitive scientist – can accept? I used to think that the answer was 'No', since I was thinking of God only as given in Metaphors 1 and 2. I thought I was an atheist, but now I realize that I am not, since I can say 'Yes' to Metaphor 3: God As Immanent, as what exists. What is sacred is the world. It has inherent and ultimate value. I take spiritual connection as empathy with the world (via mirror and canonical neurons), empathy with people, and with what David Abram calls 'the more than human world': plants, animals, soil, sea, clouds, geological formations, all of it, including the wonderful inventions of human minds. With it comes a way of life

– a commitment to nurturant morality, that is, a commitment to empathy and responsibility. That includes a commitment to a practice, a quite demanding practice of rigorous thought, finding out about and trying to comprehend the world, meditation, exploration of self and others, appreciation, connection, giving, and experiencing fully the wonders of your own mind and body and the wonders of the Other – all kinds of Other.

The study of the embodied mind and metaphorical thought is a liberating enterprise. It frees us from the many tyrannies of the disembodied literal mind:

- the tyranny of a literalist philosophy that devalues the imaginative powers of human minds and mistakenly sees only one causation;
- the tyranny of a falsely disembodied mathematics that would turn the beauty of human creation into mere discovery;
- the tyranny of a literalist science that ignores the contribution of human bodies and minds and culture in constituting knowledge;
- the tyranny of a strict morality centred on authority rather than empathy and responsibility;
- the tyranny of a disembodied spiritual life whose focus is outside the magnificence of *this* world; and
- the tyranny of an unreal disembodied 'realism' that removes from us the proper responsibility for the reality we bring into being through living by our metaphors.

An embodied realism is liberating. Recognizing metaphorical thought acknowledges what is real. Understanding how our bodies shape even mathematical and scientific thought makes human knowledge that much more stunning, worthy of awe, and worth pursuing.

Best of all, cognitive science and neuroscience explain what is unsatisfying (at least to me) in religions and spiritual traditions based around personification, infinity, and essence metaphors. At the same time, they clarify the rich spiritual and moral life of those who find what is sacred and of ultimate value in the here and now, in the connection to the Other – the human Other and the more than human Other.

Do not say God is not in the stone and the oak, the virus and the bacterium, the ant and the aardvark, you and me, houses and chairs, books and wine. Sex and eating are sacred, they unite you with the Other, hence with God under Metaphor 3. Travelling the world is sacred; it is an exploration of God under Metaphor 3. Preserving the world is sacred; it is preserving God under

Metaphor 3. Creative activity is sacred; it is creating God under Metaphor 3. All experience is sacred; it is the experience of God under Metaphor 3.

'God' has largely been defined by Metaphors 1 and 2. That is unfortunate, because it has located the sacred in a place other than in the world and in our relationships to the Other – human and more than human: animal, plant, soil, water, air. And what is not sacred is open to destruction in the name of what is.

We *are* our bodies. We don't need disembodied souls to have full moral and spiritual lives. Human bodies are more than enough.

Conclusion

Research on the embodiment of mind is anything but esoteric and irrelevant. It has the deepest consequences not just for academic fields like Philosophy, Psychology, Linguistics, Mathematics, and Literary Studies, but also for how we understand our experience, govern our societies, live our lives, and so change our lives. The new understanding of morality, politics, and religion coming out of our understanding of mind is critical if we are to live better lives and leave the world better than we found it.

References

Austin, J. H. (1999) *Zen and the Brain*. Cambridge, MA: MIT Press.

Berlin, B., and Kay, P. (1969). *Basic Color Terms: Their Universality and Evolution*. Berkeley: University of California Press.

Boroditsky, L. (2000) 'Metaphoric structuring: Understanding time through spatial metaphors', *Cognition*, 75(1): 1–28. http://www.mit.edu/~lera/papers

Brugman, C. (1981) *Story of Over: Polysemy, Semantics, and the Structure of the Lexicon*. New York: Garland.

Crick, F. (1994) *The Astonishing Hypothesis: The Scientific Search for the Soul*. New York: Charles Scribner's Sons.

Damasio, A. R. (1994) *Descartes' Error: Emotion, Reason, and the Human Brain*. New York: Putnam.

— (1999) *The Feeling of What Happens: Body and Emotion in the Making of Consciousness*. New York: Harcourt, Brace & Co.

Dehaene, S. (1997). *The Number Sense*. Oxford and New York: Oxford University Press.

De Valois, R. L., and De Valois, K. (1975) 'Neural coding of color', in Careterette, E. C. and Friedman, M. P. (eds), *Handbook of Perception*. V. *Seeing*. New York: Academic Press.

De Valois, R. L., and Jacobs, G. H. (1968) 'Primate color vision', *Science*, 162: 533–40.

Edelman, G. (1992) *Bright Air, Brilliant Fire: On the Matter of Mind*. New York: Basic Books.

Edelman, G., and Tononi, G. (2001) *A Universe of Consciousness: How Matter Becomes Imagination*. New York: Basic Books.

Fadiga, L., Fogassi, L., Pavesi, G., and Rizzolatti, G. (1995) 'Motor facilitation during action observation: A magnetic stimulation study', *Journal of Neurophysiology*, 73: 2608–11.

Fauconnier, G. (1985) *Mental Spaces: Aspects of Meaning Construction in Natural Language*. Cambridge, MA: MIT Press.

— (1997) *Mappings in Thought and Language*. New York: Cambridge University Press.

Fauconnier, G., and Turner, M. (2002), *The Way We Think*. New York: Basic Books.

Feldman, J., and Lakoff, G. (forthcoming) *From Molecules to Metaphors: The Neural Theory of Language*.

Fillmore, C. (1985) 'Frames and the semantics of understanding'. *Quaderni di Semantica*, 6: 222–53.

Gallese, V., Fadiga, L., Fogassi, L., and Rizzolatti, G. (1996), 'Action recognition in the premotor cortex'. *Brain*, 119: 593–609.

Gibbs, R. (1994) *The Poetics of Mind*. Cambridge: Cambridge University Press.

Grady, J. (1997) 'Foundations of Meaning: Primary Metaphors and Primary Scenes'. PhD dissertation, Linguistics Department, University of California at Berkeley.

Herskovits, A. (1986) *Language and Spatial Cognition: An Interdisciplinary Study of the Prepositions in English*. Cambridge: Cambridge University Press.

Iacoboni, M., Woods, R. P., Brass, M., Bekkering, H., Mazziotta, J. C., and Rizzolatti, G. (1999) 'Cortical mechanisms of human imitation', *Science*, 286: 2526–8.

Johnson, C. (1997) 'Metaphor vs. conflation in the acquisition of polysemy: The case of SEE', in Hiraga, M. K., Sinha, C. and Wilcox, S. (eds), *Cultural, Typological and Psychological Issues in Cognitive Linguistics*. 'Current Issues in Linguistic Theory'. Amsterdam: John Benjamins.

Johnson, M. (1987) *The Body in the Mind: The Bodily Basis of Meaning, Imagination, and Reason*. Chicago: University of Chicago Press.

— (1993) *Moral Imagination: Implications of Cognitive Science for Ethics*. Chicago: University of Chicago Press.

Kay, P., and McDaniel, C. (1978) 'The linguistic significance of the meanings of basic color terms', *Language*, 54: 610–46.

Lakoff, G. (1987) *Women, Fire, and Dangerous Things: What Categories Reveal About the Mind*. Chicago: University of Chicago Press.

— (1990) *Women, Fire and Dangerous Things*. Chicago: University of Chicago Press.

— (2002) *Moral Politics*. Chicago: University of Chicago Press. [1996]

Lakoff, G., and Johnson M. (1980). *Metaphors We Live By*. Chicago: University of Chicago Press.

— (1999) *Philosophy in the Flesh*. New York: Basic Books.

Lakoff, G., and Núñez, R. (2000) *Where Mathematics Comes From*. New York: Basic Books.

Lakoff, G., and Turner, M. (1989) *More Than Cool Reason*. Chicago: University of Chicago Press.

Langacker, R. (1986/1991) *Foundations of Cognitive Grammar*. 2 vols. Stanford: Stanford University Press.

— (1990) *Concept, Image, and Symbol: The Cognitive Basis of Grammar*. Berlin: Mouton de Gruyter.

Lewis, D. (1973) 'Causation', *Journal of Philosophy*, 70: 556–67. Reprinted in Ernest Sosa (ed.), *Causation and Conditionals* (Oxford University Press, 1975) and in Lewis's *Philosophical Papers* II.

Narayanan, S. (1997a) 'Embodiment in Language Understanding: Sensory-Motor Representations for Metaphoric Reasoning about Event Descriptions'. PhD dissertation, Department of Computer Science, University of California at Berkeley.

Narayanan, S. (1997b) 'Talking The Talk Is Like Walking The Walk: A Computational Model of Verbal Aspect', *Proceedings of the Nineteenth Annual Conference of the Cognitive Science Society*.

Reddy, M. (1979) 'The conduit metaphor', in Ortony, A. (ed.), *Metaphor and Thought*. Cambridge: Cambridge University Press: 284–324.

Rizzolatti, G., and Arbib, M. A. (1998) 'Language within our grasp', *Trends in Neurosciences*, 21: 188–94.

Rizzolatti, G., Fadiga, L., Gallese, V., and Fogassi, L. (1996) 'Premotor cortex and the recognition of motor actions', *Cognitive Brain Research*, 3: 131–41.

Rohrer, T. (2001) 'The Neurophysiology of Cognitive Semantics,' International Cognitive Linguistics Conference, University of California at Santa Barbara (unpublished conference presentation). For details see website: http://zakros.ucsd.edu/~trohrer/#research.

Stalnaker, R. (1968) 'A Theory of Conditionals', in Rescher, N. (ed.), *Studies in Logical Theory* (Oxford: Oxford University Press): 98–112. Reprinted in Sosa, E. (ed.), *Causation and Conditionals* (Oxford Readings in Philosophy; London: Oxford University Press, 1976); and in Jackson F., (ed.), *Conditionals* (Oxford Readings in Philosophy; Oxford: Oxford University Press, 1991).

Sweetser, E. (1990) *From Etymology to Pragmatics: Metaphorical and Cultural Aspects of Semantic Structure.* Cambridge: Cambridge University Press.

Talmy, L. (1985) 'Force dynamics in language and thought', in *Papers from the Parasession on Causatives and Agentivity.* Chicago: Chicago Linguistic Society.

— (2000) *Toward a Cognitive Semantics.* I. *Concept Structuring Systems;* II. *Typology and Process in Concept Structuring.* Cambridge, MA: MIT Press.

Wynn, K. (1992) 'Addition and subtraction by human infants', *Nature,* 358: 749–50.

Zimler, J., and Keenan, J. M. (1983) 'Imagery in the congenitally blind: How visual are visual images?' *Journal of Experimental Psychology: Learning, Memory, and Cognition,* 9 (2): 269–82.

Part III
Evolutionary Naturalism

Michael Ruse

5
A Darwinian Understanding of Epistemology

Michael Ruse

As I read David Hume, he was trying to see in what directions one would be led philosophically if one took seriously the ideas and methods of the best science of his day, most notably Newtonian physics. I intend to follow in his footsteps, and to see in what directions one is led philosophically if one takes seriously the ideas and methods of the best science of our day, most notably Darwinian evolutionary biology. Although there are certainly suggestive hints in his writings, I do not think that Hume was truly an organic evolutionist, but I do think that he would have been very sympathetic to evolutionary thinking. In a sense of humility therefore rather than arrogance, let me say that what I hope to sketch is a Humean philosophy brought up to date by the insights of Charles Darwin and his successors. Following Hume, I shall turn first (in this chapter) to questions of epistemology (theory of knowledge) and shall turn second (in the next) to questions of ethics (theory of morality). This is a logical division rather than a reflection of personal history. As it happens, again I believe, following Hume, my thinking was first about ethics and only secondarily pushed back into thinking about epistemology.

Darwinian Evolutionary Biology

Since mine is the approach of the empiricist, often today spoken
of as taking a naturalistic stance, I need to start with the real world
– that is, the world of experience. I am not going to start all the
way down with sense data (assuming that they or something
comparable exist) but higher up with the use and understanding
that we make of sense data and the rest of experience. I am going
to begin in fact with scientific understanding, most particularly
with scientific understanding about organisms, including
ourselves. I am referring of course to evolution, and without
undue argument (for I have dealt at length with these matters
elsewhere) let me say that as an evolutionist I find it convenient
and enlightening to make a threefold division, amongst the *fact*
of evolution, the *path* (or *paths*) of evolution, and the *mechanism*
or *cause* of evolution (Ayala 1985; Ruse 1982).

By the *fact* of evolution, I mean the belief that all organisms
(living and dead) are the end results of a long, slow, natural (that
is, law-bound) process of change, from just a few or even one
simple organism, and most probably ultimately from inorganic
materials. We humans are part of this picture. By the *path* or *paths*
of evolution (known technically as 'phylogenies'), I mean the
actual tracks taken by organisms through time as they evolved
from simple beginnings to the forms today. I believe that the
proper metaphor for this history is that of a tree (the tree of life)
although it may be that today's molecular findings are pointing to
some crossing over between very different branches and so in
some respects a net might be a better metaphor. Roughly
speaking, the universe is about fifteen (American) billion years
old; our planet rather more than four billion years old. Life
started here on earth about three and three-quarter billion years
ago (in other words, pretty much as soon as the earth cooled
down enough for life to exist); there was, some five or six
hundred million years ago, a real explosion of life forms and
complexity (the Cambrian explosion). Mammals came into being
about two hundred million years ago, although the Age of
Mammals when they filled the earth had to wait until after an
event about sixty-five million years ago when the giant reptiles,
the dinosaurs, went extinct (with the exception of that branch
that evolved into the birds); the first proto-human remains are
about four million years old (Lucy or *Australopithecus afarensis*,
showing that first we got up on our hind legs and only then did
our brains start to explode upwards to their present size); and our

species is about a million years old (or less according to how you measure it), with agriculture and civilization as we know it but ten thousand years in existence.

Third and finally there is the question of *mechanisms* or *causes*. With the vast majority of today's active professional evolutionists, I believe that Charles Darwin in his *Origin of Species* had the true insight. More organisms are born than can survive and reproduce. There is therefore a struggle for existence. Natural variation occurs in populations. This means that, on average, success in the struggle is a function of the differences between organisms, and that the winners (the 'fittest') will be different from the losers, these differences ultimately making for ongoing change, in the direction of improved physical characteristics or adaptations – 'contrivances', in the old language of the natural theologians. Let Darwin speak in his own words:

> A struggle for existence inevitably follows from the high rate at which all organic beings tend to increase. Every being, which during its natural lifetime produces several eggs or seeds, must suffer destruction during some period of its life, and during some season or occasional year, otherwise, on the principle of geometrical increase, its numbers would quickly become so inordinately great that no country could support the product. Hence, as more individuals are produced than can possibly survive, there must in every case be a struggle for existence, either one individual with another of the same species, or with the individuals of distinct species, or with the physical conditions of life. It is the doctrine of Malthus applied with manifold force to the whole animal and vegetable kingdoms; for in this case there can be no artificial increase of food, and no prudential restraint from marriage. (Darwin 1859: 63)

Note that, even more than a struggle for existence, Darwin needed a struggle for reproduction. It is no good having the physique of Tarzan if you have the sexual desires of a philosopher. But with the struggle understood in this sort of way, given naturally occurring variation, natural selection follows at once.

> Let it be borne in mind in what an endless number of strange peculiarities our domestic productions, and, in a lesser degree, those under nature, vary; and how strong the hereditary tendency is. Under domestication, it may be truly said that the whole organization becomes in some degree plastic. Let it be borne in mind how infinitely complex and close-fitting are the mutual relations of all organic beings to each other and to their physical conditions of life. Can it, then, be thought improbable, seeing that variations useful to man have undoubtedly occurred, that other variations useful in some way to each being in the great and complex battle of life, should sometimes occur in the course of thousands of

generations? If such do occur, can we doubt (remembering that many more individuals are born than can possibly survive) that individuals having any advantage, however slight, over others, would have the best chance of surviving and of procreating their kind? On the other hand we may feel sure that any variation in the least degree injurious would be rigidly destroyed. This preservation of favourable variations and the rejection of injurious variations, I call Natural Selection. (Darwin 1859: 80–1)

In later editions, Darwin introduced the alternative term 'survival of the fittest', which was perhaps a little unfortunate, for it has led to endless claims that selection is a tautology, reducing simply to the claim that those that survive are those that survive. But while this is obviously true, selection means more than this. It claims – for better or for worse – that on average those that survive are different from those that do not, and that success in the struggle is a function of those differences. This may or may not be true. It is not a tautology (Ruse 1973).

As is well known, Darwin in fact did not have all the pieces to the puzzle (Ruse 1979). He lacked an adequate theory of heredity. On the one hand, you need that ongoing supply of new variations, the raw stuff that makes eventually for evolution. On the other hand, you need a mechanism that will ensure that new variations can make their mark, sooner or later. You need a 'particulate' theory that guarantees that variations can be trans- mitted unchanged from generation to generation, as opposed to a blending theory (which in fact Darwin himself favoured) that has variations washing away into non-being as the generations pass. Such an adequate theory was not forthcoming until the beginning of the twentieth century, when the work of the hitherto obscure Moravian monk Gregor Mendel was rediscovered. Then, when in the second decade of the century Thomas Hunt Morgan and his co-workers at Columbia University in New York City had articulated the classical theory of the gene – with the units of heredity located on the chromosomes in the nuclei of cells, and with new variations ('mutations') under constant creation – the way was open for a 'synthesis' of Darwinism (meaning natural selection) and Mendelism (meaning particulate inheritance). This task was performed around 1930 by the great theoreticians ('population geneticists'), Ronald A. Fisher and J. B. S. Haldane in Britain, and Sewall Wright in America (Provine 1971). After that came the empiricists, particularly the Russian-born geneticist Theodosius Dobzhansky and his associates (Ernst Mayr the ornithologist and systematist, George Gaylord Simpson the palaeontologist, and G. Ledyard Stebbins the botanist) in America, and the public figure Julian Huxley and then E. B. Ford and his school of 'ecological genetics' in Britain (Ruse 1996).

This synthetic theory of evolution (or as it is more commonly known in Britain 'neo-Darwinism') has been the dominant paradigm (to use the language of Thomas Kuhn) for the past half century. It has certainly not stood still. The most obvious area of advance has come through the ideas and techniques of molecular biology. Although the double helix and its consequences were first regarded as threats, soon they were seen to be challenges and opportunities. Major advances have been made (thanks particularly to the American geneticist Richard Lewontin) on the understanding of heredity and variation in populations, and it is now seen how fully selection can act, not simply to change species in various directions but also to maintain and cherish diversity within species (Lewontin 1974). One consequence of this is to put to rest a worry that non-biologists often have about the scope and power of selection. If variation is (as has been insisted by Darwinians from the days of the *Origin*) random, not in the sense of being uncaused but in the sense of not appearing in a teleological fashion according to the needs of the possessor, how can anything needed ever appear? The problem is solved because, if a new selective pressure arises – let us say, from a climatic change or a new predator – there is, as it were, always a library of variations presently existing within populations, on which selection can begin immediate action. If an organism cannot evolve one way, then it can evolve another way – unless of course there is nothing it can do, in which case (as is the fate of us all eventually) it goes extinct.

Another major area of advance, since (let us say, in order to fix a date) the hundredth anniversary of the *Origin of Species* in 1959, has been that of the understanding of the evolution of behaviour, particularly that of social behaviour. I shall leave discussion of this topic here, for it will be a major focus of the discussion of Chapter 6 on ethics.

Now, completing this too-brief discussion of the science, I want to turn to our own species. Darwin was always convinced that we are part of the pattern, and indeed in his private notebooks of 1838, just after he had discovered natural selection, the very first mention we get of the mechanism is an application to *Homo sapiens*, and indeed to our most cherished and distinctive feature, our intelligence:

> An habitual action must some way affect the brain in a manner which can be transmitted. – this is analogous to a blacksmith having children with strong arms. – The other principle of those children, which *chance?* produced with strong arms, outliving the weaker one, may be applicable to the formation of instincts, independently of habits. (Darwin, Notebook N, 42, in Barrett *et al.* 1987: 574)

(The reader will note that, here, Darwin is toying with the inheritance of acquired characteristics, so-called 'Lamarckism'. As a matter of historical fact, like most other people of his day, Darwin never doubted that this was at least a secondary mechanism of evolutionary change. Today, in the biological world, it is totally discredited.)

Physically, we humans are obviously very much part of the animal world, the primate world in particular. We eat, sleep, defecate, and have sexual passions just like other animals. It is believed now, thanks to molecular studies, that humans are in fact very closely related to the great apes, only having diverged some five or six million years ago. Indeed, despite appearances, we humans may be closer to the chimpanzees than the chimpanzees are to the gorillas. Of course the big differences are our upright stance, probably a function of coming down from the trees of the jungle and moving out to the open plains and grasslands, and our much increased brains, from about 400 cc of the ape range to about 1200 cc of human range. (In fact, that extinct sub-species of *Homo sapiens* known as 'Neanderthals' had on average slightly bigger brains than we, although they were not necessarily more intelligent and may have lacked full linguistic skills.)

There has been and still is much debate about our immediate origins, but we do know that the cradle of humankind was Africa, and most probably our line came from just one African population about 130,000 years ago. This group spread out around the world, and the differences that we now see are due to adaptive responses to particular climatic demands. For instance, it is a well-established fact in the animal world that those members of a group living in colder climates tend to have bodies that minimize surface area to volume ratio (for the obvious reason of heat-loss control) as opposed to those that live in warmer climates. Humans seem to obey this rule. As of course they obey another rule about the darker specimens of a species tending to be found in warmer areas of the globe as opposed to lighter specimens being found in colder areas of the globe (Ruse 2000).

No one today is going to deny that humans have animal attributes, although many would downplay the connection with the apes, arguing that as intelligence has grown so also has the independence from the animal. It is often said that now we humans have entered the realm of culture, and as such biology is essentially irrelevant. Our artefacts, our language, our customs, our religions, and much much more take us up from the brute and into the atmosphere of civilization. The Darwinian – often today called the human sociobiologist or the evolutionary psychologist – thinks that this is a very one-sided picture. It is not so much that it is wrong, but that it is grossly incomplete. One needs to recognize that biology still matters and that culture in some sense sits upon the biology, reaching down into the biology as the biology reaches up. To set up biology against culture is simply a false dichotomy, like asking which sex is the more important, male or female.

Consider the question of homicide, one person killing another. There is no question but that culture is a significant factor here. Some societies are simply more violent than others, and the reasons are that such societies either are more tolerant of or approving of violence, or for various reasons make violent patterns easier to fall into. America and Canada make a good contrast, for although there is much overlap in ways of life and ethnic groupings and the like, America is far more violent and given to homicide than Canada. Detroit, Michigan and Hamilton, Ontario, comparable industrial cities just 200 miles or so apart, have very different homicide statistics with the former outstripping the latter by at least four to one. The ready availability and acceptance of handguns in the USA as opposed to Canada is a pertinent causal factor that springs at once to mind.

Yet culture is not all. There are some figures that hold up remarkably consistently across the widest range of societies, suggesting that perhaps there is an underlying genetic factor involved. For instance, homicide figures within families show that there is a persistent and steady number of murders, by fathers, of their children: rarely mothers, except the infanticide of the very new born, which is a special case calling for its own explanation. This male parental violence is a surprising and interesting phenomenon, because it would seem to be a direct violation of Darwinian principles. Surely, parents should not eliminate precisely those who carry on their genetic heritage? The evolutionary psychologists Martin Daly and Margo Wilson (1988) hypothesized that perhaps the homicides are of step-fathers killing step-children: this would make sociobiological sense (the mothers are freed to attend to the needs of the step-fathers' own biological children) and in fact is a common finding in the animal world (Hausfater & Hrdy 1984). Male lions and lemmings, to take two examples, kill off all of the young when they take over a female. This hypothesis about the involvement of step-fathers proved to be precisely true. A man is *one hundred times* more likely to kill a step-child than he is to kill a biological child! Showing how this was no explanation after the fact, it was not until Daly and Wilson started asking their questions that police forces (their investigations focused in on Detroit and Hamilton) began distinguishing in cases of homicide between biological and social parents. Previously, it had not been thought relevant.

One swallow does not make a summer, but the homicide findings at least illustrate the Darwinian's belief that both biology and culture matter. Although in another way, the homicide findings are liable to reinforce another prejudice that people have about humans and their biology, namely that inasmuch as we are driven by biology it is always in the direction of violence and antisocial behaviour. As Darwin's own great supporter Thomas Henry Huxley used to argue, we must conquer the animal within us, not go with it.

Many would stress that nature is red in tooth and claw (a sentiment expressed by the poet Alfred Tennyson in his pre-*Origin* poem 'In Memoriam') and many think that this applies particularly to *Homo sapiens*. We are often described as the murderous ape with blood dripping from our fangs, and no self-control. Here, let me simply say that this is as it may be – or perhaps as it may not be, as we shall learn in the next chapter. The point is that as a social species we need adaptations for dealing with sociality. One of the most obvious is an ability to resist disease. Animals alone are nowhere like as subject to the spread of infection as animals in groups. The latter need genetic defences against bacteria and viruses, and when they do not have them – as the sorry story of the American Plains Indians in the face of smallpox shows too well – they tend to get decimated if not wiped out entirely. The non-existence of Tasmanians is as much a function of the disease-carrying missionaries as the brutality of the white settlers.

One interesting consequence of sociality is that, for all the genetic variability that might exist in populations, it is necessary for some adaptations to be fairly standardized – those that are involved in interactions with others. An obvious example is language. There is little point in my having the best accent in the room, perfect BBC English, if you all come from the slums of Glasgow or of Birmingham and cannot understand a word of what I say. If your vocabulary is four-letter at best, there is little point in my lecturing you on the nicer points of antidisestablishmentarianism.

Epistemic Values

With the importance of shared norms or adaptations still ringing in our ears, let us turn now to questions about knowledge, the heart of epistemology. I am going to assume that the apotheosis of empirical knowledge is scientific knowledge – the touchstone against which other knowledge claims can be judged – and the question I want to ask is how such knowledge is formed and what evolutionary biology (Darwinian evolutionary biology) has to say about this. My problem is about science itself and its basis and its growth. And so let us start by putting biology on one side for a moment, and asking about the way that science is formed and structured.

At a basic level, I presume we need logic and mathematics. Without these, no science, especially no sophisticated science, is possible. But we need more than this, for the point of science is interaction and understanding of the world of empirical experience. We start with problems, be these theoretical (like trying to understand why the Galapagos finches have the peculiar distribution that they do) or practical (like trying to build a bomb that will end World War Two at a stroke). We need some way of structuring experience, using logic and mathematics as indispensable tools. It is fair to say that the general opinion of philosophers and others is that the key notion in play here is that of 'epistemic value'. There is debate today between those who think that science is a reflection of disinterested objective reality and those who think that science is pretty much purely subjective and cultural, a social construction based on society; but both objectivists (the best known of whom is Karl Popper [1959]) and subjectivists (the best known of whom is Thomas Kuhn [1977]) come together on these values. And so in particular, we need to list those values which – in the words of the philosopher and historian of science Ernan McMullin (1983: 18) – are 'presumed to promote the truth-like character of science, its character as the most secure knowledge available to us of the world we seek to understand'.

Availing ourselves of his efforts, high on our list of such values, we will want to put *predictive accuracy*: the power to make forecasts about what one will find in the unknown. It is true that every theory must tolerate some degree of inaccuracy, but overall the theory that does not predict, and do it accurately, is the theory doomed to rejection. The theory that lets us predict is the theory that suggests to us that it is not just a creation of our imagination but a reflection of something 'out there'.

Backing prediction, we cannot do without the twins of *internal coherence* and *external consistency*. If the parts of a theory do not hang together without contradiction, the theory is discarded. 'One recalls the primary motivating factor for many astronomers in abandoning Ptolemy in favour of Copernicus. There were too many features of the Ptolemaic orbits, particularly the incorporation in each of a one-year cycle and the handling of retrograde motions, that seemed to leave coincidence unexplained and thus, though predictively accurate, to appear ad hoc' (McMullin 1983: 15). Likewise with the relations between a theory and its fellows: 'When steady-state cosmology was proposed as an alternative to the Big Bang hypothesis in the late 1940s, the criticism it first had to face was that it flatly violated the principle of conservation of energy, which long ago attained the status almost of an a priori in mechanics' (McMullin 1983: 15). *Unifying power* is surely something which is very important for success in science. An excellent example is Newtonian mechanical theory that brought together in the one theory both the astronomical speculations of Kepler and the terrestrial discoveries of Galileo. Another such theory is the wave theory of light, that unifies so many different optical findings. And then there is the very significant value of *fertility*: 'The theory proves able to make novel predictions that were not part of the set of original explananda. More important, the theory proves to have the imaginative resources, functioning here rather as a metaphor might in literature, to enable anomalies to be overcome and new and powerful extensions to be made' (McMullin 1983: 16).

A lot of people would suggest that Popperian *falsifiability* is surely a (if not *the*) major epistemic value or norm. But although it has not made the above list, I take it that it is covered by predictive accuracy, perhaps with an element of coherence or consistency. A theory which is predictively powerful and which takes seriously empirical challenges to its various elements is precisely what we have in mind when we think of a theory as falsifiable. I will not, therefore, list it separately. But one other value that I will mention is that of *simplicity* or elegance – the sense of something aesthetically compelling about a theory. In the nineteenth century, the English philosopher and historian of science William Whewell (1840) rolled together unificatory power and fertility into one value which he labelled a 'consilience of inductions', and then argued that the whole package is equivalent to simplicity!

I will not digress here to argue the toss. We are not dealing with an official canon, like the books of the Bible. Rather, we have a set of rules that supposedly are taken seriously as part of good-quality objective science. And I think that for the purposes of this discussion, we can drop the somewhat doubting and cynical 'supposedly'. If you look, for instance, at one of the major theories of the twentieth century – let us say, plate tectonics in geology – you see that the satisfaction of the epistemic rules or principles was of vital importance. Negatively, continental drift simply could not get off the ground for 50 years after Alfred Wegener first proposed it. It went against all of the principles of physics and chemistry to suppose that continents – great big hunks of rock – could simply plough across oceans, themselves sitting on even greater big hunks of rock. A lump of sandstone cannot sail across a plain of granite, like a ship across a sea. It was not until it was seen that the continents could themselves sit on plates that slip around the globe, diving above and beneath each other, that drift became an open option. Positively, when plate tectonics was accepted, it was then that geologists first truly had a unifying, consilient theory: one could explain why there are earthquakes on the West coast and not the East coast of the USA; one could show why Africa and South America seem to fit so nicely together; one could say something about the strange distributions of animals and plants around the globe; one knew why there are massive trenches down the centres of Oceans, as with the Atlantic. And much more. Geology was integrated as never before (Ruse 1989).

Innate Dispositions

The Darwinian's move now is easy to see and grasp. One assumes simply that the rules of mathematics and logic, the basic beliefs about causality and the like, the epistemic values or principles, are not simply cultural ephemera that were invented by people (either at the time of the Greeks or 2000 years later during the Scientific Revolution) but at some level are ingrained in our biology (Ruse 1986). They are part of our genetic heritage just as much as our physical features or our emotional inclinations such as sexual desires. One thinks mathematically because one is biologically disposed to do so, and one is attracted to simple and elegant theories for the same reason. And why should this be so? Very straightforwardly because those of our would-be ancestors who thought mathematically and logically and preferred the simple over the complex tended to survive and reproduce and those that did not, did not.

The great twentieth-century American philosopher W. V. O. Quine, writing about causality and why we think the future is going to follow the same rules as the past (the philosophical problem of induction), put his finger right on the problem and the solution:

> One part of the problem of induction, the part that asks why there should be regularities in nature at all, can, I think, be dismissed. *That* there are or have been regularities, for whatever reason, is an established fact of science; and we cannot ask better than that. *Why* there have been regularities is an obscure question, for it is hard to see what would count as an answer. What does make clear sense is this other part of the problem of induction: why does our innate subjective spacing of qualities accord so well with the functionally relevant groupings in nature as to make our inductions tend to come out right? Why should our subjective spacing of qualities have a special purchase on nature and a lien on the future?
>
> There is some encouragement in Darwin. If people's innate spacing of qualities is a gene-linked trait, then the spacing that has made for the most successful inductions will have tended to predominate through natural selection. Creatures inveterately wrong in their inductions have a pathetic but praiseworthy tendency to die before reproducing their kind (Quine 1969: 126).

I am not arguing now for innate knowledge in the sense that John Locke (1959 [1690]) considered and dismissed, but more for capacities that lead one to think in various ways (something that Locke considered and accepted). The claim that we have these innate principles (as the capacities manifest themselves in development) – or as they have sometimes been called, 'epigenetic rules' (Lumsden & Wilson 1981) – is an empirical one. As is the claim that the reason we have these principles is because they are adaptively advantageous. At the rough and ready level, there is much plausibility in these claims, and this is surely the reason why many biologists and philosophers have been attracted to the position. Darwin himself set the pattern and saw the way:

> Plato says in *Phaedo* that our 'necessary ideas' arise from the pre-existence of the soul, are not derivable from experience. — real monkeys for preexistence. (Notebook M, 128, in Barrett *et al.* 1987: 551)

The fact is that an intelligent primate that could see that three oranges were more than two oranges, or that thought that where two tigers were seen to enter a cave and but one emerged was a place of danger, or that simplicity is a virtue when a lion approaches, was ahead of a primate that did and thought none of these things. The proto-human who saw beaten down grass and blood stains and heard growls and who yet said, 'Tigers, just a theory not a fact', was less biologically fit than the proto-human who started running and who is still at it.

Note what is not being said here. Obviously, at some broad level, the Darwinian believes that science and its child, technology, have adaptive value. Humans succeed as they do because of their abilities to build houses and to find appropriate medicines and to print books and papers and much more. (Although the Darwinian might well think also that this could all come crashing down as we build ever more potent weapons of mass destruction – no one ever said that adaptations are forever.) But at the more narrow and more immediate level, no one is saying that every scientific theory automatically confers biological fitness on its supporters. This is clearly false. Darwin had the mistaken genetical belief ('pangenesis') that the body gives off little particles and that thus the inheritance of acquired characters is supported. Gregor Mendel saw correctly that the units of heredity get passed on entire from generation to generation, and that there is no need of the inheritance of acquired characters ('Lamarckism'). Darwin, a good Victorian family man, had eight children. Mendel, a Catholic monk, had none.

The point rather is that the basic tools for building science (and technology) are given by the genes, or at least the dispositions that then come to fruition in the course of development are innate and adaptive, and then from these humble beginnings the most sophisticated edifices of science get built right up. There are those who find this position implausible – how can biology lead to such insights as Fermat's Last Theorem, let alone its proof? Indeed, some think the position so implausible that the only alternative is to opt for a theological solution – there must be an intelligence standing behind science to make possible its triumphs (Polkinghorne 1989; Ruse 2001). There is little need to comment here on this inference, except to note that it is generally not a good policy to assume that because we find something implausible natural selection will be likewise handicapped. The point is that even if you do not accept evolution at all, you have to agree that science is built up from humble beginnings with initially simple tools, and you are stuck with this fact whether or not you think that it points to bigger things. The Darwinian is simply accepting things as they are and trying to understand them at the scientific level.

Of course, since the position is empirical, this is not the end of the job for the Darwinian. There is still the work of trying to decide what the actual dispositions are like (e.g., is falsifiability something in its own right or a consequence of other beliefs?) and how and why they were acquired and operate. Because I am writing now as a philosopher rather than as an active working scientist – I am merely trying to sketch out the overall picture and its implications for a satisfactory theory of knowledge – I shall say little here about the actual labours that are engaging evolutionary psychologists and others. Except to note that such labours are ongoing and widespread, ranging from studies with other animals, especially chimpanzees (de Waal 1982), to detailed examinations of the nature of language (Pinker 1994), to more traditional-type experiments with the psychology of learning and reasoning (Cosmides 1989), through attempts to understand the nature of the innate dispositions and to build formal systems of the working of the innate rules of reasoning (Lumsden & Wilson 1981), and on to speculative exercises in the nature of the brain and its connections to rational thinking (Pinker 1994; Deacon 1997).

Metaphor

There is, however, something to be said by a philosopher about the connection between biology and culture. Let us assume now, if only for the sake of argument, that it is indeed true that the basic principles of reasoning – logic, mathematics, epistemic rules of scientific judgement – are embedded in our biology. And let us assume also, in a fairly uncontroversial way, that science is produced by the application of these principles to the information yielded by observation, whether this be of a fairly straightforward kind produced by the naked senses (as for instance might be the case of a biologist studying some particular organism in the wild) or of a more and more sophisticated and complex kind as given up through experimentation and controlled manipulation of nature (as might be the case of a physicist studying the nature and behaviour of very small particles of matter).

A more traditional philosophy of science – for instance that of the logical empiricists, a movement popular in the two decades after the Second World War – would probably leave things at that. In fact, a more traditional philosophy of science would probably insist that one leave things at that (Nagel 1961; Hempel 1966). Of course, genius is required to build and extend and apply the really great theories of science, but the theories (or models or hypotheses) themselves are things unto themselves, mappings (however close or adequate) of the empirical world, of reality. Since this real world exists independently of the observer – it is the same world whether one be Ancient Greek or modern-day American, whether black or white, young or old, Jew or Gentile, gay or straight, male or female – in an all-important sense one can say that science (perhaps uniquely) is culture free. It is an attempt to describe an independent, disinterested objective reality, and inasmuch as it is good science or mature science or professional science this is what it does. Science is produced *in* a culture of course, and some cultures are more science production-friendly and fertile than others, but science itself is not *of* the culture.

This traditional picture of science, often today referred to as the Received View (meaning Not Received by Me or Anyone of Philosophical Respectability), has been much criticized since the publication of Thomas Kuhn's *Structure of Scientific Revolutions* in 1962, which (if it did not absolutely start) made explicit the growing realization that there has to be more to science than the somewhat sterile and eviscerated picture given by the logical empiricists. It is now realized that science is a much more full-blooded activity than appreciated hitherto, and that one cannot dismiss the influence of culture as readily as previously confidently assumed. There are some indeed, the social constructivists, who want to argue that science is truly purely a reflection of, an epiphenomenon on, culture, and that rules of method and constraints of the empirical findings have little or no influence on the finished product. Better to look for power relations in the laboratory and to religious and political and other social factors without the scientific community for the real causes of and influences on science and its creations (see Ruse 1999).

I do not think we need to go this far. For all that it has found much favour in Scotland's capital city – being indeed known as the doctrine of the 'Edinburgh School' – such extremism is almost a priori false. But we can still agree that there is something to the reaction against logical empiricism, and that at least some aspects of culture cannot be ignored quite so readily as was the custom some half a century ago. Moving straight from generalities to specifics, let me say that my conviction is (as Kuhn himself stressed) that a major player in the game of science – a player that in an overwhelmingly significant way brings in the cultural – is *metaphor*, the use of ideas from one domain of understanding to throw light on issues in another domain of understanding (Black 1962; Lakoff & Johnson 1980).

That metaphor is an important element of science as it actually occurs can be denied by no one. Consider, perhaps somewhat self-reflectively, evolutionary biology itself. Before Darwin, one had such notions as the 'balance of nature', the 'division of labour', the 'function' of the hand, the eye, the nose, and every other adaptation, or 'contrivance' as such organic features were called. All of these notions are metaphorical. The division of labour (itself somewhat metaphorical) was taken from the world of manufacturing – one workman makes one piece and another workman makes another piece – and applied to the world of organisms, especially by the Belgian-born Henri Milne-Edwards, who saw how the various parts of the body perform their own and separate functions. Then Darwin took over these metaphors – the division occurs again and again in his writings – and added more of his own: 'struggle for existence', 'natural selection', 'tangled bank'. And since Darwin the metaphors have if anything proliferated: 'adaptive landscape', 'selfish gene', 'arms race' (as lines of organisms co-evolve, with one line throwing up adaptations and then the other counteradaptations). And this is not to mention related areas of science. Think of the significance of the 'genetic code'.

As many readers will know, the whole place and significance of metaphor, especially as it occurs in science, is a topic surrounded by controversy. There are those who think that metaphorical thought is a sign of weakness and that as science matures the metaphors fall away. I will not argue in detail on this matter here, for I have done so at length elsewhere, but I will state flatly that I do not see that metaphor ever could or (more importantly should) be eliminated from science, from science that is of the most vigorous and important kind (Ruse 1999). As a matter of empirical fact, metaphors do not go. I have just pointed out that evolutionary biology today is as metaphorical as it ever was, more so in fact. Without the notion of an arms race, much of the exciting work on the relations between different species would grind to a halt. Without the notion of an adaptive landscape, most of twentieth-century American evolutionary biology would not have occurred at all. Moreover, as a matter of heuristic fact, without metaphors most of the epistemic rules could never get into action. Consider the metaphor of the division of labour. Not only was it crucial for Darwin, it is likewise crucial for today's evolutionists. Edward O. Wilson has performed heroic studies on the caste structure of Amazonian ants, showing the different functions performed by the different morphs (Hölldobler & Wilson 1990). Throughout his labours his tool of inquiry has been the division of labour, as he struggles to find the reasons for the varied evolution of forms within the same nests. As Wilson has used Darwinian theory in an incredibly predictively fertile manner – as he has striven to exemplify one of the key epistemic values – he has turned for aid to the oldest metaphor in the evolutionist's book.

Let me say, to counter the extreme social constructivists, that this use of metaphor does not now mean that science – contemporary evolutionary biology in particular – is drenched with reflection and approval of societal values. The eighteenth-century industrialists and economists certainly thought that the division of labour was a good thing. I strongly suspect that Darwin agreed. He was the grandson of Josiah Wedgwood, who made his fortune out of applying the division to the pottery industry, and if you look at the *Descent of Man*, in particular, you will find that Darwin thought that the likes of Wedgwood were a very good thing for humankind generally, let alone Charles Darwin specifically (Darwin's wife Emma was another grandchild of Wedgwood and also benefited from the industrialist's monetary successes). But I have no reason to think that Wilson thinks the division something of value, at least as it applies to humans. It is something that seems to work for ants, but they are (to all intents and purposes) automata – they are not thinking beings. Today, many argue that the division as applied to humans is soul-deadening – doing the same monotonous work day in and day out – and in fact counterproductive precisely because it is so boring. Better to adopt other patterns of work (as in the Japanese auto industry), where a team is responsible for many different tasks and the worker can stay alive and alert as he or she faces many diverse jobs in the course of the day or the week. I see no reason why Wilson should not accept this line of thought completely.

I do not mean either – with my support for the significance of metaphor – that this means that science is now beyond check. Or that we must now drop the epistemic values that lead to control of the material as it veers from the empirical. I do not mean that fondness for some cultural institution or idea – say some religious belief like the idea of the immortal soul – can simply ride roughshod over the empirical facts or their significance as encased in epistemic criteria. A metaphor may throw up an attractive empirical hypothesis, but it has still got to meet the challenge of empirical adequacy, the test of falsifiability for instance, and the risk of falsification. Take, for example, the question of the level at which selection is supposed to operate. Cultural factors have played a crucial role in the positions that people have taken. Charles Darwin was influenced deeply by the thinking of eighteenth- and nineteenth-century political economy, especially those aspects which were congenial to the successful industrialists. For him, ultimately, the struggle always pits individual against individual (Ruse 1980). Hence, adaptations are always for the benefit for the individual.

Others have seen things differently. They have seen the struggle as occurring much more between groups than between individuals, or between a group and the environment. The co-discoverer of natural selection, Alfred Russel Wallace, was one such person. He was much influenced by his early experiences as a land surveyor: he saw the conflicts between the social classes, as those in power enclosed and took away the land from those beneath them. Given this, and his powerfully favourable exposure to the socialistic teachings of Robert Owen, he had always a tendency to see genuine alliances within groups and conflict between them (Wallace 1905).

Likewise Russian evolutionists in the nineteenth century were more inclined to a group perspective. Russia was late in industrializing: indeed, one might fairly say that it did not ever do so truly under the tsarist regime. For it, the whole Adam Smith and Robert Malthus tradition was alien and irrelevant (Todes 1989). One looked for other philosophies such as socialism or, as in the case of Prince Petr Kropotkin, anarchism. As importantly, Russia was so vast and with a climate so cruel that no one could ever think that a struggle between organisms was a significant factor. There was always going to be space enough. The key problem was the horrendous effect of the natural conditions. This was where the struggle would occur: between organisms and the elements:

> The terrible snow-storms which sweep over the northern portion of Eurasia in the later part of the winter, and the glazed frost that often follows them; the frosts and the snow-storms which return every year in the second half of May, when the trees are already in full blossom and insect life swarms everywhere; the early frosts and, occasionally, the heavy snowfalls in July and August, which suddenly destroy myriads of insects, as well as the second broods of birds in the prairies; the torrential rains, due

to the monsoons, which fall in more temperate regions in August and September – resulting in inundations on a scale which is only known in America and in Eastern Asia, and swamping, on the plateaus, areas as wide as European States; and finally, the heavy snowfalls, early in October, which eventually render a territory as large as France and Germany, absolutely impracticable for ruminants, and destroy them by the thousand – these were the conditions under which I saw animal life struggling in Northern Asia. They made me realize at an early date the overwhelming importance in Nature of what Darwin described as 'the natural checks to overmultiplication', in comparison to the struggle between individuals of the same species for the means of subsistence. (Kropotkin 1955 [1902]: vi–viii)

Clearly the only way that people, or organisms, could survive was by banding together against the elements. It was no chance that it was Kropotkin, living in exile in London, who penned the greatest-ever paean to a natural form of altruism, mutual aid:

In the animal world we have seen that the vast majority of species live in societies and that they find in association the best arms for the struggle for life: understood, of course, in its wide Darwinian sense – not as a struggle for the sheer means of existence, but as a struggle against all natural conditions unfavourable to the species. The animal species, in which individual struggle has been reduced to its narrowest limits, and the practice of mutual aid has attained the greatest development, are invariably the most numerous, the most prosperous, and the most open to further progress ... The unsociable species, on the contrary, are doomed to decay. (Kropotkin 1955 [1902]: 293)

Kropotkin was not peculiar in this. Indeed, he stood firmly in the Russian tradition.

Here we have rival theories, representing rival views of the world. Different metaphors have been incorporated into evolutionary theorizing. One the one side, we have the metaphors of British industrialism. On the other side, we have the metaphors of socialism, bureaucracy, and of a peculiarly Russian experience. But, however deeply the culture may run, scientists do have rules of proper scientific conduct which they share with those scientists of other cultures: rules of conduct incorporated in the epistemic values. And this means that the two perspectives – the individual selection and the group selection views – can be compared – as indeed they were, and, notwithstanding some technical exceptions, the one was found satisfactory and the other lacking.

Most importantly, the individual selection hypothesis has been found predictively fertile in ways that the group selection hypothesis simply is not. Most notably, the late William Hamilton (1964a; 1964b) showed that, from an individual selection perspective, one could work out how close relatives aid each other (because they are thereby passing on copies of genes held in common) and how therefore adaptation for helping others – adaptations for altruism – could be produced by natural selection and refined and promoted. Selfish genes can lead to non-selfish animals. Hamilton's success in applying this idea (that came to be known as 'kin selection') to the long-festering problem of the sterility of workers in the Hymenoptera (the ants, the bees, and the wasps) is well known. By pointing to the odd reproductive patterns in the Hymenoptera (males have only mothers, whereas females have two parents, meaning that sisters are more closely related to each other than are mothers to daughters), he was able to show that an individualistic perspective can explain the sterility (better to raise fertile sisters than fertile daughters) and that a group perspective says nothing – or rather, points the wrong way.

My point is made. Science is an intimate and inextricable fusion of the biological and the cultural, brought to bear on empirical experience. The biology gives the underlying rules of method, the norms of good science. The cultural gives the means of applying the rules and of bringing the labours to fruition. But just as the biologically based norms remain in the science, a testament to their importance, so also does the cultural remain in the science, as the metaphors bear witness to the people and societies that produced the theories and models and metaphors of under-standing.

Limits to Understanding

I draw to a conclusion. Trying to accentuate the positive, it has not really been arrogance or indifference that has led me to ignore the other side of my brief, namely that of the limits to understanding. But redressing the balance a little, let me mention three areas where I think the Darwinian position may leave gaps, if such things are truly to be considered gaps.

The first has been touched on already. I do not think that one can say much about why everything does work – at least, at the level of the Darwinian, the empiricist, I do not think one can say much. Why is it that one can peer so far into the mysteries of nature, given the rather crude principles that selection throws up? How can elementary principles of reasoning lead to higher mathematics (which may just be a fiction but which often turns out to have empirical application) or to the understanding of the largest and smallest elements of possible experience? I think that that is simply something that the Darwinian has to accept as a given. Perhaps religion can say something useful here, but that is another matter, and not within my present brief. I also think, conversely, that one should not assume that one is going to be able to solve all of the problems of experience. There is no guarantee that tools forged by natural selection to help us to survive and reproduce are going to be able to see and understand everything. Perhaps the body–mind problem ultimately will flounder here; although, showing that the last thing I intend is to downplay new research, I think that at one level at least the past two or three decades have seen more action and advance on the body–mind problem than the two or three thousand years previously, and that this advance has been primarily if not exclusively thanks to empirical investigation (computers, brain science, and the like).

Second, I do not think that we can ever claim to have the definitive and only perspective on experience. My relativism puts me with the social constructivists here. If the culture of the West had not been as it was, I do not see that evolutionary theory as we understand it would have been produced. The very question about origins was alien to the Greeks and came with the Jewish elements incorporated into Christianity. And the metaphors of the eighteenth, nineteenth, and twentieth centuries infused and informed and made the theory as we have it. I do not mean that without the culture we would all deny evolution and be Creationists. That is our way of thinking and false. I mean that we might simply think in other ways, and divide experience in other fashions – whether more or less profitably, I cannot say: just that the ways would be different. (Rather as something like Buddhism looks upon the world in a way very different from Christianity: in a sense, they are so different they do not really clash.) Of course, my relativism is limited – perhaps too limited for the hardcore constructivist – because I have said that I do not think that anything goes. There is the test of experience. But I do think that one cannot privilege just one society. (Perhaps also one cannot privilege just one thought pattern in society. Although group selection has gone, other rival metaphors persist – those separating the enthusiasts for form and those for function, perhaps. It could be that some issues will never be solved, just ongoing and dropping away when people get bored.)

Whether my relativism extends to the biological, I hesitate to pronounce. I suspect that there is no such relativism on this earth (which may be why even things like Buddhism and Christianity can be brought to some interaction). We humans all tend to think in terms of the same maths and logic and epistemic rules. But whether on Andromeda, say, things would all be the same as here on earth seems to be speculative (Ruse 1989). Not that the Andromedans would have $2 + 2 = 5$, for again that is earthly mathematics and false, but that they might not think in such mathematical terms at all. Dare one nevertheless say, as Immanuel Kant would have said, that such people are irrational? (Actually, Kant thought that some denizens of other planets are significantly brighter than us.) Perhaps some patterns would persist, especially those connected with bodily functions. Could one have a rational being that was totally without and indifferent to artefacts, for instance? If not, is a kind of teleological thought – thinking in terms of functions or final causes – something which always goes with rationality? Perhaps so, perhaps not. Beware of philosophers making predictions about what can or cannot be. We have certainly reached the limits of my understanding at this point.

Third and finally, I do not think that the Darwinian can throw much light on some of the ultimate metaphysical questions, especially those about ontology (Ruse 1999). Can the Darwinian say that there is or is not an absolute reality, what is often known as a metaphysical reality, the reality of the tree falling in the forest when no one is around? The Darwinian is obviously committed to some kind of commonsense reality – chairs and tables, dinosaurs and *drosophila* (fruitflies). But ultimate reality is beyond his or her ken. Which may or may not mean that questions about ultimate reality, metaphysical reality, are genuine questions (soluble by non-empirical means), or pseudo-questions without real solution. I have my opinions, but let me now leave it as an exercise for the reader as to whether the failure of Darwinism at this point is truly a limit to our understanding.

6
A Darwinian Understanding of Ethics

Michael Ruse

From the earliest days of evolutionary speculation in the eighteenth century, people were using their theories as a basis for ethical thinking. In the mid-nineteenth century, before Charles Darwin published his *Origin of Species* in 1859, Herbert Spencer was pushing a moral code based on what he thought were historical principles based on the nature and causes of life's origins. Like other evolutionists, Spencer felt that in a modern age, where one saw rapid urbanization, industrialization, the rise of an educated middle class living by its abilities rather than its heritage, the ethics of the past – particularly the ethics of Christianity – was no longer adequate. One had to replace it with a new, forward-looking, scientific ethics appropriate for the age. Evolution was the key. (See Spencer 1851, 1892; Richards 1987; Ruse 1994, 1996, 2000.)

Evolutionary ethics – or, as it came to be called, 'Social Darwinism' – was a powerful and wide-ranging doctrine or set of beliefs. It was also something criticized severely from its very inception: not just by theologians and like thinkers, but also by secular philosophers. G. E. Moore in his *Principia Ethica* (1903) dealt severely with Spencer's own ideas. Nevertheless, even to this day, there are those (particularly biologists) who put forward a modified form of Social Darwinism, if not by that name. Most prominently in our own age, the world's leading authority on the social insects, the Harvard biologist Edward O. Wilson (1984, 1992, 1998), has been arguing for an updated evolutionary ethics of a Spencerian ilk. Although as criticized in our time as Spencer was in his time, Wilson has persisted with dogged determination. Indeed, today one finds many who sympathize with his point of view.

Although I have myself on many occasions criticized Social Darwinism, both the traditional form and the updated version (Ruse 1985, 1986), I think that there is much more to be said for it than is often allowed in the traditional critique. But I think also that today one can do better. And so, after some historical remarks by way of contrast, I want to put forward an alternative evolutionary ethics: one which pays as much attention to evolutionism, particularly modern-day evolutionism, as does Social Darwinism. Specifically, I want to offer an evolutionary ethics which uses the modern-day Darwinian evolutionism that deals with social behaviour. As in the previous chapter, I think of my position as being one very much in the tradition of David Hume. If the critic objects that what little I have to say of philosophical importance is to be found in the *Treatise of Human Nature,* I shall take this as praise rather than condemnation.

As always in philosophical discussions about ethics and morality, it is useful to make a twofold distinction: between 'substantive' or 'normative ethics' and 'meta-ethics'. By the former, I mean that domain asking questions about what one ought to do, as in, 'Love your neighbour as yourself', or 'Treat others as ends rather than as means'. By the latter, I mean that domain asking questions about why one ought to do what one ought to do, as in, 'Follow the Sermon on the Mount because that is God's will', or 'Act only in ways which avoid social contradictions'. I realize that there are those who question the substantive/meta-ethical distinction, but for the rather broad purposes I have here it will serve well.

Social Darwinism

Social Darwinism, although truly it might better be called Social Spencerianism, derives its substantive ethics from the nature of the evolutionary process. This is the way that things have been; therefore, this is the way that things ought to be. One ferrets out the nature of the evolutionary process – the mechanism or cause of evolution – and then one transfers it to the human realm (if this has not already been done), arguing that that which holds as a matter of fact among organisms holds as a matter of obligation among humans (Ruse 1986).

Herbert Spencer, for instance, started with the struggle for existence and the consequent selective effects: a connection which he made in print in 1852, years after Darwin made the connection but years before Darwin published. He then applied his theory to the human realm: not much to do here, actually, since Spencer speculated on selective effects showing themselves in the different natures and behaviours of the Irish and the Scots. He concluded that struggle and selection in society translate into extreme laissez-faire socioeconomics: the state should stay out of the way of people pursuing their own self-interests and should not at all attempt to regulate practices or redress imbalances or unfairnesses. Libertarian licence therefore is not only the way that things are but the way that they should be. In fact, Spencer was far from convinced that mid-Victorian Britain was a laissez-faire society, but this is what he fervently hoped it would become:

> We must call those spurious philanthropists, who, to prevent present misery, would entail greater misery upon future generations. All defenders of a Poor Law must, however, be classed among such. That rigorous necessity which, when allowed to act on them, becomes so sharp a spur to the lazy and so strong a bridle to the random, these pauper's friends would repeal, because of the wailing it here and there produces. Blind to the fact that under the natural order of things, society is constantly excreting its unhealthy, imbecile, slow, vacillating, faithless members, these unthinking, though well-meaning, men advocate an interference which not only stops the purifying process but even increases the vitiation – absolutely encourages the multiplication of the reckless and incompetent by offering them an unfailing provision, and *discourages* the multiplication of the competent and provident by heightening the prospective difficulty of maintaining a family. (Spencer 1851: 323–4)

Spencer could sound positively brutal about those who would help the unfortunate within society: 'Besides an habitual neglect of the fact that the quality of a society is physically lowered by the artificial preservation of its feeblest members, there is an habitual neglect of the fact that the quality of a society is lowered morally and intellectually, by the artificial preservation of those who are least able to take care of themselves ... For if the unworthy are helped to increase, by shielding them from that mortality which their unworthiness would naturally entail, the effect is to produce, generation after generation, a greater unworthiness'

(Spencer, quoted in Richards 1987: 303). Yet one should not assume that everyone would have agreed with Spencer on this. Just as Christians differ on the interpretation of Jesus' moral dicta, so also evolutionists differed on the interpretation of evolution's moral dicta. There were those who argued that, far from evolution supporting capitalism and denying socialism, it promotes a strong state and the attempt to diminish inequality through its controls.

One who falls into this category of using evolution to bolster moral claims about the virtues of strong, centralized control was Darwin's great supporter, Thomas Henry Huxley. In the years after the *Origin of Species*, as Huxley and his fellow scientists were increasingly successful at finding themselves and their students positions of authority and power within universities and the civil service, he grew correspondingly sceptical of extreme laissez-faire. Rather he saw the virtues of a bureaucracy and of state intervention, in education and elsewhere (Huxley 1871). It is true that Huxley oscillated between favouring an evolutionarily justified ethics and denying that evolution has anything to do with ethics, and that thus one must combat the biological beast within oneself (Huxley 1893). But no such qualms were felt by others who favoured his conclusions about the importance of central control.

As we learnt in Chapter 5, Alfred Russel Wallace was ever an ardent socialist, thinking that the state can and should regulate people's lives for the better (Wallace 1905; Marchant 1916), and he justified his beliefs in the name of evolution. Believing that selection favours groups as well as individuals, he argued that a state founded and run on socialist principles would be better now and more prepared for the future than one which simply bowed before market forces. (See also Jones 1980.) Similar sorts of reasoning motivated the Russian Prince Petr Kropotkin (1955 [1902]), although somewhat paradoxically far from being in favour of state control, he was led in the very opposite direction towards anarchism. Kropotkin believed that there is a natural sympathy existing between people (and animals) – 'mutual aid' – and although unlike Wallace he wanted to lift state controls, he too was much influenced by a group selection perspective on the evolutionary process. As we saw in Chapter 5, coming from nineteenth-century Russia, a vast pre-industrial society where the chief threat to life lay in the elements, it seemed self-evident to someone like Kropotkin that evolution must work for good and sympathy rather than harm and competition. (I am sure also that Kropotkin's early Russian experiences of an overly regulated and policed state, rather than the liberal state of Britain, was a major psychological factor in his move towards anarchism.)

War and Oppression

What about the really vile aspects of evolution and its social consequences? Today we associate Social Darwinism with ruthless cunning and force, not to mention other factors that have led to the appalling happenings and systems of the last century. 'Might is right' and that sort of thing. Is it not the case that Darwin's ideas were taken up on the continent, in Germany in particular, leading to warlike sentiments as struggle between nations was justified as 'natural' in the name of Darwin? And that they provided a rationale for the militarism which led to the First World War, as well as a theoretical justification for the vile philosophies which followed in its wake, Communism and National Socialism?

Actually, however, as in the social sphere, matters are mixed, both with respect to influences and to consequences. Start with militarism. It is true that you can find force and expansion justified in the name of Darwin. Huxley was one who thought that force and violence tend to be natural, even though he was explicit that this is not morality but rather to be combated in the name of morality. Others went farther down the savage bloodstained-ape path, recognizing our nature as the way things are and are destined to be. One writer, in a passage which admittedly perhaps owes as much to Hegel as it does to Darwin, claimed that war is 'a phase in the life-effort of the State towards completer self-realization, a phase of the eternal nisus, the perpetual omnipresent strife of all beings towards self-fulfilment' (quoted in Crook 1994: 137). Even if not this enthusiastic, others saw it as 'more or less normal for men at times to plunge back down the evolutionary ladder ... to break away from the complex conventions and routine of civilized life and revert to that of the troglodytes in the trenches'. And added: 'Man has always been a fighter and his passion to kill animals ... and inferior races ... is the same thing which perhaps in the dark past so effectively destroyed the missing link between the great fossil apes of the tertiary and the lowest men of the Neanderthal type. All these illustrate an instinct which we cannot eradicate or suppress, but can best only hope to sublimate' (Crook 1994: 143–4).

Some however stressed that war is only a temporary primitive phase and urged peace in the name of evolution. Spencer was in the forefront of this group. He always tended to put the inheritance of acquired characters ahead of natural selection, thus it was the essence of Spencer's position that Lamarckian strife means a rise up the chain of being with a consequent decline in fertility (as effort goes into brainpower rather than reproduction), with a falling away of the struggle and universal peace. This fitted in with his belief that what is best for business and unrestrained laissez-faire is free trade and open frontiers: the last thing Spencer wanted was the waste of military spending and the erection of barriers to unrestricted commercial intercourse. And others felt the same way down and through the First World War (Mitman 1990).

But what of the ideologies? Start with Communism. Both Engels and Marx liked the *Origin* (although thinking it crudely empirical and English), and, at the grave of Marx, Engels went so far as to say that Marx did in the social world what Darwin did in the biological world (Young 1985). There was, therefore, always a warm place for Darwinism in the Soviet system, although one should note that much of the thinking was more Germanic than Darwinian: Engel's posthumously published *Dialectics of Nature* shows strong Hegelian-*Naturphilosoph* influences. And, when it came to practical agriculture, the sorry story of Lysenko (who single-handedly destroyed twentieth-century Russian agriculture) shows that the Darwin-complementing Mendelism counted for little (Joravsky 1970). Lamarckian change through effort has a natural appeal that Darwinian change through selection does not. One can, therefore, hardly say that Darwinism really influenced Marxism or its consequent Communism: it was more used as justification. Scholarship shows, however, that, particularly in America, many who called themselves 'Marxists' owed more to evolutionism – to Spencer particularly – than they did to Marx (Pittenger 1993). To this often was added a dash of the biogenetic law – that ontogeny recapitulates phylogeny – as it was argued that societies go from primitive (and homogeneous) up to the most developed (and heterogeneous) which are communistic (Richards 1987).

National Socialism likewise bears an ambiguous relationship to evolutionary ideas. Ernst Haeckel favoured a group perspective on evolution. He used this to argue the virtues of the integrated state with strong military, efficient civil service, and well-supported universities: Prussia under Bismarck in fact! One can see here the outlines of the Third Reich and to this one can add other elements: a cherishing of the highest form of human who just so happens to be Nordic and who excludes other races, including blacks and Jews. There were other ideas which were to resurface in the 1930s, including views about the virtues of selective breeding and the elimination of the unfit (eugenics), as well as a strong opposition to Christianity as the religion of the weak. Hitler notoriously was contemptuous of Christianity, arguing that it tried to put humankind outside of or beyond nature when we must realize that we are all part of the living flow of nature. He even condemned Christianity for its opposition to evolution (Gasman 1971: 168). And there are times when Hitler sounds like the paradigmatic Social Darwinian. 'He who wants to live must fight, and he who does not want to fight in this world where eternal struggle is the law of life has no right to exist' (quoted in Bullock 1991: 141).

But this is only a very small part of the story about the relationship of Darwinism to Nazi ideology. The overlaps frequently owe more to common cause than to cause and event (Kelly 1981). Hitler's philosophy owed most to the Volkish ideology of the nineteenth century, which saw Germans uniquely as the supreme race, threatened by outsiders: threatened above all by the Jew. This led to what has been called 'redemptive' or 'apocalyptic' anti-Semitism: an anti-Semitism that has a kind of ontological or religious status (Friedlander 1997). Haeckel, by contrast, may not have much cared for Jews, but his solution was to assimilate them. This was the farthest thought from Hitler's mind. Moreover, evolution – as most of the Nazis saw quite clearly – was fundamentally opposed to the ideology of National Socialism. Within the theory, there is no warrant for saying Germans are uniquely the superior race, there is denial that this can be a permanent state of affairs, there is the connection of all peoples including Aryans and Jews, there is the simian origin, and much more. There is little surprise that Nazi celebrations of Haeckel's centenary were muted in the extreme and that evolutionary works were among those proscribed by the Party. The Nazis knew who were their friends and who were not.

Justification

One could continue this historical discussion with coverage of many more evolutionists who have used their biological theorizing to inform their moral prescriptions. In the middle of the twentieth century, for instance, one had Julian Huxley (the

grandson of Thomas Henry Huxley), who – much impressed by
such New Deal activities as the Tennessee Valley Authority –
argued in the name of evolution for state-sponsored major feats
of civil engineering (Maienschein & Ruse 1998). And then, more
recently, we have had Edward O. Wilson (1984) arguing that we
humans live in an evolved symbiotic relationship with the rest of
nature and that therefore we ought to preserve biodiversity. He
himself is much involved in the preservation of the Brazilian
rainforests. But, while others could be added to the names of
Huxley and Wilson, the main historical moral can be drawn
already. The prescriptions of Social Darwinism – its normative
ethics – are nowhere like as black as often claimed, nor is there
the unanimity of thought that many assume. One can find as
much good (and as much ill) in Social Darwinism as in most of
the other major ethical systems, not excluding Christianity. To a
certain extent, you pay your money and you take your choice. The
main point is that I do not think you can, as many are wont to do,
condemn Social Darwinism simply on the grounds that it has a set
of repellent normative claims at its heart. The truth is more
complex than simple black and white, let alone simple black and
black.

This turns us then to the meta-ethical heart of Social
Darwinism. Here of course is where the traditional philosophical
criticisms lie. Moore accused the neo-Spencerians of committing
the so-called naturalistic fallacy, justifying the good (a non-
natural property) in terms of the evolutionarily successful (a
natural property). And this of course is a variant of the sin identified by David Hume, namely justifying moral claims ('ought'
claims) in terms of factual claims ('is' claims). One is going from
the way that evolution acts, to the way that one thinks humans
ought to act. Let me say at once that I think this is a valid line of
criticism, one spotted by Thomas Henry Huxley among others.
Because nature makes lions and tigers violent, it is not to say that
we humans should be violent. But let me say also that I find the
average evolutionary ethicist supremely unworried by the
criticism. He or she agrees that generally one cannot go from 'is'
to 'ought' but argues that there are exceptions and that evolution
supremely is one such exception. One can go from the way that
evolution works to the way that one ought to behave.

Why the confidence in this move? Simply, I suspect, because
evolutionary ethicists are progressionists – they think that the
course of evolution is upwards, from the bad or the non-moral to
the good and the moral and the worthy of value. Hence, to keep

this progress going is in itself a good thing. Listen, for instance, to Herbert Spencer. For him, evolution was a transition from the undifferentiated or what he called the 'homogeneous', to the thoroughly mixed up or what he called the 'heterogeneous'. Progress was not just a biological or a social phenomenon – it was an all-encompassing world philosophy:

> Now we propose in the first place to show, that this law of organic progress is the law of all progress. Whether it be in the development of the Earth, in the development of Life upon its surface, in the development of Society, of Government, of Manufactures, of Commerce, of Language, Literature, Science, Art, this same evolution of the simple into the complex, through successive differentiations, holds throughout. From the earliest traceable cosmical changes down to the latest results of civilization, we shall find that the transformation of the homogeneous into the heterogeneous, is that in which Progress essentially consists. (Spencer 1857: 1)

Likewise Julian Huxley (1942). For him, the key question was always, not whether biological progress had ever occurred, but what form it generally took. Much ink was spilled in defences of candidates for the true criterion: complexity, intelligence, flexibility, and more. Huxley liked the idea of *complexity* – 'High types *are* on the whole more complex than low' – but what really excited him were the notions of *control* and *independence*. In his opinion, the more the organism is capable of exercising control over its particular environment and the greater its independence of this environment, the higher is such an organism up the scale of improvement. Mammals, for instance, with their methods of maintaining a constant body temperature, are more in control and more independent than reptiles without such methods – and they are clearly higher up the scale. Humans, Huxley saw as right at the pinnacle of being. More than any other organism, they have 'increased control over and independence of the environment', or in other words, they have raised 'the upper level of all-round functional efficiency and of harmony of internal adjustment' (1942: 564–5). Seeing progress in the evolution of organisms up to our own species and believing progress to be a social phenomenon also, Huxley also saw social progress as being that which has taken up from biological progress. 'True human progress consists in increases of aesthetic, intellectual, and spiritual experience and satisfaction' (1942: 575).

One could continue with the theme of progress, particularly in the work of Edward O. Wilson: 'the overall average across the history of life has moved from the simple and few to the more complex and numerous. During the past billion years, animals as a whole evolved upward in body size, feeding and defensive techniques, brain and behavioral complexity, social organization, and precision of environmental control – in each case farther from the nonliving state than their simpler antecedents did' (Wilson 1992: 187). He concludes: 'Progress, then, is a property of the evolution of life as a whole by almost any conceivable intuitive standard, including the acquisition of goals and intentions in the behavior of animals.' The point is made.

And here I think is the reason to be dubious about Social Darwinism. Popular though it may be, the very idea of progress in evolution is clouded in problems. It is far from obvious either that natural selection promotes progress or that progress actually occurs, at least in any clear definable and quantifiable way. One can of course label humans as the pinnacle of being – I myself am inclined to do just this – but such an act is arbitrary, at least as applied to evolution. Why not label a dog the pinnacle of being or a buttercup? From a biological point of view, the AIDS virus is far more successful than the gorilla, but does anyone truly want to say that the former is superior in a moral or other value sense to the latter? In a typically hyperbolic fashion, Stephen Jay Gould (1988) writes: 'Progress is a noxious, culturally embedded, untestable, nonoperational, intractable idea that must be replaced if we wish to understand the patterns of history.' With respect to human evolution, he writes: 'Since dinosaurs were not moving toward markedly larger brains, and since such a prospect may lie outside the capabilities of reptilian design ... we must assume that consciousness would not have evolved on our planet if a cosmic catastrophe had not claimed the dinosaurs as victims. In an entirely literal sense, we owe our existence, as large and reasoning mammals, to our lucky stars' (Gould 1989: 318). Even if one thinks that this is perhaps a little extreme, there is surely enough truth to make one very wary about biological progress as a basis for one's moral code. Normatively, perhaps, Social Darwinism has much going for it; meta-ethically, the justification seems shaky.

On Being Social

So how are we to do better, convinced that the Social Darwinians may have been wrong in execution but were certainly right in conviction, that evolution – specifically Darwinian evolution – has to be important in the understanding of morality? As in the case of epistemology, let us start with the empirical case and then try to tease out the philosophical implications. And to start the empirical case let us go back to the fact that humans are members of a highly social species, and that human social behaviour must be seen as a product of natural selection. We survive as a species because we work together. But remember the survival is not for the benefit of the species: we survive as individuals because by working cooperatively we do better as individuals than we would otherwise. We humans are not particularly fast, we are not particularly strong, we are not particularly ferocious or any of these things, but because we work together we do very well. Of course there is violence between humans. We have seen that in the case of the brutality of some men towards their step-children (Daly & Wilson 1988). But the violence notwithstanding, we humans are still capable of much social interaction, far more so in fact than most other mammals. The question now becomes, how it is that humans act together so well socially. I think there are at least three possible answers to this question, and that in some respects we humans answer positively to all three. Let me explain.

The first way in which humans might interact socially is purely innately, that is to say purely by instinct. I take it that this is the way that much if not most social behaviour in the animal kingdom comes about. No one thinks, for instance, that the ants are thinking beings, and yet they cooperate in the most marvellous ways (Wilson 1971). They do everything entirely by instinct. They are, to use a modern metaphor, hard-wired in their behaviour. Fairly obviously, humans follow this pattern to a certain extent also. Parents and children often interact on an instinctive basis: the love that a mother feels for her child has nothing to do with reason or rationality in any way. It is something which comes about naturally, as it were. It is part of human nature, meaning that it is part of instinctive or biological human nature. However, this is not the only way in which humans interact socially, and there is a very good reason why we humans must have taken a different evolutionary route from lower organisms such as ants. Their instinct has both strengths and weaknesses. The strengths are that one can start action immediately. There is no need for training or education or anything like that, so the ants can work with fairly simple brains, and do not need any instructing as to what they ought to do. But there are major drawbacks. In particular, there is the big problem that if something goes wrong instinctive behaviour is (generally speaking) unable to respond and put things right immediately. If, for instance, a stream of ants is out foraging — doing all of this instinctively — and then it starts to rain, it is more than likely that many of these ants will fail to find their way back to the nest. To this point, they have been guided out and back by chemical (pheromone) trails. The rain washes these trails away, and consequently because of the disruption many of the nest members are lost.

A queen ant can afford to lose many offspring, because she is turning out literally millions. Humans do not have this luxury. We have evolved in such a way as to produce only a few offspring, and we simply cannot afford to lose them if something goes wrong. (The difference I am referring to is known technically as the distinction between r-selection and K-selection. With the former, you produce lots of offspring but do not put too much parental care into matters. With the latter, you produce very few offspring, but do put a lot of parental care into matters. Humans are K-selected organisms; although again one has one of those feedback, selective loops. As we have developed our social adaptations, in the way that we have, we have become K-selected and conversely have become better at K-selection strategies.) The point I am making is that instinct simply will not do as the exclusive cause of the social interactions of humans.

What then would be a second option? The most obvious is to go completely the other way. Instead of being purely instinctive, we might be hardly instinctive if at all, forever calculating the payoff in social interactions (Axelrod 1984). Two humans meet and (for some reason) the issue arises as to whether they should interact socially or not. Remembering now that in the modern biological context everything is done from the individual perspective, what these two individuals will do is reason together or apart, deciding whether cooperation is in their interests or not. If it is, then they will cooperate, and if it is not then they will not cooperate. (It is often thought that purely rational beings, that is to say humans with superbrains, would necessarily be really nasty beings like Darth Vader before his reformation. In fact, this is not necessarily so. Because everybody is a superbeing, each will recognize that it is going to be impossible to be universally nasty, because everyone else is in the same condition. Hence, each will have to cooperate.)

In respects, as with the first option (instinct), humans have taken this causal path towards sociality. Many of our dealings with our fellow humans are done in a purely reasonable or rational way. I go to buy a shirt from L. L. Bean. I give him money for the shirt; he gives me the shirt. I do this not because I like L. L. Bean, nor does he reciprocate because he likes me. Rather, it is in our own self-interest to interact socially together here. However, again there are limits to this mode of interaction. There are good biological reasons why we have not become just superbrain, rational calculators, even were this biologically possible. The big drawback to being a supercalculator is that it takes time, and in the evolutionary world time is money. Often, one simply does not have the temporal luxury available to make the perfect calculations. Suppose you and I are out on a savannah and a lion is coming at us. If I spend much time deciding whether or not it is in my interests to let you know that the lion is coming and that we should cooperate in escaping, before the decision is made we will both be in the lion's stomach. What we need, therefore, is some kind of quick and dirty solution in order to cooperate rapidly together, a method that will usually work quickly on a day-to-day basis, even though it is not failsafe.

The analogy which comes to mind here is that of a chess-playing machine. The early chess-playing machines calculated every move. They were like the superbrains of the second option. But of course, as we all know, the early chess-playing machines were virtually useless. They took so long after two or three moves to make the next move that no one got anywhere. What happened then was that the designers of such machines started to 'build in' certain strategies: when a configuration of pieces came up on the board, the machine could run through its various options and come up with a quick solution. Initially, the early machines were not very good and could be beaten easily by human beings. But as we all know from the story of Deep Blue (the chess machine that beat the human World Champion), before very long the machines became so very sophisticated that, although they could in fact be beaten, generally they were not. I think that humans have taken this third option. We are hard-wired in some sense to act socially together, but we are not hard-wired in such a way that we never make mistakes. The point is that we use this hard-wiring in order to deal with particular situations on a day-by-day basis.

Less metaphorically, what I am suggesting is that we humans have built-in innately, or instinctively if you like, a capacity for working together socially. And what I want to suggest is that this capacity manifests itself at the physical level as a moral sense.

Hence, what I am arguing – on purely naturalistic, Darwinian grounds – is that morality or rather a moral sense is something which is hard-wired into humans. It has been put there by natural selection in order to get us to work together socially or to cooperate. This is not to say that we do not have freedom in any sense. I am not saying that we never disregard our moral sense, but rather that we do have the moral sense and we have the moral sense not by choice or decision, but because we are human. (Of course, there are going to be psychopaths without a moral sense, but in biology you know that there are going to be exceptions for every rule.) My claim, therefore, is that when that when humans find themselves in a position where cooperation might pay, morality kicks into place. This is not to say that we always will cooperate or be moral. We are influenced by many factors, including selfish and other sorts of desires. But morality is one of these factors, and overall we humans do generally work together. Sometimes the morality backfires. I might go to the aid of a drowning child, and drown myself. This is hardly in my self-interest. But on balance it is in my interests to have the feeling that I ought to help people in distress, particularly children in distress. This is both because I myself was at some stage of my life a child, and also because I myself will probably have or be going to have children. I want others to be prepared to take a risk on my behalf or on the behalf of my children.

Let me stress that the biological claim (I am not yet talking philosophically) is that humans have a genuine sense of morality. It is the kind of morality that someone like Immanuel Kant (1949[1788]) talks about. This is not a scientific position of pure ethical egoism in the sense that we are all selfish people just simply calculating for our own ends. That is the second option. We are rather people with a real moral sense, a feeling of right and wrong and obligation. Admittedly, at the causal level this is brought about by individual selection maximizing our own reproductive ends. But the point is that, although humans are produced by selfish genes, selfish genes do not necessarily produce selfish people. In fact, selfish people in the literal sense tend to get pushed out of the group or ostracized pretty quickly. They are simply not playing the game. In a way, therefore, we have a kind of social contract. But note that it is not a social contract brought about, in the long-distant past, by a group of grey-bearded men sitting around a campfire. It is rather a social contract brought on by our biology, that is to say, by our genes as fashioned and selected by natural selection.

This then is the Darwinian perspective on the evolution and current nature of morality. Let us now see how this plays out when we try to put things into a philosophical context, asking the questions that we asked earlier about Social Darwinism.

Substantive Ethics

I am arguing that humans cooperate for biological ends, namely their own biological ends. I am arguing that human moral behaviour has to be such that it is going to serve the individual. That is not to say that it is going to serve the individual on every occasion, nor is it to say that the human will be thinking about the personal gain every time one acts morally. In fact the whole point about morality is that one tends not to think in such a way. Perhaps by definition morality excludes such thinking. But it is to say that morality must be such that it will be of personal benefit. I have referred above to a social contract, and while I am denying a social contract in the traditional sense, it is pretty clear that the kind of substantive ethics to which Darwinian biology leads is an ethics very much akin to what one would expect to find in a social contract. More than this. I would argue that this is the kind of ethics that we do have in real life. So, remembering that I am offering a naturalized position (that is, one consciously based on the methods and results of the physical sciences), we have here the kind of empirical backing that is demanded by the kind of position I am proposing and endorsing. The best-known contemporary exposition of the social contract theory is that offered by John Rawls in his 1971 book *A Theory of Justice*, and I would say that this is very much the kind of morality that one would expect from a Darwinian perspective. It is, incidentally, interesting and significant that Rawls himself acknowledges this fact. He agrees that the social contract was hardly an actual event, but was rather something which was brought on by the struggle for existence working on our innate biology. Let us explore this point.

As is well known, Rawls argues for a position that he calls 'justice as fairness'. He argues that in order to be just one ought to be fair. For Rawls, being fair does not necessarily mean giving everybody absolutely equal shares of everything. Rather, he invites us to put ourselves behind what he calls a 'veil of ignorance', not knowing what position we might find ourselves occupying in society: whether we will be male or female, rich or poor, black or white, healthy or sick, or any of these things. Then he asks what position self-interest dictates as the best kind of society to find oneself in, and Rawls' answer is that it is a society where in some sense everybody does as well out of the society as one might possibly expect, given our various talents. It may well be that we will be born male and rich and powerful and healthy and so forth. If we knew we were going to find ourselves in that position, then we would want maximally to reward people in that position. But of course we may be female and poor and helpless, in which case we would lose out. So there is an initial presumption of equality. Yet this is overthrown as soon as one recognizes that something like the availability of good medical care is going to be of benefit to everybody. And if in fact the only way that you can get the best talented people to become doctors is by paying them more than twice what you pay university professors, then 'justice as fairness' dictates the propriety of this kind of inequality. So what Rawls ends up with is a society with inequalities, but in some sense a society where the inequalities benefit each and every individual in the group.

I would suggest that this is very much the kind of society that one expects evolutionary biology to have produced. That is to say, a group of people who think that one ought to be just, meaning that one ought to be fair. A group which will recognize that there will be inequalities, but will also recognize that these inequalities will in some sense be of benefit to all. I am not suggesting that every actual society has turned out like this, but that is not really the point. One recognizes there are going to be all sorts of ways in which biology will fail to match what the genes might dictate as best. There may be inequalities brought about by particular circumstance or fortune or whatever. But the point is, how do we think that a society ought to be, even if it is not necessarily always that way. That is to say, how we think morally that a society ought to be, even though it does not always work out that way. (Although note how unstable are societies, like the Third Reich, that blatantly and egregiously violate rules of fairness.)

Even societies that we may (properly) judge as unfair in some overall sense, societies based on a slave system for instance, usually flourish only if and inasmuch as everyone gets some kind of break. If you mistreat your slaves, you are going to get rebellion and worse. And this point about societies – the distinction between what one might think morally ought to be, and what actually comes about – reflects down to the same point about individuals. The way that things actually come about is because of individuals, but nobody is ever saying that people always act morally or follow the dictates of their conscience. Morally, it is a question of how you ought to behave not how you do behave. If, for instance, I find myself rich and powerful, then from a purely selfish point of view I might simply ignore the call of morality or suppress it or educate myself or my children to ignore our biology. No one, certainly no Darwinian is saying that this sort of thing might never happen. At times of great social stress because of a natural disaster like a plague, one might well find the rich and powerful looking after themselves alone. As Christians remind us when they talk of original sin, the existence of a moral code does not preclude selfishness by the individual, even by the individual who accepts the blinding validity of the code.

There are many moral systems other than those focusing on a social contract. However, as a Darwinian I would suggest that these alternatives do not necessarily refute or repudiate what has just been said in favour of a social contract theory. The simple fact of the matter is that most moral systems agree on the basics and only come apart on the kinds of esoteric, artificial examples that philosophers delight in. Everybody, whether a Kantian or a utilitarian or a Christian or whatever, thinks that one ought to be kind to small children, and that gratuitous cruelty towards the aged is wrong, and that there is something to be said for honesty and decency in business and relationships, and so on and so forth.

Most morality in fact is a fairly common-sense morality, rather than a well-articulated system as produced by philosophers (Mackie 1977). And this point is precisely what the Darwinian would insist on. Real human beings have a commonsense morality – just as they have a commonsense rule of reasoning – that guides them in their everyday life. Of course, there are certainly real cases where it is less than obvious to know what one ought to do in a particular case, or where one runs into contradictions as one tries to put things together. If one is in favour of abortion, does this mean that one ought to be in favour of capital punishment also? If one is in favour of free speech, does this mean that tobacco manufacturers ought to be allowed to advertise? Should anti-Semites be allowed to educate their own children in their beliefs? So in some ultimate sense, I am not denying the virtues of what is done by philosophers and other theoretical moralists. What I am saying is that most everyday morality, or what I call commonsense morality – something which is shared by all lasting moral systems – is backed by Darwinian biology. Be kind to others. Don't let your friends down. Try to be as truthful as you can. Care about your kids. (Let me stop at once one of the most popular counterarguments to the Darwinian at this point. Is not the soldier going over the top in the Battle of the Somme putting duty and country above self-interest? Well, yes, but note what one account after another about the First World War always stresses [Ferguson 1998]. What drove men forward was not God or country or glory. Padres were pathetic, generals distant, and gongs were for the regulars. The real force was the desire not to let down your pals on either side of you. That and revenge for the Canadian sergeant who had been crucified by the Hun. Pure Darwin!)

Indeed, I press my defence of a Darwinian commonsense morality. Sometimes one encounters moral systems that, at the substantive level, urge upon you behaviour which is surely counter to the selfish-gene perspective of sociobiology (Singer 1981). For instance, one sometimes finds calls to give everything one has to the poor and to give up on any kind of self-regard or preferential favouritism for one's family or friends. This clearly goes against Darwinian biology. Such biology does not say that you should never care for the stranger, because apart from anything else you may well find yourself a stranger at some point. It does not say that one should never worry about international relations and the well-being of children in Africa. In this day and age particularly, we have what has been called the 'Global Village'. There are good reasons, therefore, from a biological perspective, for some kind of regard for even the most distant human. However, from a biological point of view you are clearly going to do better for yourself if you look after your own children rather than other people's children, and if you are nice to your own friends who might in turn be nice to you than if you care about people far distant. The fact is that the sociobiological approach at the substantive level puts the emphasis on the individual rather than the individual's close acquaintances, and in turn on the individual's close acquaintances rather than the group.

I would say, however, that here is a point in favour of Darwinism rather than otherwise. It is one thing for people to say one ought to care about others. It is another to feel genuinely that one ought to care about others and act upon it. As David Hume pointed out perceptively, our passions follow our relationships: 'A man naturally loves his children better than his nephews, his nephews better than his cousins, his cousins better than strangers, where every thing else is equal. Hence arise our common measures of duty, in preferring one to the other. Our sense of duty always follows the common and natural course of our passions' (Hume 1978[1739–40]: 483–4).

Following the same line, Charles Dickens in his brilliant novel *Bleak House* savagely criticized Mrs Jellyby because she spent all her time worrying about the benighted heathen in Borrioboola-Gha. She should have concerned herself with her own neglected family. Then, after that, with people in her own social group, particularly people like poor Jo the crossing sweeper. Dickens is saying that charity begins at home, and this is the commonsense morality that we all have. If you learned that Michael Ruse was giving three-quarters of his salary to Oxfam, while at the same time his wife and children were having to shop at the Salvation Army and go to the food bank for food, you would have good reason to think that Michael Ruse was trying to buy his way into the Kingdom of Heaven at the expense of others. God will not buy this and neither should we. Darwinism is definitive here and so it should be.

Meta-ethics

There is more one could say about substantive ethics, particularly things about culture that parallel the things said in the realm of epistemology. Certainly much that we do or think at the practical level is much affected by the science and technology of the day. Take, for instance, the question of relations between the sexes and the proper ethical attitude to be taken towards rights of women. We today in the West generally agree that it is right and proper that our daughters receive the education open to our sons, and that our wives and other women have the same opportunities in employment as our husbands and other men. This has not always been so; but, before we rush to condemn our parents and grandparents, reflect first that they did not have the luxury to choose as do we – childbearing and rearing for them was far more onerous (and the need of a man to have an income to support a family more pressing) – and reflect second that they did not have the understanding that we have about men and women. It was not long ago that the best scientific and medical thought was that women (especially middle- and upper-class women) were more delicate than men and hence less able to withstand the rigours of strenuous labour. As with epistemology, I am not saying that culture makes it impossible to judge rival claims, but I am saying that in ethics as in epistemology one can see that whatever the significant role of the genes, there is still place – crucial place – for culture.

Let us now move on. What kind of meta-ethical justification can one give for such claims as that one ought to be kind to children and that one ought to favour one's own family over those of others? I would argue, paradoxically but truthfully, that ultimately there is no justification which can be given! That is to say, I argue that at some level one is driven to a kind of moral scepticism – a scepticism, please note, about foundations rather than about substantive dictates. What I am saying, therefore, is that, properly understood, the Darwinian approach to ethics leads one to a kind of moral non-realism (Ruse 1986). In this respect, the Darwinian ethics I am putting forward in this chapter differs very dramatically from traditional Darwinian ethics, Social Darwinism. There, the foundational appeal is to the very fact of evolution. Herbert Spencer and Edward O. Wilson (among others) argue that one ought to do certain things because by so doing one is promoting the welfare of evolution itself. Specifically, one is promoting human beings as the apotheosis of the evolutionary process – a move condemned by philosophers as a gross instance of the naturalistic fallacy, or as a flagrant violation of Hume's Law (which denies that one can move legitimately from the way that things are, to the way that things ought to be). My kind of evolutionary ethics agrees with the philosopher that the naturalistic fallacy is a fallacy and so also is the violation of Hume's Law. My kind of evolutionary ethics also agrees that Social Darwinism is guilty as charged. But my kind of evolutionary ethics takes this failure as a springboard of strength to its own position. The Darwinian ethics described here avoids the naturalistic fallacy, not so much by denying that the fallacy is a fallacy, but by doing an end run around. There is no fallacious appeal to evolution as foundations because there are no foundations to appeal to!

To be blunt, my Darwinian says that substantive morality is a kind of illusion, put in place by our genes, in order to make us good social cooperators (Ruse & Wilson 1985, 1986). I would add, incidentally, that the reason why the illusion is such a successful adaptation is that not only do we believe in substantive morality, but we also believe that substantive morality does have an objective foundation. An important part of the phenomenological experience of substantive ethics is, not just that we feel that we that we ought to do the right and proper thing, but that we feel that we ought to do the right and proper thing because it truly is the right and proper thing. As John Mackie (1979) argued before me, an important part of the moral experience is that we objectify our substantive ethics. There are in fact no foundations, but we believe that there are in some sense foundations. There is a good biological reason why we do this. If, with the emotivists, we thought that morality was simply a question of emotions without any sanction or justification behind them, then pretty quickly morality would collapse into futility. I might dislike you stealing my money, but ultimately why should you not do so? It is just a question of feelings. But in actual fact, the reason why I dislike you stealing my money is not simply because I do not like to see my money go, but because I think that you have done wrong. You really and truly have done wrong in some objective sense. This gives me and others the authority to criticize you. Substantive morality stays in place as an effective illusion because we think that it is no illusion but the real thing. Thus, I am arguing that the epistemological foundation of evolutionary ethics is a kind of moral non-realism, but that it is an important part of evolutionary ethics that we think it is a kind of moral realism.

In a way, what has been given thus far in this section is just statements rather than proofs. What justification can I offer for my position? Why should one not say that there truly is a moral reality underlying what I have said about morality at the substantive level, and that our biology has led us to it. After all we would surely want to say that, because of our biology, we are aware of a speeding train bearing down on us, but this in no sense denies the reality of the speeding train (Nozick 1981). Why should we not say, in a like fashion, that we are aware of right and wrong because ultimately there is an objective right and wrong lying behind moral intuitions?

However, things are rather different in the moral case from the speeding train case. A more insightful analogy can be drawn from spiritualism. In the First World War, when so many young men were killed, the bereaved – the parents, the wives, the sweethearts, on both sides of the trenches – often went to spiritualists, hoping to get back in touch with the departed dead. And indeed they would get back in touch. They would hear the messages come through the Ouija boards or whatever assuring them of the happiness of the deceased. Hence, the people who went to spiritualists would go away comforted. Now, how do we explain this sort of thing? Cases of fraud aside, we would say that people were not listening to the late departed, but rather were hearing voices created by their own imaginations which were in some sense helping them to compensate for their loss. What we have here is some kind of individual illusion brought about by powerful social circumstances. No one would think that the late Private Higgins was really speaking to his mum and dad. Indeed, there are notorious cases where people were reported killed and then found not to be dead. How embarrassing it would be to have heard the late departed assure you of his well-being, and then to find out that the late departed was in fact lying injured in a military field hospital.

In the spiritualism case, once we have got the causal explanation as to why people hear as they do, we recognize that there is no further call for ultimate foundations. I would argue that the biological case is very similar. There are strong biological reasons for cooperation; naturally, we are going to be selfish people but as cooperators we need some way to break through this selfishness; and so our biology has given us morality in order to help us do it. Once again I stress that this is not to say that we are always going to act morally: in fact, we are an ambivalent mixture of good and bad, as the Christian well knows. It is to say that we do have genuine moral sentiments which we think are objective, and that these were put in place by biology. Once we recognize this, we see the sentiments as illusory (although, because we objectify, it is very difficult to recognize this fact). But still you might protest that does not mean that there is no objective morality behind all of this: either an objective morality of a Platonic ilk that actually exists out there, or an objective morality of the Kantian form that is a kind of necessary condition for rational beings getting along. Here, however, the Darwinian can come back with a further argument, namely one based on the doubts expressed earlier about biological progress. There is no natural climb upwards from the blob up to the human, from the monad to the man, as people used to say in the nineteenth century. Rather, evolution is a directionless process, going nowhere rather slowly. What this means in this particular context is that there is really no reason why humans might not have evolved in a very different sort of way, without the kind of moral sentiments that we have. From the Darwinian perspective, there is no ontological compulsion about moral thinking.

It is true that, as Kant stressed, it may possibly be that social animals may necessarily have to have certain formal rules of behaviour. But it is not necessarily the case that these formal rules of behaviour have to incorporate what we would understand as commonsense (substantive) morality. In particular, we might well have evolved as beings with what I like to call the 'John Foster

Dulles system of morality', so named after Eisenhower's secretary of State during the Cold War in the 1950s. Dulles hated the Russians, and he knew that the Russians hated him. He felt he had a moral obligation to hate the Russians because if he did not everything would come tumbling down. But because there was this mutual dislike, of a real obligation-based kind, there was in fact a level of cooperation and harmony. The world did not break down into war and destruction. As a Darwinian, it is plausible to suggest that humans might have evolved with the John Foster Dulles kind of morality, where the highest ethical calling would not be 'Love your neighbour', but 'Hate your neighbour'. But remember that your neighbour hates you and so you had better not harm them because they are going to come straight back at you and do the same.

Now, at the very least, this means that we have the possibility not only of our own (substantive) morality but of an alternative, very different kind of morality: a morality which may have the same formal structure but which certainly has a different content. The question now is, if there is an objective foundation to substantive morality, which of the two is right? At a minimum, we are left with the possibility that we humans now might be behaving in the way that we do but that what is truly objective morality is something quite else from what we believe. We believe what we do because of our biology, and we believe that because of our biology our substantive morality is objectively justified. But the true objective morality is something other than what we have. Obviously, this is a sheer contradiction to what most people mean by objective morality. What most people mean by objective morality incorporates the fact that it is going to be self-revealing to human beings. Not necessarily to all human beings but – like Descartes' clear and distinct ideas – certainly self-revealing to all decent human beings who work hard at it. So, given Darwinism, we have a refutation of the existence of such a morality. Darwinian evolutionary biology is non-progressive, pointing away from the possibility of our knowing objective morality. We might be completely deceived, and since objective morality could never allow this, it cannot exist. For this reason, I argue strongly that Darwinian evolutionary theory leads one to a moral scepticism, a kind of moral non-realism. (And if you point out that, having rejected the Kantian option, my whole position starts to sound very much like that of David Hume, who likewise thought that morality was a matter of psychology rather than reflection of non-natural objective properties, I shall take this as a compliment not a criticism. As I said at the beginning of Chapter 5, I regard what I am about as bringing David Hume up to date via the science of Charles Darwin.)

Limits

As in Chapter 5, I come to the question of limits to understanding. And you will not be surprised to learn that I think that in ethics there are things to be said roughly parallel to those said in the realm of epistemology. First, why are things as they are and why do things work as well as they do? You might think that in ethics things hardly do work as well as they do in epistemology, in science for instance, and there is perhaps truth in this. But if you look at today's large societies, especially those that do function reasonably well (I would pick out those from the West if I were not at danger of being accused of chauvinism about others), it is surely remarkable that they are simply based on rules of conduct forged in times and places very different from our own. And here, all I can say is that remarkable or not this is as it may be, and an empirical approach – an approach based on Darwinism – can say little or nothing more. If you are to seek supposedly deeper answers, you must seek elsewhere.

Second, there is the relativism of ethics as there is the relativism of epistemology. Being part of the system as we humans are, I do not think we can ever properly privilege one system absolutely over all others. Just as we can dismiss phlogiston theory as false, so we can dismiss National Socialism as evil; so we are not moral cretins or totally amoral subjectivists. But I doubt we can ever achieve some kind of total and absolute objectivity or finality in these matters. If there is any plausibility to my example of a Dulles morality, then you will know what I mean and why I argue as I do.

Third, there is the question of realism. Now, I have just been arguing against realism, so in a sense I am perhaps taking a somewhat stronger stand than I took in the realm of epistemology. But of course it is always open to someone to complain that his or her realism is immune to my charges. Such a person might object that no one today believes (as did Moore) in nonnatural properties, the good, somewhat akin to the natural property of being red or cold. Such a person might object that Platonic Forms are no more convincing today than other aspects of Plato's philosophy. Thus, such a person might claim that perhaps the realism is embedded in the will of God who (as supposed by Saint Augustine) saw all that would happen as soon as the first thought of the possibility and desirability of creation at all. The progress supposedly needed to get to the right end thus becomes otiose, for God knew that the end would be achieved whatever the mechanism. And the fact that we humans cannot discern, directly or clearly, the will of God is irrelevant to its true existence. God's will is, after all, clouded in mystery (Ruse 2001).

To which, in reply, all I can say is that if this is indeed the case, then we have reached beyond Darwinian understanding in the realm of ethics. As before, I have my opinions, but let me now leave it as an exercise for the reader as to whether the failure of Darwinism at this point is truly a limit to our understanding.

References

Axelrod, R. (1984) *The Evolution of Cooperation.* New York: Basic Books.

Ayala, F. J. (1985) 'The theory of evolution: recent successes and challenges', in McMullin, E. (ed.), *Evolution and Creation.* Notre Dame, IN: University of Notre Dame Press: 59–90.

Barrett, P. H., Gautrey, P. J., Herbert, S., Kohn, D., and Smith, S. (eds) (1987) *Charles Darwin's Notebooks, 1836–1844.* Ithaca, NY: Cornell University Press.

Black, M. (1962) *Models and Metaphors.* Ithaca, NY: Cornell University Press.

Bullock, A. (1991) *Hitler and Stalin: Parallel Lives.* London: HarperCollins.

Cosmides, L. (1989) 'The logic of social exchange: has natural selection shaped how humans reason? Studies with the Wason selection task', *Cognition,* 31: 187–276.

Crook, P. (1994) *Darwinism: War and History.* Cambridge: Cambridge University Press.

Daly, M., and Wilson, M. (1988) *Homicide.* New York: De Gruyter.

Darwin, C. (1859) *On the Origin of Species.* London: John Murray.

— (1871) *The Descent of Man.* London: John Murray.

Deacon, T. W. (1997) *The Symbolic Species: The Co-Evolution of Language and the Brain.* New York: W. W. Norton.

De Waal, F. (1982) *Chimpanzee Politics: Power and Sex Among Apes.* London: Cape.

Ferguson, N. (1998) *The Pity of War.* London: Allen Lane.

Friedlander, S. (1997) *Nazi Germany and the Jews: The Years of Persecution 1933–39.* London: Weidenfeld & Nicolson.

Gasman, D. (1971) *The Scientific Origins of National Socialism: Social Darwinism in Ernst Haeckel and the Monist League.* New York: Elsevier.

Gould, S. J. (1988) 'On replacing the idea of progress with an operational notion of directionality', in Nitecki, M. H. (ed.), *Evolutionary Progress.* Chicago: University of Chicago Press: 319–38.

— (1989) *Wonderful Life: The Burgess Shale and the Nature of History.* New York: W. W. Norton.

Hamilton, W. D. (1964a) 'The genetical evolution of social behaviour I', *Journal of Theoretical Biology,* 7: 1–16.

— (1964b) 'The genetical evolution of social behaviour II', *Journal of Theoretical Biology,* 7: 17–32.

Hausfater, G., and Hrdy, S. (eds) (1984) *Infanticide: Comparative and Evolutionary Perspectives.* New York: Aldine.

Hempel, C. G. (1966) *Philosophy of Natural Science.* Englewood Cliffs, NJ: Prentice–Hall.

Hölldobler, B., and Wilson, E. O. (1990) *The Ants.* Cambridge, MA: Harvard University Press.

Hume, D. (1978) *A Treatise of Human Nature.* Oxford: Oxford University Press. [1739–40]

Huxley, J. S. (1942) *Evolution: The Modern Synthesis.* London: Allen & Unwin.

Huxley, T. H. (1871) 'Administrative nihilism', in Huxley, T. H., *Methods and Results.* London: Macmillan: 251–89.

— (1893) 'Evolution and ethics', in T. H., Huxley, *Evolution and Ethics'.* London: Macmillan: 46–116.

Jones, G. (1980) *Social Darwinism and English Thought.* Brighton: Harvester.

Joravsky, D. (1970) *The Lysenko Affair.* Cambridge, MA: Harvard University Press.

Kant, I. (1949) *Critique of Practical Reason.* Chicago: University of Chicago Press. [1788]

Kelly, A. (1981) *The Descent of Darwin: The Popularization of Darwinism in Germany, 1860–1914.* Chapel Hill: University of North Carolina Press.

Kropotkin, P. (1955) *Mutual Aid.* Ed. A. Montague; Boston: Extending Horizons Books. [1902]

Kuhn, T. (1962) *The Structure of Scientific Revolutions.* Chicago: University of Chicago Press.

— (1977) 'Objectivity, value, judgement, and theory choice', in Kuhn, T. *The Essential Tension: Selected Studies in Scientific Tradition and Change.* Chicago: University of Chicago Press: 320–39.

Lakoff, G., and Johnson, M. (1980) *Metaphors We Live By*. Chicago: University of Chicago Press.

Lewontin, R. C. (1974) *The Genetic Basis of Evolutionary Change*. New York: Columbia University Press.

Locke, J. (1959) *An Essay Concerning Human Understanding*. New York: Dover. [1690]

Lumsden, C. J., and Wilson, E. O. (1981) *Genes, Mind, and Culture*. Cambridge, MA: Harvard University Press.

McMullin, E. (1983) 'Values in science', in Asquith, P. D. and Nickles, T. (eds), *PSA 1982*. East Lansing, MI: Philosophy of Science Association: 3–28.

Mackie, J. (1977) *Ethics*. Harmondsworth: Penguin Books.

— (1979) *Hume's Moral Theory*. London: Routledge & Kegan Paul.

Maienschein, J., and Ruse, M. (eds) (1998) *Biology and Ethics*. Cambridge: Cambridge University Press.

Marchant, J. (ed.) (1916) *Alfred Russel Wallace: Letters and Reminiscences*. London: Cassell.

Mitman, G. (1990) 'Evolution as Gospel: William Patten, the language of democracy and the Great War', *Isis*, 81: 44–93.

Moore, G. E. (1903) *Principia Ethica*. Cambridge: Cambridge University Press.

Nagel, E. (1961) *The Structure of Science, Problems in the Logic of Scientific Explanation*. New York: Harcourt, Brace & World.

Nozick, R. (1981) *Philosophical Explanations*. Cambridge, MA: Harvard University Press.

Pinker, S. (1994) *The Language Instinct: How the Mind Creates Language*. New York: William Morrow.

— (1997) *How the Mind Works*. New York: W. W. Norton.

Pittenger, M. (1993) *American Socialists and Evolutionary Thought, 1870–1920*. Madison: University of Wisconsin Press.

Polkinghorne, J. (1989) *Science and Providence: God's Interaction with the World*. Boston: Shambhala.

Popper, K. R. (1959) *The Logic of Scientific Discovery*. London: Hutchinson.

Provine, W. B. (1971) *The Origins of Theoretical Population Genetics*. Chicago: University of Chicago Press.

Quine, W. V. O. (1969) *Ontological Relativity and Other Essays*. New York: Columbia University Press.

Rawls, John (1971) *A Theory of Justice*. Cambridge, MA. Harvard University Press.

Richards, R. J. (1987) *Darwin and the Emergence of Evolutionary Theories of Mind and Behavior*. Chicago: University of Chicago Press.

Ruse, M. (1973) *The Philosophy of Biology*. London: Hutchinson.

— (1979) *The Darwinian Revolution: Science Red in Tooth and Claw*. Chicago: University of Chicago Press.

— (1980) 'Charles Darwin and group selection', *Annals of Science*, 37: 615–30.

— (1982) *Darwinism Defended: A Guide to the Evolution Controversies*. Reading, MA: Benjamin/Cummings.

— (1985) *Sociobiology: Sense or Nonsense?* 2nd edn. Dordrecht: Reidel.

— (1986) *Taking Darwin Seriously: A Naturalistic Approach to Philosophy*. Oxford: Blackwell.

— (1989) *The Darwinian Paradigm: Essays on its History, Philosophy and Religious Implications*. London: Routledge.

— (1994) *Evolutionary Naturalism: Selected Essays*. London: Routledge.

— (1996) *Monad to Man: The Concept of Progress in Evolutionary Biology*. Cambridge, MA: Harvard University Press.

— (1999) *Mystery of Mysteries: Is Evolution a Social Construction?* Cambridge, MA: Harvard University Press.

— (2000) *The Evolution Wars: A Guide to the Controversies*. Santa Barbara, CA: ABC–CLIO.

— (2001) *Can a Darwinian be a Christian? The Relationship between Science and Religion*. Cambridge: Cambridge University Press.

Ruse, M., and Wilson, E. O. (1985) 'The evolution of morality', *New Scientist*, 1478: 108–28.

— (1986) 'Moral philosophy as applied science', *Philosophy*, 61: 173–92.

Singer, P. (1981) *The Expanding Circle: Ethics and Sociobiology*. New York: Farrar, Straus & Giroux.

Spencer, H. (1851) *Social Statics; Or the Conditions Essential to Human Happiness Specified and the First of them Developed*. London: J. Chapman.

— (1852) 'A theory of population, deduced from the general law of animal fertility', *Westminster Review*, 1: 468–501.

— (1892) *The Principles of Ethics*. London: Williams & Norgate.

— (1857) 'Progress: Its law and cause', *Westminster Review*, 67: 244–67.

Todes, D. P. (1989) *Darwin Without Malthus: The Struggle for Existence in Russian Evolutionary Thought*. New York: Oxford University Press.

Wallace, A. R. (1905) *My Life: A Record of Events and Opinions*. London: Chapman & Hall.

Whewell, W. (1840) *The Philosophy of the Inductive Sciences.* 2 vols; London: Parker.
Wilson, E. O. (1971) *The Insect Societies.* Cambridge, MA: Harvard University Press.
— (1984) *Biophilia.* Cambridge, MA: Harvard University Press.
— (1992) *The Diversity of Life.* Cambridge, MA: Harvard University Press.
— (1998) *Consilience.* New York: Vintage.
Young, R. M. (1985) *Darwin's Metaphor: Nature's Place in Victorian Culture.* Cambridge, MA: Cambridge University Press.

Part IV
Must Science Validate All Knowledge?

Lynne Rudder Baker

7
First-Person Knowledge

Lynne Rudder Baker

On 11 June 2001, Timothy McVeigh was executed for the Oklahoma City bombing that killed 168 people. Two days prior to the execution, many people, including McVeigh, knew that McVeigh was going to be executed in two days. But McVeigh knew something that the rest of us did not. He had first-person knowledge: '*I* am going to be executed in two days.' Moreover, his first-person knowledge was something that he experienced: he knew how it felt to know that he was going to be executed in two days. This is something that the rest of us could not have known.

What I intend to do in this chapter is to discuss the peculiar sort of knowledge that McVeigh had, but that the rest of us lacked, two days before the execution. I choose to speak of McVeigh's first-person knowledge, not to exploit a solemn and momentous occasion, but to illustrate the existential and cognitive significance of first-person knowledge to the knower. The contrast between first- and third-person knowledge in the case of McVeigh strikes me as particularly vivid.

Let me begin by stating my aim in these two chapters. They are chapters entitled 'First-Person Knowledge' and 'Third-Person Understanding'. Each of these is a piece of a philosophical picture. What is distinctive about the philosophical picture, and what each of these chapters illustrates, is a rejection of what has been called 'scientific naturalism' or 'scientism'. By 'scientism' I mean the view that all knowable reality is knowable by science. According to this view, if there is any question about reality that no science could ever answer, then the question is defective: science must validate all claims to knowledge. Scientism is not itself a scientific claim; it is a philosophical claim *about* science.

Each of my chapters is intended to be a counterexample to scientism. In the first, I'll argue that there is first-person knowledge that is not accessible to the methods of science. In the second, I'll argue that there is third-person understanding that amounts to a full-blown commonsense conception of the world; the entities and properties recognized by the commonsense conception cannot be systematized into anything like a domain for scientific understanding. My overall goal in the two is to show that not everything that is both knowable and important is visible to science.

The first chapter has four parts. In the first, I shall begin with some background on what I call 'the first-person perspective'. I begin with the first-person perspective, because all first-person knowledge, from the most significant to the most mundane, presupposes that the knower has a first-person perspective. In the second, I shall work out the details of first-person knowledge, knowledge expressed by first-person sentences like 'I know that I am thinking that I am in Scotland', or 'I know that I am in Scotland', or 'I am in Scotland'. In the third, I shall argue for an Irreducibility Thesis, to the effect that first-person knowledge cannot be replaced by third-person knowledge without cognitive loss. Finally, I shall discuss the implications of first-person knowledge for the scope of science.

The First-Person Perspective

We read frequently that the biological differences – differences in DNA, in morphology, in neural structure – between human and nonhuman animals are very slight. Yet, the differences between human and nonhuman animals in behaviour and in social organization are enormous: only human societies have philosophy, science, art, religion. What makes this enormous difference in complexity between human and nonhuman animals, I believe, is that only human animals have what I call 'first-person perspectives'. A first-person perspective is the ability to conceive of oneself as oneself, from 'within' so to speak, without any name or description or demonstrative (Baker 2000, 1998).

The importance of a first-person perspective is easily overlooked because it is both so familiar and so difficult to articulate. But its importance can hardly be overestimated. The first-person perspective makes it possible for us to know that we have goals and to evaluate them and to change them (and thus it underwrites our rational agency). The first-person perspective makes possible self-consciousness, and thus underwrites the fact that we matter to ourselves (Baker 2000, 2002). I believe, but cannot yet prove, that only beings with first-person perspectives can develop sciences and other cultural institutions. The idea of a first-person perspective touches on many philosophical issues – from the ethical issue of what a moral agent is, to the logical issue of what a proposition is, to the existential issue of what it is to prepare for one's own death. (Nothing lacking a first-person perspective could even conceive of its own death.) So, my interest in the first-person perspective is not solely as a counterexample to scientism.

On my view, a first-person perspective is not just a matter of sentience. To have a first-person perspective is to be able to entertain a certain kind of thought about oneself. It is a conceptual ability, not just a discriminative ability of the sort that chimpanzees can acquire by training (Gallup 1977). To have a first-person perspective is not just to be able to think about someone who happens to be oneself, without knowing that it is oneself that one is thinking about. Oedipus thought about the murderer of Laius without realizing that the murderer of Laius was himself. When Oedipus pronounced a malediction upon the murderer of Laius, he was not thereby manifesting his first-person perspective. But when he discovered the truth and said, 'I myself am accursed by my own ignorant edict', he was manifesting a first-person perspective. He not only was thinking about himself, but he was thinking about himself as himself – not thinking of himself as Oedipus, or as the murderer of Laius. A first-person perspective, on my view, is the ability to think about oneself in this unique first-person way and to think about one's thoughts as one's own.

In English, the ability to conceive of oneself as oneself is marked grammatically by a sentence with a first-person subject of a psychological or linguistic verb and an embedded first-person reference (Castañeda 1966, 1967). We English speakers not only use first-person pronouns to refer to ourselves (as in 'I'm happy'), but also to attribute to ourselves first-person reference (as in 'I wonder whether I'll be happy in ten years'). The second occurrence of 'I' in 'I wonder whether I'll be happy in 10 years' makes it obvious that the *content* of my thought includes a first-person reference. The thought directs attention to the person *per se*, without recourse to any name, description or third-person referential device to identify who is being thought about. When I wonder whether I'll be happy in ten years, I am wondering about myself as myself; from a first-person perspective, I do not need to pick myself out as one object among many. I could still have this thought even if I had total amnesia. To hope that I will have a painless death is not, I believe, the same as hoping that Lynne Baker will have a painless death, even though I am Lynne Baker. Use of first-person pronouns embedded in sentences with linguistic or psychological verbs – (e.g., 'I hope that I will have a painless death') – provides linguistic evidence of a first-person perspective.

Borrowing from Hector-Neri Castañeda and from Gareth Matthews, I shall call thoughts of this kind 'I*-thoughts' (Castañeda 1966; Matthews 1992). Examples of I*-thoughts are 'I hope that I* will have a painless death', 'I believe that I* am in good health', and 'I insist that I* am not guilty'. In English, I*-thoughts are expressed grammatically in the first person. The main verb is a psychological verb (like 'wish', 'hope', 'desire', 'expect', 'believe', and so on) or a linguistic verb (like 'say', 'insist', 'swear', and so on). I*-thoughts contain two occurrences of the first-person pronoun, 'I'; the second occurrence of the pronoun 'I' – the one signalled by an asterisk – indicates that my first-person concept of myself is part of the content of the thought. So, 'I am glad that I* am back in Scotland', and 'I swear that I* put the cheque in the mail', indicate that I am thinking of myself from a first-person perspective. The thinker of I*-thoughts has a first-person perspective. You can attribute a first-person perspective to me by saying, 'She is glad that she* is in Scotland'. (And you can attribute a present-time reference to me – a thought that I would express as 'I'm glad that I'm in Scotland now' by saying, 'She was glad that she* was in Scotland then*'. 'She*' attributes a first-person reference).

All forms of self-consciousness, I believe, require a first-person perspective. Self-consciousness is the ability to think about oneself in the way afforded by the first-person perspective. Without the use of any name or description or other third-person referential device, a being with a first-person perspective can know that she* is thinking about herself. Let me emphasize that the first-person perspective is not a substance; it is a property, not a thing, and it is a property that distinguishes persons from everything else. The first-person perspective may well be the product of natural selection, and if it is, then it is still unlike any other kind of property that we know of. Only beings with first-person perspectives can have an inner life; only such beings can be self-reflective. The first-person perspective, as I mentioned, is the basis of all forms of self-consciousness. Now, let us turn to first-person knowledge.

First-Person Knowledge

On my view, the defining characteristic of a person is a first-person perspective, and first-person knowledge is rooted in this view of what a person really is. It is only because we have first-person perspectives that we can have first-person knowledge. The objects of knowledge as well as of belief are propositions.[1] On the view of propositions that I favour, propositions contain concepts. To believe a proposition requires that one have at least partial mastery of the concepts contained in it. The propositions of concern here are those canonically expressed by sentences containing first-person pronouns – whether simple sentences like 'I am happy' or I* sentences like 'I know that I am happy'. Call such propositions 'first-person propositions'. First-person knowledge, as I shall construe it, is knowledge of first-person propositions, where knowledge of a first-person proposition requires that the knower have a first-person concept of himself by means of which to think the proposition known. To have knowledge of a first-person proposition, one must be in a position to formulate the first-person proposition: and if one is in a position to formulate the first-person proposition, then one has the conceptual resources to think an I*-thought. So, anyone who has knowledge of even a simple first-person proposition ('I am happy') has the conceptual resources to entertain an I*-thought ('I know that I* am happy'), and thus has a first-person perspective.

There are two kinds of knowledge that have first-person propositions as objects: (1) knowledge of propositions known as self-justifying (e.g., I exist [as thought by me now]); and (2) knowledge of propositions justified for the knower by evidence or observation (e.g., 'I am in Scotland' [as thought by me now]). What the first-person perspective makes possible is not just knowledge of first-person propositions, but conscious awareness of one's knowledge. One cannot only know that he* exists (or

1 Neither Lewis (1979) nor Chisholm (1981) takes the objects of belief to be propositions. Rather, they construe belief as self-ascription of properties. Instead of first-person propositions expressed by I* sentences, they will have to countenance first-person properties expressed by I* predicates. (Perhaps: I self-ascribe the property of being a person who self-ascribes the property of existing.) Self-ascribing the property of self-ascribing any property presupposes a first-person perspective. The Lewis and Chisholm views, in effect, take 'I*' as primitive.

that he* is going to die in two days), but one can also be consciously aware of knowing these things.

Unlike Descartes, I am not claiming transparency or infallibility about conscious first-person thoughts. I may be mistaken in thinking that I fear that I* shall be interrupted from work this afternoon; without realizing it, I really hope that I* will be interrupted. So, my sincere and comprehending utterance 'I fear that I* will be interrupted from work this afternoon' may be false, a case of self-deception, and thus not a case of knowledge at all. Perhaps you know me well enough to convince me that I really want to be interrupted. I am not claiming that all I*-sentences are true or that I have infallible access to my own mind. So, the first way that I depart from approaches spawned by Descartes is that, as Freud made vivid, in some cases we may be mistaken about our own mental states.

A second way that I depart from Cartesian approaches is that I take those first-person propositions about which I could not be wrong to be part of a broader class of first-person propositions. It is customary to focus on first-person propositions to which the thinker has 'privileged access' or for which the thinker has special authority.[2] These are propositions that are known without observation or evidence – propositions like those expressed by 'I exist' or 'I am now thinking that it's cold in here'. But all first-person knowledge requires that the knower have a first-person perspective, whether the knower has a privileged position with respect to the knowledge or not. On the one hand, knowledge to which a person has privileged access (expressed by, e.g., 'I exist'), and on the other hand, first-person knowledge to which a person has no privileged access (expressed by, e.g., 'I won the lottery') are in the same boat with respect to the first-person perspective. Descartes would have emphasized an epistemological difference between these cases with respect to justification; however, I want to emphasize the metaphysical similarity between them with respect to requiring a first-person perspective.

Theories of knowledge generally agree that, in some sense, knowledge requires justification. It cannot be a fluke or an accident that the knower has a correct belief. A proposition that one knows must, in some sense, be justified. In the example with which I started, Timothy McVeigh had first-person knowledge of his impending execution, which was justified for him by his

2 There is a large literature on first-person authority. See Burge 1996; Wright, Smith & MacDonald 1998.

observations: the trial judge had pronounced the sentence, the appeals were not successful, and McVeigh himself had called off further resistance to execution. McVeigh's knowledge that he was going to be executed was not self-justifying, but was justified on the basis of evidence. The evidence for him was evidence for the proposition that he* was going to be executed in two days.

In general, the evidence that justifies a proposition for a person also justifies her claim to know the proposition. Evidence that justifies for me the proposition that I am in Scotland also justifies for me the proposition that I know that I am in Scotland. So, we have a first-person version of a general transfer-of-justification principle: For any first-person proposition P, if P is justified for a subject S at a time t, then the proposition that S would express by asserting 'I know P' is also justified for S at time t. Whatever justifies, for example, 'I am in Scotland' for me also justifies 'I know that I* am in Scotland'. This transfer-of-justification principle underwrote McVeigh's first-person knowledge of his impending execution. If the proposition that McVeigh would have expressed on 9 June by 'I am going to be executed in two days' was justified for him by evidence or observation, then so was the proposition that he would have expressed on 9 June by 'I know that I* am going to be executed in two days'.

It is well known that there is a special class of first-person propositions for which no evidence or observation is needed for justification. As Descartes persuasively argued, every time I think 'I exist' my thought is true and I know that it is true. Indeed, I am absolutely certain that I* exist when I think that I do. My thinking at some time that I exist guarantees that I do exist then. I am using 'thinking' here as something that I do and am aware of doing at a particular time. I'll appropriate the phrase 'to think assertively at t' to capture this active and conscious thinking. To think P *assertively* at t is to think P sincerely and comprehendingly at t, and with the same illocutionary force as an assertion of P in natural language, and in such a way that one has the experience of thinking P. Self-justifying thoughts are sometimes called 'occurrent'. One who assertively thinks P at t believes P at t and is aware at t that she* is thinking P then*. She has the experience of thinking P at t; she is conscious that she* is thinking P while she is thinking it. There is something that it is like at t for her to be conscious of P then, and she knows at t what it is like to think P then*. With this notion of 'assertively thinking P at t', we can define 'self-justifying proposition' as follows:

P is a self-justifying proposition for a subject S if and only if S's assertively thinking P at t guarantees that P is true at t.

Examples of self-justifying propositions are familiar cases like those expressed by 'I exist', 'I am now judging that snow is white', 'I intend to raise my arm now'. Self-justifying propositions have this special feature: every time that S thinks assertively a self-justifying proposition, S has knowledge of it. If I think assertively at t 'I exist now', then I know at t that I* exist then*. Of course, there may be self-justifying propositions for S that S is not even aware of. A proposition P is self-justifying for S just in case, if S were to think P assertively, S would know P; but S may not know P because S never thought P assertively. What makes a proposition self-justifying for S is that if S were to think that proposition assertively, that proposition would be true. Only first-person propositions (and not all of them) are self-justifying.

On the traditional conception of knowledge (found in Plato), knowledge is thought of as belief that is both true and justified. In 1963, my colleague, Edmund Gettier, showed that this conception was defective, and started an industry of attempts to repair the notion of knowledge as justified true belief (Gettier 1963). Since I think that the notion of justified true belief is a deep insight into the nature of knowledge, and since clauses may be added to the traditional conception to make it adequate, I shall advert to the traditional conception, at least provisionally. The traditional conception of knowledge straightforwardly applies to first-person propositions, whether self-justifying or justified by evidence or observation: If P is a first-person proposition – one that S would express by a first-person sentence – then S knows P at time t if and only if S believes P at t, P is true at t, and P is justified for S at t. Thus, we have a unified view of first-person knowledge that does not sever self-justifying knowledge from other first-person knowledge. First-person knowledge is of a piece.

Wittgenstein famously denied that the sentence 'I am in pain' expresses a proposition that can be known (Wittgenstein 1953). Wittgenstein held that where there was knowledge, there was the possibility of doubt. Saying 'I am in pain', Wittgenstein thought, is just a linguistic replacement for natural behaviour like groaning. 'I am in pain' cannot be doubted any more than groaning can be. But I see no reason why natural non-linguistic behaviour (which, I agree, is not subject to knowledge or doubt) cannot be replaced by linguistic behaviour that can be known, whether it can be doubted or not. And it is not even clear that 'I am in pain' is always immune to doubt. There are borderline cases of pain, in which I've been given a painkiller for excruciating pain and it is beginning to take effect. I might even wonder: Am I in pain?

Moreover, there is another reason to think that the sentence 'I am in pain' expresses a proposition that can be known. There are inferential connections between first-person expressions like 'I am in pain' and third-persons expressions that undoubtedly express propositions that can be known. If I say 'I am in pain', then someone has said that someone is in pain. 'Someone is in pain' surely expresses a proposition that can be known. Similarly, if I sincerely say 'I am in pain' and you sincerely say 'I am in pain', then an observer who does not doubt our sincerity may correctly infer, 'Two people are in pain' – again a proposition that can be known. Such inferential connections between first- and third-person propositions seem to me to override Wittgenstein's considerations of undoubtability.

An additional reason, I think, that Wittgenstein denied that 'I am in pain' is subject to being known is that my relation to my pain seems more intimate than one of knowledge or doubt. I agree that my relation to my pain is maximally intimate; but we need not on that account deny that I can know 'I am in pain'. On my view, the difference between my being in pain and my knowing that I am in pain is that the latter but not the former requires a first-person perspective. But the first-person perspective – which, on my view, is what makes me me – can hardly distance me from my pain. My knowledge of my pain is as intimate as my pain. A dog can be in pain, but, lacking a first-person perspective – a dog does not know that he* is in pain. Nor does a dog have a concept of pain. (Wittgenstein was utterly convincing that one could not acquire the concept 'pain' merely by feeling pain.)

Hence, we should discard Wittgenstein's view that 'I am in pain' is something that I can not know. We can and should discard Wittgenstein's view that I do not know that I am in pain (when I am) without discarding Wittgenstein's valuable insight that the mind cannot be a Cartesian theatre at which a ghostly self is a spectator. So, 'I am in pain' expresses a proposition that I can know.

As I have mentioned, I have been thinking of first-person knowledge on the traditional model of knowledge as justified true belief. But since W. V. O. Quine, we have a new, more empirical model for knowledge. This new approach – called 'naturalized epistemology' – conjoins theory of knowledge with science.[3] Knowledge is still considered to be a kind of true belief, but old-fashioned justification by evidence or self-justification is replaced (in one popular version) by the idea that justification of a belief depends on its having been produced by a reliable psychological mechanism – that is, a mechanism that tends to produce true belief. I shall focus on this version, called 'reliabilism'. On the traditional model, the knower has access to what entitles him to claim to know something (e.g., evidence), and not just to believe it; on reliabilism, the knower does not have such access. The scientist will determine which mechanism actually caused a belief, and whether mechanisms of its kind are reliable.

I do not want to dismiss reliabilism as merely an example of the scientism that I oppose. My objection to scientism is not any objection to science; the objection to scientism is rather an objection to regarding science as a kind of closure principle on knowledge that says, in effect, that there is no knowledge beyond the reach of science. So, the question that I would ask about reliabilism is this: how could reliabilism handle first-person knowledge?

In the non-self-justifying cases, naturalized epistemology would usually return the same results as the traditional model of knowledge. If the reliabilists are right, then reliable belief-forming mechanisms generate beliefs for which we have good evidence in the traditional sense. (Otherwise, on what grounds would we call a mechanism reliable? An uncharitable observer might note that reliabilism thus seems to presuppose the traditional view of knowledge.) But knowledge of self-justifying propositions presents a problem for reliabilism, I believe. Most of the time when I think 'I exist now' my thought is no doubt produced by a reliable mechanism; and hence on those occasions, reliabilism would agree that I have first-person knowledge. But suppose that I have taken LSD, which causes random chemical changes in my brain that at t produces the thought 'I exist now'. Clearly, LSD-induced beliefs are not produced by reliable mechanisms. 'Even a tautology can be believed unjustifiably if one arrives at that belief through inappropriate psychological processes,' says Alvin Goldman, a prominent proponent of reliabilism (Goldman 1992). It seems that a reliabilist of this kind must deny that there are any self-justifying

3 For an excellent introduction to naturalized epistemology, see the essays in Kornblith (1985).

propositions. So, according to reliabilism, my true belief at t that I* exist then* is not justified, and hence not knowledge: it was not produced by a reliable mechanism.

Although I take this case to be a counterexample to reliabilism, the reliabilist can just bite the bullet and say that on the occasion when my belief that I* exist then* is caused by LSD, I do not know that I* exist then*. Instead of trying to get the reliabilist to break her teeth on this bullet, however, let me just note that the traditionalist and the naturalized epistemologist can disagree about which cases count as first-person knowledge without disagreeing about the irreplaceability of first-person knowledge by third-person knowledge. And it is the irreplaceability of first-person knowledge by third-person knowledge that I am concerned with here. So, I now turn to showing that first-person knowledge is irreplaceable: it cannot be assimilated to third-person knowledge.

The Irreducibility of First-Person Knowledge

First-person knowledge is unique. First-person knowledge – knowledge expressed by first-person sentences – cannot be replaced by (or translated into, or reduced to) any wholly third-person knowledge without cognitive loss. That is, I want to argue for what I shall call 'the irreducibility thesis':

> *The Irreducibility Thesis:* First-person knowledge (i.e., knowledge that a knower would express by a first-person sentence) cannot be replaced by third-person knowledge (i.e., knowledge that does not require or presuppose that a knower have a first-person perspective) without cognitive loss.

The Irreducibility Thesis implies that a complete account of third-person knowledge would not be a complete account of all knowledge. I say that first-person knowledge cannot be reduced to third-person knowledge for two reasons. The first concerns the uniqueness of the first-person way of thinking of oneself afforded by the first-person perspective; the second concerns the relation between first-person and third-person propositions.

1 To see the uniqueness of the first-person way of thinking of oneself, consider my thought that I exist now. Since 'I exist now' is self-justifying for me now, it is true. Since I believe that I exist now, and 'I exist now' is justified for me, and is true, I

have first-person knowledge that I* exist now. There is no third-person way to express my knowledge that I* exist now. My knowledge that I* exist now is not knowledge that Lynne Baker exists now, as Descartes would be the first to remind us. I cannot assertively think 'I exist now' without knowing that it is true; I can assertively think, 'Lynne Baker exists now' without knowing that it is true. My knowledge that I* exist now cannot be replaced without cognitive loss by my knowledge that Lynne Baker exists now, and I see no other candidates for third-person replacement of my knowledge that I* exist now. Hence, the uniqueness of my first-person way of thinking of myself insures that my knowledge that I* exist now is not reducible to a third-person proposition.

2 The second kind of argument for the Irreducibility Thesis concerns the relation between first-person and third-person propositions. The relation between first- and third-person propositions is such that no purely third-person premises could license the first-person conclusion, say, that I am going to be executed in two days. There are three kinds of points to be made here: one epistemic, one psychological, one logical.

First, consider the epistemic point. The propositions 'McVeigh is going to be executed in two days' and 'I am going to be executed in two days' were justified for McVeigh in different ways. When McVeigh read stories about his impending execution in the papers, he had the same evidence that everyone else had, on 9 June, for the conclusion that McVeigh was going to be executed in two days. All newspaper readers drew the conclusion on 9 June that McVeigh was going to be executed in two days. But McVeigh had an additional premise that did not – indeed, could not – appear in the papers. The additional premise was that he* was McVeigh, a premise that McVeigh would express as 'I am McVeigh'. Only with the addition of that premise was McVeigh justified – not only in concluding what we all concluded, viz., the proposition expressed by 'McVeigh is going to be executed in two days' – but also in concluding (as none of the rest of us did), 'I am going to be executed in two days'.

In short, all readers of the newspapers, including McVeigh, had the same justification on 9 June for the proposition that McVeigh expressed by 'McVeigh is going to be executed in two days'. But we did not all have the same justification on 9 June for the proposition that McVeigh expressed by 'I am going to be executed in two days'.

The second point is psychological: McVeigh's mental state of consciously knowing on 9 June 'I am going to be executed in two days' was a different mental state from his mental state of consciously knowing on 9 June 'McVeigh is going to be executed in two days'. McVeigh's consciously knowing that he* was going to be executed in two days caused him, as the headlines said, to 'prepare to die'. But if McVeigh had been in an accident that had resulted in amnesia, he may have known that McVeigh was going to be executed in two days; but not realizing that he* was McVeigh, McVeigh would not have known that he* was going to be executed in two days. In that case, he would not have prepared to die. If kinds of mental states are individuated by their causes and effects, then McVeigh's knowing that he* was going to be executed is a very different kind of mental state from his knowing that McVeigh was going to be executed (if he hadn't realized that he* was McVeigh).

The third point is logical. No purely third-person propositions entail any first-person proposition (Baker 1981, 2000). One can infer from the first to the third person (from, e.g., 'I am in pain' to 'Someone is in pain') but not, as I am now pointing out, from the third to the first person. In order for McVeigh to make a valid inference from what he read in the papers to the conclusion that he could express on 9 June by, 'I am going to be executed in two days', the premises would have to include one that McVeigh knew that he* was McVeigh. But, of course, that premise is not a wholly third-person proposition since it attributes to McVeigh a first-person reference: it attributes to McVeigh a proposition that he would express by saying, 'I am McVeigh'. If no wholly third-person propositions entail any first-person propositions, then first-person knowledge is not reducible to third-person knowledge.

Let me briefly discuss an alternative to this line of thought. On the alternative, there are no irreducible first-person propositions. There are first-person sentences, or ways of knowing propositions, but all propositions can be expressed in the third person. Propositions, so regarded, contain no tensed or indexical elements (like 'will be' or 'I'). We can distinguish absolute propositions that are the objects of belief from belief-states (or ways of believing or sentences believed or modes of presentation of propositions). There are several accounts of belief that distinguish between proposition believed and what I shall call ways of believing the proposition. John Perry, whose concern is the semantics of belief, distinguishes between belief-state and proposition (1979); David Kaplan, whose concern is the semantics of indexical terms like 'I', 'now', 'here', and demonstrative terms like 'this' and 'that', distinguishes between character and content (1989). Character is a concept close to traditional meaning (e.g., that 'I' means the speaker); content gives the referent. If Adam says 'I am happy', the character of 'I' is a function from the context to the speaker; its content is a function from the speaker to Adam. For purposes here, I am going to lump these views together and call the result 'the 3-place view' since all these views take a belief to be a 3-place relation among a believer, a proposition believed, and some third element (like a belief-state, or as I shall usually say, a way of believing).

On the 3-place view, the term 'first person' applies not to propositions, but rather to ways of believing propositions: the third element of belief. If I say at t 'Sam is tall', and Sam says at t 'I am tall', then, on the 3-place view, the object of both Sam's and my belief is the same proposition: that Sam is tall at t. The difference between us is that Sam is in a first-person belief state, and I'm in a third-person belief state. Sam believes the proposition in a first-person way, and I believe it in a third-person way. But there is just one proposition that we both believe in different ways. On the 3-place view, there are no propositions that are really first-person propositions; there are only first-person ways of believing propositions that are essentially third-person and timeless. Although I do not believe that any 3-place view has been explicitly applied to the topics that concern me here, I want to try to apply a 3-place view to first-person knowledge.

Interestingly, the 3-place view – though it does not countenance irreducible first-person *propositions* – does countenance irreducible first-person *knowledge*. Knowledge, on a 3-place view, has two objects (Lewis 1979): the proposition known and the way of knowing it. The first-person ways of believing (1) are ineliminable without cognitive loss, and (2) take precedence over the object of belief (i.e., the third-person proposition) with respect to knowledge accessible to the knower. On the 3-place view, it is the first-person way of believing (not the proposition or object of belief) that is cognitively significant for the knower. To see the cognitive dominance of (first-person) ways of knowing over (third-person) propositions known on a 3-place account of knowledge, consider four things:

1 Knowledge requires justification. On a 3-place view, the items to be justified must be, in the first instance, ways of knowing, not propositions known. This is so, because a proposition expressed one way may be justified for S at t and that same proposition expressed another way may fail to be justified for S at t. The proposition that I express when at t I think 'I exist now' is justified for me; what, according to the 3-place view, is the very same proposition expressed by 'Lynne Baker exists at t' may not be justified for me: I may not know that I am Lynne Baker, or that now is t. If an advocate of the 3-place view takes justification to pertain primarily to propositions instead of ways of believing them, there will be a contradiction: One and the same proposition could be both justified and unjustified for S at t (justified if expressed at t as 'I exist now', unjustified if expressed at t as 'Lynne Baker exists at t); but if we take justification to pertain primarily to ways of knowing, there is no contradiction. So, we should take justification to apply, in the first instance, not to propositions known but to ways of knowing. Then, secondarily, a proposition itself is justified for S at t if and only if there is some way of believing the proposition that is justified for S at t. (The advocate of the 3-place view would also have to modify the definition of 'self-justifying' to apply not directly to propositions, but to ways they are presented.) Granted, on the 3-place view, the truth of a belief depends on the proposition believed; but the justification of a belief depends on the way of believing or belief-state. So, on the 3-place view, what makes a true belief a bit of knowledge directly concerns the way that it is believed, not the proposition believed.

2 What guides action, on the 3-place view, are not the propositions known, but the ways of knowing them. In Kaplan's famous example, suppose that you are walking down the street, look in a store window and see a person whose pants are on fire. You think 'That person's pants are on fire', but you don't do anything until you realize that the person is you, and it is your pants that are on fire. Then, your behaviour immediately changes. On the 3-place view, there is no change of proposition known (that a particular person's pants were on fire); all that changed was the way that you knew that proposition. You had to know the proposition in a first-person way in order for it to guide your behaviour.[4] Then, in terms of knowledge that can

4 Perry (1979) has a similar example that he treats similarly.

be used to guide action, what matters, on the 3-place view, is the way the proposition is believed (in the first-person way), not the identity of the proposition.

3 When a proposition is presented in a first-person (or other indexical) way, on the 3-place view, the knower is typically ignorant of which proposition, according to the 3-place view, is the proposition known. If Descartes had had total amnesia, he would still have known that he* existed, even if he had no third-person way to express his knowledge. But, on the 3-place view, without a third-person way to express his knowledge, he would have been ignorant of which proposition he expressed by 'I exist'. Indeed, he might well have denied the very proposition that, according to the 3-place view, was the object of his knowledge. With amnesia, Descartes may well have sincerely affirmed, 'I exist but Descartes does not'. The identity of the proposition that Descartes would thus both affirm and deny on the 3-place view is concealed from him. What a knower has access to, on the 3-place view, is the way that the proposition is presented, not the (third-person) identity of the proposition known. Thus, on the 3-place view, one may rationally affirm and deny a single proposition presented to one in different ways. Again, what carries the water on the 3-place view are ways of knowing, not propositions known.

4 Proponents of the 3-place view explicitly identify the cognitive significance of a word or phrase with the way that it is presented to the knower, and not with the proposition known. As we have seen, there are two parts to knowledge on the 3-place view: a proposition known, and a way of knowing it. From the point of view of the knower, the way of knowing has the upper hand over the proposition known. Cognitive significance pertains to ways of knowing, and the first-person way of knowing a proposition cannot be eliminated in favour of third-person ways of knowing without cognitive loss.

The ways of believing (the third element on the 3-place view) have the same features that I attribute to first-person propositions. On the 3-place view, it is ways of knowing, that are: (1) what in the first instance are subject to justification; (2) what guide action; (3) what the knower has access to and thus can use in thought; and (4) what have cognitive significance for the knower. On my view, it is the propositions known that have these features, including first-person propositions. On the 3-place view, it is not propositions, but ways of knowing propositions that have these features. This difference aside, these important first-person features are ineliminable on both views. My conclusion is that, even if we accept the 3-place view, first-person knowledge – understood as what has cognitive significance for the knower – cannot be replaced by third-person knowledge without cognitive loss. So, the uniqueness and importance of first-person knowledge is preserved by the 3-place view as well as by my view.

However, I reject the 3-place view. First, it seems unintuitive to hold that 'I am Lynne Baker' expresses the same proposition as 'Lynne Baker is Lynne Baker'. I do not hold that my thinking 'I am Lynne Baker' is just a different way of my thinking 'Lynne Baker is Lynne Baker'. It seems to me that 'I am Lynne Baker' expresses one proposition and 'Lynne Baker is Lynne Baker' expresses another, even when they are both thought by me. Since I realize that these intuitions cut no ice with those who do not share them, I simply offer them for consideration. A second reason that I reject the 3-place view is that, although it is technically elegant as a semantics of indexicals generally, it is not integrated with what I think is the best metaphysical view – a view that construes persons in terms of the first-person perspective, and that privileges 'I' and 'now' over other indexicals. But I do not hope to unseat the 3-place view here. I am content to show that it is no threat to the Irreducibility Thesis, construed as a thesis about ways of knowing.

With this, I conclude that the Irreducibility Thesis is true: first-person knowledge cannot be replaced by third-person knowledge without cognitive loss.

Implications for Scientific Knowledge

The straightforward conclusion that I would draw from the Irreducibility Thesis is that scientism is false. Here is a valid Aristotelian syllogism for that conclusion:

All scientific knowledge is third-person knowledge.
Some genuine knowledge (i.e., first-person knowledge) is not third-person knowledge.

∴ Some genuine knowledge is not scientific knowledge.

The discussions of first-person knowledge and the Irreducibility Thesis support the second premise of the syllogism – that some genuine knowledge is not third-person knowledge – and I shall take the first premise that all scientific knowledge is third-person knowledge on authority for now. Not everyone, however, would accept the premises. For example, Daniel Dennett, on whose authority I am provisionally accepting the premise that all scientific knowledge is third-person knowledge, vehemently rejects the second premise that some genuine knowledge is not third-person knowledge. It is a central tenet of Dennett's that 'objective physical science' is characterized by an 'insistence on the third-person point of view'.[5] Even a theory of consciousness, Dennett says, 'will have to be constructed from the third-person point of view since *all* science is constructed from that perspective' (Dennett 1991a: 71).

Although Dennett affirms the first premise – that all scientific knowledge is third-person knowledge – he would dismiss with a flick of the wrist everything that I have said in support of the second premise that some genuine knowledge is not third-person knowledge. Far from taking it to be obvious that we have rich inner lives and conscious first-person knowledge, Dennett believes that we can 'trade in the first-person perspective of Descartes and Kant for the third-person perspective of the natural sciences and answer all the questions – without philosophical residue' (Dennett 2001). Wielding his relentlessly third-person approach, Dennett requires that anything that counts as a phenomenon be publicly observable. Nevertheless, Dennett has devised a method – he calls it 'heterophenomenology' – which he claims to be a way to 'do justice to the most private and ineffable subjective experiences, while never abandoning the [third-person] methodological principles of science' (Dennett 1991a: 72). Heterophenomenology, he says, is adequate to explain all first-personal phenomena that need explaining. The data to be explained are not subjective experiences, but rather a subject's reports of subjective experiences and of how things seem to her. The (putative) subjective experiences themselves never come into the picture.

5 Dennett 1991a: 72. On the other hand, David Chalmers, an opponent of Dennett's, vigorously argues for a first-person science – a science that takes consciousness, or experience as a fundamental feature of the world, like electromagnetic force, and hence rejects the first premise that all scientific knowledge is third-person knowledge (see Chalmers 1996). However, neither Dennett nor Chalmers displays any sympathy for the conclusion that some genuine knowledge is not scientific knowledge.

Here is how heterophenomenology works. The theorist asks a subject to report how things seem to her. The theorist makes a sound tape, perhaps accompanied by an electroencephalograph, of the first-person reports of the subject. From the taped sounds, a transcript is prepared. Then the theorist interprets the transcript as a record of speech acts. Both these transitions – from tape of noises to direct-quotation transcript and from direct-quotation transcript to interpreted text – require the theorist to adopt an intentional stance. The intentional stance is a stance that we take towards phenomena for which explanations in terms of beliefs, desires, and intentions is useful (Dennett 1991a: 76). The data to be explained are a subject's verbal reports about how things seem to her. We grant that these verbal reports are expressions of belief. What heterophenomenology is to explain is the etiology of beliefs that things seem a certain way to the subject. Dennett pronounces it 'a simple mistake' to insist 'that conscious experiences themselves, not merely our verbal judgments about them, are the primary data to which a theory must answer' (Dennett 2001, quoting Joseph Levine).

Heterophenomenology cannot, by Dennett's own strictures, recognize any non-observable phenomena to be explained. Dennett dispenses with any putative phenomenon that is inaccessible to an observer. So, there are no data of first-person knowledge; the closest one gets are such data as a subject's reports about how things seem to her. And the scientific explanations of these data consist only of explanation of the etiology of the subject's beliefs, the 'why does she say these things?'

But this is surely unsatisfactory. Suppose that a high-school student, Ann, is to recite Hamlet's famous soliloquy in front of the class. On the bus, she practises the soliloquy silently. On the view that I have proposed, she has first-person knowledge that she* is reciting Hamlet's soliloquy to herself. Dennett cannot countenance any such knowledge, or even the phenomenon of Ann's silent recitation of Hamlet's soliloquy. The only datum for science is Ann's report that she* was reciting Hamlet's soliloquy silently on the bus.

But confining attention to Ann's report misses the phenomenon. It is her recitations of the soliloquy, whether silent or aloud, that account for her flawless performance in front of the class, not her report or belief that she was reciting the soliloquy. Moreover, the only thing about her belief that heterophenomenology explains is how she came to have that belief. And no part of that explanation can advert to the (putative) fact that she actually was silently reciting the soliloquy. To advert to the fact that she actually was silently reciting the soliloquy as part of the explanation that she believed that she was silently reciting the soliloquy would make the (putative) fact that she was actually reciting the soliloquy part of the explanatory apparatus of her belief. However, Dennett will not even recognize such an unobservable fact as something to be explained, much less as part of an explanation. Ann's silent recitation, on Dennett's view, is not a phenomenon at all.

I take the case of the silent recitations to be a decisive counterexample to Dennett's claim that heterophenomenology can 'answer all the questions – without philosophical residue' from the third-person perspective of natural science. To refuse to recognize a phenomenon like Ann's silent recitations of Hamlet's soliloquy is to leave out a phenomenon about which Ann had first-person knowledge: 'I just finished reciting Hamlet's soliloquy to myself.' Heterophenomenology is no substitute for old-fashioned consideration of first-person phenomena. If the only challenge to the claim that some genuine knowledge is not third-person knowledge comes from replacement of first-person phenomena by heterophenomenology, then I am confident that that claim is true: either science will have to countenance first-person phenomena, or scientific knowledge is essentially incomplete. Although I tend towards the view that scientific knowledge is essentially incomplete, I shall make the more modest conditional claim here: if science is inherently third-personal, then scientific knowledge is essentially incomplete.

Let me conclude with a thought experiment in which Mephistopheles offers someone – Bob, say – a Faustian bargain.

MEPHISTOPHELES: How would you like to be scientifically omniscient? I can let you know everything that could be known by perfected third-person total science. All I require in return is to take away from you all your first-person thoughts. You will know nothing about yourself from a first-person perspective, but you will know of every existing thing, including yourself, that it existed, and you would know all the third-person properties of each thing.

BOB (echoing Faust himself): I'd love to have limitless scientific knowledge.

MEPHISTOPHELES: Sure you would. You would know every third-person timeless proposition – you would even know that many of the existing things used first-person sentences. What you would not know is which one of those things is you, and of course you would not know anything that follows from knowing which person you were. You would know everything about Bob that could be known by third-person science – as you would also know about Jill and Fran and everyone else. You would know every detail about Bob's health and physical condition; you would know who Bob loved, what kind of car Bob drove, whether Bob had been sentenced to be executed, and so on.

BOB (getting the hang of it): But I would not know whether I was Bob. I would not know who *I* loved, what kind of car *I* drove, whether *I* had been sentenced to be executed, and so on. I could only watch Bob and the others from 'outside' so to speak. I could not conceive of my having a place in the world. Wait a minute; this is not such a good deal after all. Not all the scientific knowledge in the world would compensate for not being able to conceive of myself as a participant in the world. I might as well be dead.

VOICEOVER: Wily fellow that he is, Mephistopheles has misled Bob into thinking that, although the bargain may be a bad one for Bob, there really is a bargain to be made: he has led Bob to believe that he would lose everything connected with his sense of self, in return for which he would be an unengaged scientific observer of third-person truth. But this is not really what is on offer. What Bob – or you, if you were offered the bargain – would lose is not just your ability to enjoy the popcorn while you watched the show. On the view that is under discussion, it is a first-person perspective that makes you you. If you accepted the Faustian bargain, there would no longer be you at all. Lose your first-person perspective and you go out of existence. Not only would you lose touch with most of the things that would matter to you (like whether you are sentenced to death), but without your first-person perspective, there would be no you there at all. Far from being a totally unengaged scientist if you accepted the Faustian bargain, you would simply cease to exist altogether. If Mephistopheles took away your first-person perspective, you would be gone.[6]

---

[6] I am very grateful to Gareth Matthews, Edmund Gettier, and Katherine Sonderegger for comments on drafts of this chapter and for many helpful discussions.

8
Third-Person Understanding

Lynne Rudder Baker

In Chapter 7 I argued that to know everything knowable by third-person science is not to know everything that there is to know. What is left out is first-person knowledge. In this chapter, I want to suggest that, even in the third-person realm, science is not cognitively exhaustive.

I am now shifting from speaking of knowledge, as I did in 'First-Person Knowledge', to speaking of understanding, as I do here in 'Third-Person Understanding'. Although I am not going to try to make the distinction between knowing and understanding precise, there is an intuitive contrast. A mathematical novice, presented with Gödel's proof of the incompleteness of arithmetic, may well know that it is a proof of the incompleteness of arithmetic without understanding it at all. Or someone may know a piece of music in the sense of being able to give an analysis of it – here is the tonic, followed by the dominant seventh, which is resolved in the last chord – but it does not follow that the person understands the piece of music; she may even be tone-deaf.

Understanding is more comprehensive than knowledge. To understand something is to know what it is and to make reasonable sense of it. For example, one has to know what money is, in at least a pretheoretical sense, in order to understand a bank transaction. Although third-person understanding has a subjective aspect, it is not independent of knowledge. In general, a person must have true beliefs about the things that reasonably make sense to her. (The paranoid who makes sense of things in terms of imagined conspiracies has only the illusion of under-standing.) Nevertheless, someone understands something, in contrast to merely knowing it, only when she makes reasonable sense of it.

We make sense of the world that we encounter – Husserl's *Lebenswelt* or life-world – in terms of what I call 'the commonsense conception'. My overall aim is to show that the commonsense conception, the home of our third-person understanding of the world, is cognitively legitimate. I shall first argue that the commonsense conception is not just useful, not just a *façon de parler*, not something to be accompanied by winks. Rather, it provides the framework for making true descriptions and genuine explanations. Moreover, the justification of the commonsense conception does not depend on legitimation by science. Then, I shall try to fend off two important challenges to my argument for the cognitive legitimacy of the commonsense conception. Finally, I'll discuss science and scientism and propose the commonsense conception as another counterexample to scientism.

The Commonsense Conception

According to the commonsense conception, the world is populated in part by medium-sized objects – people, nonhuman animals, artefacts, artworks, and natural objects. To these are attributed various properties – properties such as being round or being blue, of course, but also properties such as being dangerous and being edible and properties such as deserving respect. To people and to some nonhuman animals, we attribute beliefs, desires, and intentions. Beliefs, desires, and intentions are in a very special class of properties, known as propositional attitudes.

Propositional attitudes are attributed in English by means of 'that-clauses' which express propositions. Propositional attitudes differ from ordinary physical properties like shape or hardness in two important ways. (1) Propositional attitudes are identified by the contents of their 'that'-clauses (a belief that snow is white is different from a belief that grass is green); and (2) propositional attitudes are susceptible to a kind of failure: beliefs may be false, desires unfulfilled, intentions miscarried, expectations thwarted, hopes dashed, and so on. It may be true that you have a certain belief, even if the belief is false. Propositional attitudes are directed upon states of affairs in the world – states of affairs that you believe or expect or fear obtain, or that you desire to obtain. In philosophical parlance, the phenomenon of being directed upon states of affairs in the world is called 'intentionality'. ('Intentionality' in the philosophical sense is not to be confused with intending to do something, or with doing something on purpose – although intending to do something is an example of an intentional phenomenon in that it is directed upon a state of affairs that someone intends to bring about.) Brentano introduced the term 'intentionality' into contemporary use.

I shall use the term 'intentional' very broadly, so that any phenomenon is intentional if it would not exist or occur in a world lacking beings with propositional attitudes. Intentional phenomena stand in contrast to physical phenomena (e.g., bodily motions, vocal emissions, marks on paper), which could exist or occur in a world lacking beings with propositional attitudes. Skills, rules, and practices are intentional phenomena; in a world without propositional attitudes, there would be no experts, no conventions or institutions. Writing a cheque is an intentional phenomenon because there would be no such thing as writing a cheque in a world lacking the social and economic conventions (like owing money) that presuppose that people have beliefs, desires, and intentions. But many kinds of things are intentional: events (e.g., a baseball game), objects (e.g., a passport), actions (e.g., voting), properties (e.g., being in debt), dispositions (e.g., being honest), activities (e.g., reading your mail), institutions (e.g., a national bank), artworks (e.g., Michelangelo's *David*), artefacts (e.g., clocks) – all these are intentional. Intentional language contains terms (e.g., 'disobeyed the order', 'was elected president', 'paid her taxes') whose application presupposes that there are beings with propositional attitudes (beliefs, desires, intentions).

I shall continue to say that what the commonsense conception takes to be real are medium-sized objects and intentional phenomena. To do so is not very elegant, however, since some medium-sized objects are intentional (e.g., my driver's licence) though, of course, some intentional phenomena are not medium-sized objects (e.g., my driving record).

For purposes here, we can contrast intentional phenomena with physical phenomena. The commonsense conception recognizes both: hills and streams are physical; rocking chairs and footballs are intentional. The sine qua non of the commonsense conception are intentional phenomena – in a rich sense that includes rule-governed activities, institutions, and the other phenomena just mentioned. The physical sciences are notable for not appealing to anything intentional. If there are sufficient physical conditions for intentional properties, philosophers' valiant attempts to find them have failed. In any case, the commonsense conception is intentional through and through.

The commonsense conception in a thin sense is universal in that all peoples have concepts that apply to medium-sized objects and to intentional phenomena. In this thin sense, I shall argue, the commonsense conception is not a scientific theory, nor is it replaceable by scientific theory. Although human beings share a core commonsense conception of medium-sized objects and intentional phenomena, cultures may differ in their 'thick' commonsense conceptions. A language may lack a concept of email or of blackmail, but (I would wager) a language would not lack a concept of obeying authorities. Different languages may well have different concepts, but no language, I believe, could do without intentional concepts altogether; otherwise, it could not serve its purpose of communication and facilitation of human interaction.[1] The phenomena that our thick commonsense conception describes and explains (e.g., the causes of World War One, Jane's being denied tenure, Al Gore's campaign for President of the USA, Henry's being declared ineligible for the team, Fran's being indicted) are intentional. The commonsense conception – with its concepts of medium-sized objects, including people, with intentional and non-intentional observable properties – is a cognitive background of all our activities. It is the sea in which we all swim, scientists and nonscientists alike.

It may not be obvious that the commonsense conception needs defence. However, many philosophers challenge the cognitive legitimacy of the commonsense conception, on either scientific or metaphysical grounds. What appear to be tables and chairs are really something else. For example, some scientistically inclined philosophers hold that everything that really exists can be reductively understood in terms of fundamental physics. On this approach, all that really exists is what is recognized by

1   An anthropologist who reports of a culture that has no concept of belief also speaks of 'the received ideas to which [the] people subscribed' (Needham 1972). But if they really had no beliefs, they would be in no position to subscribe to received ideas. Needham's doubts about belief concerned an ethnographer's saying 'that people believed something when he did not actually know what was going on inside them'. But obviously knowing that Ann believes that the key is in her pocket does not require knowing anything about what is going on inside of her.

fundamental physics. And some metaphysicians think that the sum (or combination) of your right shoe, my nose, and the electrons in this page is an object in the same sense as my passport, say, is an object. The only difference between the two 'objects' is that we find it useful to give a name to the sum of metaphysical simples that make up my passport; but there is no ontological difference between my passport and that sum of simples (Lewis 1991). On this approach, all that really exists are simples and sums of simples.

Such views contrast sharply with the one that I shall defend here. If I am right, then reality is not exhausted by simples and sums of simples, nor by what is recognized by fundamental physics. And the conception of the world in terms of things like portraits and passports could not be replaced by a conception in terms of quarks and leptons without drastic loss of understanding. Now let us turn to the vindication of the commonsense conception.

Vindication of the Commonsense Conception

When I say that the commonsense conception is cognitively legitimate, I mean that the picture of reality that it affords – in terms of medium-sized objects, including people, and intentional phenomena – is correct. Thick commonsense conceptions may be wrong in detail, but there really are medium-sized objects and intentional phenomena. Another way to put it is that the core concepts of the commonsense conception (the concepts of medium-sized objects, including people, and intentional phenomena) are non-empty. There really are such things. Chairs are as real as electrons.

I have two kinds of arguments to vindicate the commonsense conception. The first kind of argument is that the categories of the commonsense conception are confirmed by ordinary observation daily by everyone. The second kind of argument is much more controversial. It is that the commonsense conception is reliable and indispensable and serves non-optional interests; and if so, then it is cognitively legitimate. This second more pragmatic argument has been challenged in two ways. Although I want to meet those challenges head-on, I'll begin with the first and less controversial argument to vindicate the commonsense conception.

The commonsense conception is verified piecemeal by ordinary observation. In its terms, we make empirically true and false statements. It is true that the local office of the Department of Motor Vehicles is about to move to Hadley, and this can be confirmed by observation available to anyone who drives on a certain section of Route 9. It is true that women are waiting longer to get married than they used to, and this can be confirmed by statistical evidence available to anyone who studies the results of the census. Without the commonsense conception, there would be no Department of Motor Vehicles, and no institution of marriage. Without the commonsense conception, there would be no such truths. Without the commonsense conception, we could not even doubt these truths. The very concept of doubt is part of the commonsense conception.

Anyone can confirm everyday descriptions like these: the pie is in the oven; payment of the electric bill is overdue. Anyone can confirm causal explanations like these: her jumping on the hood is causing dents in the car; overcooking the fish caused it to get too dry. And anyone can confirm commonsense generalizations like these: insults make people angry; running into wooden furniture causes bruises; traffic to the beach is heavier in the summer than in the winter. All of these – commonsense descriptions, singular causal explanations, and generalizations – are confirmed by observation from everyday life. When David went out to slay Goliath, he was as justified in choosing stones for his slingshot instead of twigs as a twenty-first century physicist would be.

Not only do the activities of individuals confirm the commonsense conception, but also groups come to intersubjective agreement about commonsense facts. It is much more common for juries to reach a verdict than to be 'hung'. And for more mundane matters, we all agree that trees have leaves, that bowling balls are harder than soccer balls, and that soccer balls are more durable than balloons. The life-world is the object of massive intersubjective agreement – which, in turn, further confirms our commonsense understanding. This is not to say that everything agreed on is true. Perhaps in the late fifteenth century, there was general commonsense agreement that indigenous people of the so-called New World were incapable of civilization. Such a belief – disconfirmed by evidence that indigenous New-World people had produced civilizations – was 'local' in that it could be abandoned without disturbing the commonsense conception as a whole. Our understanding of the life-world is empirical – verified by experience – even if not systematic. Naive empiricism justifies the commonsense conception. And it is a good thing too: without the commonsense conception, the idea of making sense would not make sense, and understanding would be impossible.

My second argument to vindicate the commonsense conception is that the commonsense conception is indispensable, reliable, and serves our non-optional interests; and if so, then the categories of the commonsense conception are cognitively legitimate. The commonsense conception is a reliable source of reasonable expectations. Some people are masters of conventions of camel travel, court etiquette, and peace conferences. Others, including me, are more secure with conventions of air travel, dinner parties, and deans' meetings. We can rely on the fact that if a dean calls a meeting, she will be there or else there will be an explanation of her absence – the president called her in; or she forgot it; or maybe she was struck by lightning. But if she did not show up at the appointed time, there will some explanation within a given range of possible explanations for failure. Moreover, we count on the commonsense conception all the time. Every time we get in a car, we bet our lives that the other drivers will behave in predictable ways that are describable in terms of the commonsense conception.

Not only is the commonsense conception reliable in the way just described, but also it is indispensable. Without it, you would have no food on the table; you could not get to the lab. You could not get on in the world at all – go to the cleaners, change jobs, respond to a jury summons, plan a vacation. Indeed, without the commonsense conception – and in particular, intentionality – there could be *no* social, political, legal, religious, scientific, or any other kind of institution at all.

Finally, the commonsense conception serves our non-optional interests, prominent among which is an interest in understanding the world, in making reasonable sense of it. That we conceive of reality in terms of commonsense categories is not a matter of choice. Most obviously, conceiving of reality in terms of commonsense concepts serves biologically given goals like survival and reproduction; but there are further universal human interests – such as an interest in having satisfying relationships with others, or an interest in having a measure of control over one's own life and environment – that are intelligible only in terms of the commonsense conception (Baker 1995). At bottom, the commonsense conception is not expendable because such interests, borne of a first-person perspective, are not optional.

Many people agree that the commonsense conception is reliable, indispensable, and tied to non-optional interests, but they still have doubts about the truth of the commonsense conception. Usefulness, it is urged, may diverge from truth. I want to respond to two such criticisms. The first is the sceptical worry that reliability and indispensability do not entail truth. The second is an appeal to Quine's 'double standard' of truth.

From Usefulness to Truth

Hume proposed a sceptical scenario in which there is a system of beliefs about laws of nature that contribute to practical success in the present, but in the future these putative laws are discovered to be false. Because of the apparent coherence of this scenario, says one critic (Hill 1997: 135): 'we must suppose that there is a gap between practical success and truth even when practical success is measured in terms of ability to serve interests that are nonoptional. The question of whether an interest is optional for human beings has no obvious connection with the question of whether beliefs that serve that interest are trustworthy guides to reality – that is, no obvious connection that is non-problematic from the point of view of epistemology.'

The critic here is asking how appeal to non-optional interests can provide epistemic justification of the commonsense conception. Epistemic justification for something gives a reason to think it true. (If you were offered a million dollars to believe P, you would have a reason to believe P, but this kind of reason would not be epistemic justification of P. Being offered a million dollars to believe P gives no reason to think P true.) The critic is suggesting that practical success of the commonsense conception may give us a (practical) reason to believe it, without giving a reason to believe that it is true.

Pragmatist that I am, I think that this objection is misguided. It is obvious to me that practical success in, say, driving a car does provide reason to believe that one's beliefs about where the brakes are, what will happen when you apply them, and so on, are true. Be that as it may, I have a kind of pragmatic-transcendental argument to show that there is a bridge from a non-optional interest to epistemic justification of a belief – in this case from our interest in inquiry to the correctness of the commonsense conception. Following Aristotle, who famously said 'Man by nature desires to know', I take it that inquiry is a nonoptional interest. If something is a non-optional interest, it will be pursued unless something prevents its pursuit. Since nothing prevents engagement in inquiry, we may infer that:

1. There is inquiry.

If an activity is engaged in, then the necessary conditions for engaging in that activity are satisfied. For example, if vegetable gardening at a certain place is an activity engaged in and the presence of dirt is a necessary condition for engaging in vegetable gardening, then there is dirt present in that place. If there were no dirt in that place, it would be impossible to engage in vegetable gardening there. Necessary conditions for engaging in inquiry include the existence of medium-sized objects and the existence of people with intentional states. If there were no medium-sized objects, then there would be no gauges or maps or electron microscopes or telescopes or any other kinds of scientific instruments needed for inquiry. Nothing would count as engaging in inquiry without people with intentional states. If there were no people with intentional states, then there would be no scientific experiments, no hypotheses, no tests – no inquiry. So:

2. If there is inquiry, then there are medium-sized objects and people with intentional states.

Therefore:

3. There are medium-sized objects and people with intentional states.

Since medium-sized objects and people with intentional states are core features of the commonsense conception, it follows from the fact that we engage in inquiry – a non-optional interest for us – that the core commonsense conception is correct.

I can think of three ways that a critic can respond to this argument. First, he may deny that inquiry is a non-optional interest for us. I think that since inquiry is such a central feature of human life – no doubt for good evolutionary reasons – this challenge is implausible; so, I'll put it aside. Second, the critic may challenge the move from saying that inquiry is a non-optional interest to saying that there is inquiry. This challenge, too, is implausible: it is perfectly obvious that there is inquiry of all sorts, and its being a nonoptional interest explains why there is inquiry at all. Third, the critic may challenge the claim that the existence of medium-sized objects and people with intentional states is a necessary condition of inquiry. Perhaps a critic would claim that we only must suppose or pretend that medium-sized objects and people with intentional states exist. But this won't do. To suppose or pretend something is to be in an intentional state. So, if we suppose or pretend that there are intentional states, then there *are* intentional states – viz., our state of supposing or pretending. So, I think that the above pragmatic-transcendental argument bridges the gap between what is useful and what is true or correct.

The rebuttal of the third challenge to the pragmatic-transcendental argument suggests another angle from which to defuse the critic of the cognitive legitimacy of the commonsense conception. Say that a first-person proposition P (or, if you hold the 3-place view that I discussed in Chapter 7, a first-person way of knowing) is self-defeating if and only if its being assertively thought at t guarantees that it is false at t. For example, the proposition that you would assertively think by 'I am not thinking now' is self-defeating. If you are thinking it, it is false. (Self-defeating propositions are the opposite of self-justifying propositions like Descartes' cogito: assertively thinking 'I exist now' guarantees that your thought is true; assertively thinking 'I do not exist now' guarantees that your thought is false.) Now consider the hypothesis that there are no intentional phenomena. If the core commonsense conception is false, then there are no intentional phenomena, and the hypothesis that there are no intentional phenomena is true. But the hypothesis that there are no intentional phenomena is self-defeating in the same way as 'I am not thinking now'. Your entertaining the hypothesis that there are no intentional phenomena falsifies it – since your having the thought that there are no intentional phenomena is itself an intentional phenomenon. So, denial of this key part of the commonsense conception is self-defeating: if the hypothesis that there are no intentional phenomena can be entertained, then it is false.

Therefore, the hypothesis that the core commonsense conception is false cannot be assertively thought or meaningfully entertained. That is, it is inconceivable that the commonsense conception is wholesale false. Again, to conceive of ourselves as beings without intentional states is to be in an intentional state. It is not self-defeating to conceive of a world without persons in intentional states – our own world a million years ago, for example – but we cannot conceive of our being in such a world. And it is unintelligible to affirm what we cannot conceive of. If it is unintelligible to affirm that the core commonsense conception is false, then we need no further reason to reject the possibility of its being false.

Here is the methodological issue between my imagined critic and me. I say: if it is inconceivable that the core commonsense conception is false, then it is not false. (This is at the heart of pragmatism.) However, the critic (rightly) insists that what we can meaningfully entertain or conceive of depends on the limits of our conceptual abilities; but surely reality itself does not depend on the limits of our conceptual abilities. (This is at the heart of realism.)

I agree with the realist here that reality itself does not depend on the limits of our conceptual abilities. There may be a great deal of reality that is simply beyond our abilities to conceive, just as it is beyond the abilities of a dog to entertain the thought that the Cold War is over. But our philosophy – what we can say, or write, or argue about – most assuredly does depend on the limits of our conceptual abilities. (Realists get into trouble when they try to describe what they take to be beyond their conceptual abilities.) If we cannot conceive of something, we cannot meaningfully assert it or deny it – much less argue about whether it is true or false. If P cannot be meaningfully asserted, then we cannot be called upon to argue against it.

To conclude this section: For any proposition P, if one asserts P (or rather attempts to assert P), but one is unable to conceive of P, then one is in a pragmatically untenable situation. My methodological suggestion is to discard, denounce or otherwise repudiate any proposition that leads to such pragmatic paradox. To hold that the commonsense conception is useful but false is to be in such a pragmatically untenable position. The commonsense conception is thus cognitively vindicated by the fact that denial of its correctness leads to pragmatic paradox. For further arguments, see Baker (1987).

Rejection of Two-Tiered Truth

Now turn to the second important challenge to my defence of the commonsense conception: Quine's 'double standard'. Many critics affirm the reliability and indispensability of the commonsense conception, but take it to be genuinely false nonetheless. Since the commonsense conception does have all these pragmatic virtues, these critics advise us not to give up commonsense concepts of, say, persons with intentional states, but rather to regard such concepts as applying to things in a second-class sense. Without taking issue with the point that we cannot conceive of a situation in which we would give up concepts of medium-sized objects or of persons with intentional states, a critic may advise us to retain these commonsense concepts in contexts of ordinary life, but not to take them with full epistemic seriousness. Here is one critic (Hill 1997: 135): '[T]he claim that we will not abandon a concept does not by itself imply that we will continue to believe that propositions involving that concept are literally true. To think otherwise is to neglect the possibility ... of adopting a "double standard" – that is, the possibility of continuing to use a concept in everyday life, but of setting it aside in contexts in which we are concerned to limn "the true and ultimate structure of reality" '.

W. V. O. Quine is famous for this position (Quine 1960). Without giving up the concepts of persons with intentional states and medium-sized objects, we can just 'cross our fingers' so to speak when we use such concepts. One follower of Quine who has tried to work out a two-tiered approach to truth in detail is Daniel Dennett. Dennett coined the phrase 'truth "with a grain of salt" ' to apply to intentional phenomena (Dennett 1987). In Chapter 7, I showed that Dennett's attempt to capture first-person phenomena by third-person science (his heterophenomenology) was unsuccessful. Now I want to show that his overall approach to intentionality is self-defeating.

Dennett recognizes different 'stances', from which different kinds of things are discerned. From the physical stance, we discern physical phenomena – phenomena within the purview of the physical sciences. From the intentional stance, we discern intentional phenomena – not only propositional attitudes, but all the intentional phenomena that I canvassed at the beginning.

There is also an intermediate design stance, but Dennett has recently aligned the design stance with the intentional stance. Dennett comments that 'biology depends, in the end, on adopting the intentional stance towards the evolutionary process itself' (Dennett 1993: 224). The design stance, characterized by a distinction between function and malfunction, has occupied an unstable middle ground throughout Dennett's work. (For a discussion of the instability of the design stance, see Baker [1987].) I follow Dennett and do not consider the design stance separately here.

What is important for understanding Dennett is that we discern different kinds of things from the stances, and that the kinds of things discerned from the different stances are not on a par. The physical phenomena would occur even if no one took a stance at all. But the intentional phenomena are stance-dependent; their existence depends on being discerned from the intentional stance. Moreover, physical phenomena could occur in a world without intentional phenomena, but not conversely: intentional phenomena could not occur in a world without physical phenomena (Dennett 1991b).

Anything that is intentional is a matter of interpretation, where interpretation is, in Dennett's words, a 'heuristic overlay' (Dennett 1998: 360). To be intentional on Dennett's view is to be interpretable in a certain way. That is all. Dennett thinks that he has given a unified naturalistic account of intentionality that applies equally to natural selection (interpretable as aiming to produce survivors and reproducers), to genes (interpretable as aiming to replicate themselves), as well as to people (interpretable as aiming to get tenure). All of these are intentional in exactly the same way: they are interpretable as intentional. All intentionality is 'as if' intentionality. What makes an intentional phenomenon what it is is nothing but interpretation; what makes a physical phenomenon what it is has nothing to do with interpretation.

What are genuinely true are propositions about the world discerned from the physical stance, in contexts where we are concerned to limn the 'true and ultimate structure of reality'. Propositions about the world discerned from the intentional stance can only be 'true with a grain of salt'. The commonsense conception, since it prominently countenances intentional phenomena, is the home of second-class truth. So, on Dennett's view, we have two ontological tiers (physical and intentional) mirrored by two-tiered truth (genuine truth and truth with a grain of salt).

Now I want to show that Dennett's view cannot be sustained. In the first place, Dennett's interpretationist theory cannot make sense of ordinary human interpreters. Here is the problem. If, as Dennett has it, to be an interpreter is to be interpretable as an interpreter, then the role of interpreting is subordinated to the role of being interpreted. To put it metaphorically, Dennett collapses the active into the passive. Putting it this way brings to mind Socrates' analogy in the *Euthyphro*: being carried presupposes carrying, being seen presupposes seeing, being loved presupposes loving. Socrates' point is that the passive state (e.g., being seen) is dependent on the active state (e.g., seeing). I would like to say to Dennett something similar to what Socrates said to Euthyphro: Just as being seen presupposes seeing, being interpreted presupposes interpreting; and just as there is no such thing as being seen unless there is seeing, there is no such thing as being interpreted unless there is interpreting. Interpreting is logically prior to being interpreted.

But on Dennett's view, interpreting cannot be logically prior to being interpreted inasmuch as to interpret is to be interpretable as interpreting and to be interpretable as interpreting is to be interpretable as interpretable as interpreting. And so on – without end. On Dennett's view, doing something intentionally (interpreting) is not in any way prior to being regarded as doing something intentionally (being interpretable as interpreting); indeed, they are one and the same thing. But surely there is a distinction: when a scientist interprets evidence, she is *doing something* (interpreting), not just being regarded as doing something, not just being interpretable as interpreting. (Of course, she is interpretable as interpreting; but that's not all that's going on.) So, I do not believe that Dennett's theory can accommodate a tenable notion of an interpreter.

To raise the ante, let me suggest that Dennett's interpretationism is self-defeating (Baker 1987). If his interpretationism is true, Dennett could not have thought it up. Or rather, it would be incoherent to say that Dennett thought it up – since to say that he thought it up would only amount to saying that he is interpretable as having thought it up. It is true that if Dennett thought up the theory, he can be interpreted as having thought it up; but thinking it up does not *consist in* being interpretable as having thought it up. There is no logical space in Dennett's interpretationism for the difference between thinking up a theory and being interpretable as thinking it up. (Nor, for that matter, between discovering the Higgs particle and being interpretable as discovering the Higgs particle. They would be one and the same thing.)

I conclude that the conception of reality behind Dennett's view of two-tiered truth can make no sense of what we do when we engage in interpretation. Even worse, it is self-defeating in that if true, then Dennett could not have thought it up. The idea of two-tiered truth, of a double standard, that denigrates intentional truth cannot be sustained. In some cases, we do have a kind of double standard of truth: 'Juliet is the sun' may be metaphorically, but not literally, true. 'My house is full of right angles' may be true even if Euclidean geometry is false of the universe. I do not deny such cases; rather, what I deny is that there is a global distinction between first-class physical truth and second-class intentional truth. Since Dennett's development of the view of two-tiered truth is the most refined one that I know of, I suspect that it is impossible to make out such a distinction without falling into pragmatic paradox.

Before leaving my vindication of the commonsense conception, I should like to propose a consideration that many philosophers would take as disreputable. In evaluating metaphysical positions, I think that moral considerations are relevant. Thus I reject Hume's view: 'There is no method of reasoning more common, and yet none more blameable, than, in philosophical disputes, to endeavour the refutation of any hypothesis, by a pretence of its dangerous consequences to religion and morality' (Hume 1977 [1748]). *Pace* Hume, it seems to me perfectly reasonable to reject a proposition on the basis of moral consequences if you are more certain of your knowledge of morality than of the proposition in question. Many people suppose that it is a merely psychological fact that we must believe the commonsense conception. Psychological or not, the fact remains that we have no choice in believing the commonsense conception. Indeed, it seems to me deeply hypocritical to deny the truth of what one cannot avoid believing. The reason that we cannot get along without the commonsense conception is that the commonsense conception is the source of our making sense of things; the commonsense conception is the arena of understanding the world that we encounter. Ordinary concepts of the commonsense conception do a lot of heavy lifting in our cognitive lives. And I think that it is a moral maxim that: Whatever does the work gets the credit.

On the double-standard approach, we would be fully entitled to say: 'In terms of the true and ultimate structure of reality, you do not really exist. It is a mere psychological fact that I can't help thinking of you as a person; but I know that there's no real "you" since there really are no persons or anything with intentional states. So, of course, there's no real me either but I [the emitter of these sounds] am powerless to deny my own existence.' Unlike many of my fellow philosophers, I simply cannot believe that such a morally repugnant view is true. Although I realize that this moral consideration will leave many philosophers unmoved, I think it important to see the moral consequences of denial of the truth of the commonsense conception. However, I am content to rest my case for the cognitive legitimacy of the commonsense conception on the argument from everyday observation, the argument from usefulness to truth, and, especially, the argument against the 'double-standard' view.

So far, I have argued that the commonsense conception is universal, indispensable, reliable, in the service of non-optional interests, and finally cognitively legitimate. Some commonsense descriptions are true, and some commonsense explanations are correct. I now want to argue that the commonsense conception cannot be assimilated wholesale by science. If I am right on that score, then the commonsense conception is another counterexample to scientism.

Science and Scientism

I should explain more carefully what I mean by scientism. Scientism is a metaphysical commitment that is captured nicely by Wilfrid Sellars' aphorism: 'In the dimension of describing and explaining the world, science is the measure of all things, of what is that it is, and of what is not that it is not' (Sellars 1963: 173). Everything that we legitimately claim to know is subject to vindication by science.

We can distinguish a stronger and a weaker version of scientism, depending on how 'science' is understood. On the stronger version, 'science' means physical science. Quine was an influential proponent of this strong version of scientism, according to which all science is physical science. It was obvious to Quine that there is no intentional science. Citing the thesis that 'there is no breaking out of the intentional vocabulary by explaining its members in other terms', Quine was struck by 'the baselessness of intentional idioms and the emptiness of a science of intention' (Quine 1960: 221). Closely allied with this strong version of scientism is a thesis of the unity of science. Physics is the foundational science, and the legitimacy of any other science depends on its relations to physics. On the strong version of scientism, all knowledge claims – from common sense to metaphysics – are susceptible to empirical disconfirmation by physical science.

The weaker version of scientism construes science as including not only physical sciences, but the social and behavioural sciences as well. Much of psychology and all of the social sciences employ intentional concepts (e.g., concepts of belief, of consumer goods, of crime, of voting data). The weaker version of scientism makes no demand that such concepts be replaced by non-intentional concepts. Nor, on the weaker version, are sciences legitimated by their relation to physics; rather, we can think of a science in terms of method (of data gathering, of testing hypotheses) aimed at systematic explanation of phenomena in some specifiable domain. So, the strong and weak versions of scientism differ on what they would count as vindication by science. The strong version would hold that the commonsense conception was vindicated only if its core concepts were explained ultimately in terms of a physical science, without intentionality; the weaker version would allow the commonsense conception was vindicated if its core concepts were explained ultimately in terms of an intentional science.

On the strong version of scientism, all phenomena are ultimately explainable in terms of physical science. Proponents of the strong version like Paul Churchland think that physical science not only sits in judgement of the commonsense conception, but that it is likely to unseat the commonsense conception altogether. Persons with intentional states will go the way of witches and the vital spirit. Indeed, Churchland sees the commonsense conception itself as a proto-scientific theory ripe for replacement by a more mature physical science. He says, '[T]he network of principles and assumptions constitutive of our commonsense conceptual framework can be seen to be as speculative and as artificial as any overtly theoretical system' (Churchland 1979: 2). According to Churchland, the commonsense conception may be wholesale false, and shown to be so by physical science.

But this view comes at too high a cost. I have already discussed the problem of pragmatic paradox. There are other costs as well. Strong scientism can be endorsed only by denying the existence of the phenomena that we are most familiar with. Physical science is not fit for explaining phenomena whose very existence depends on rules, practices, and conventions. (Of course, since endorsing anything is an intentional phenomenon, if strong scientism were true, it could not be endorsed. But this is another instance of pragmatic paradox.) Here are some commonsense explanations that are not replaceable by physical explanations: 'Our team lost the game because the quarterback fumbled in the last second.' 'The price went up because the painting has been authenticated as a Vermeer.' What makes something a fumble is not just a matter of bodily movements but of the rules of the game; what makes something an authentication as a Vermeer depends on our conventions of expertise. There are no physical theories in which we can describe fumbles and authentications in terms that make sense of them. Without the rules and practices of the life-world described in terms of the commonsense conception, not only would explanations in terms of fumbles and authentications disappear, but even the phenomena being explained – our team's loss, the increase in price – would vanish. Without the thin version of the commonsense conception, every thick version would disappear. To endorse strong scientism would be to commit cognitive suicide.

The weak version of scientism fares somewhat better in that it allows vindication of the commonsense conception by the intentional psychological and social sciences. I readily admit that large parts of any thick commonsense conception can be disconfirmed by intentional sciences; for example, received ideas about what causes crime may be disconfirmed by a more mature sociology and/or economics and/or psychology. I think that we just must wait and see how much of the commonsense conception the intentional sciences confirm or disconfirm. But even weak scientism is false, because the ontology of the commonsense conception does not stand in need of vindication by even the intentional sciences. Our justification for believing that the concepts of medium-sized objects, including people, and intentional phenomena does not depend on its connection to any science, intentional or physical.

Another reason to think that science, even construed as including intentional as well as physical sciences, will not fully assimilate the commonsense conception is that theories are propositional; if true, they provide knowledge-that. But our third-person understanding includes knowing-how, which is not just a species of knowing-that. As I have argued elsewhere, the commonsense conception is not itself a theory (Baker 1995: ch. 3 and ch. 8). Nor can it be replaced by a theory: a theory cannot serve the purposes of negotiating the life-world. Much of our know-how – knowing how to get a driver's licence, knowing how to read, knowing how to search the web – is integrated with knowing-that in our thick commonsense conception.

In light both of first-person knowledge and of third-person understanding in terms of the commonsense conception, then, I would not endorse Sellars' aphorism. It is not the case that 'In the dimension of describing and explaining the world, science is the measure of all things, of what is that it is, and of what is not that it is not'.

My opposition to scientism should not be construed as opposition to science. It is important to distinguish scientism (both strong and weak) from respect for the sciences (Baker 1995: 85ff). Scientism is not just the thesis that if the best science appeals to quarks, then we should recognize the reality of quarks. Rather, scientism is a closure principle on knowledge. It is not just the thesis that science reveals the truth, but that science reveals *all* the truth. Like other closure principles, scientism does not meet the standards it imposes. That science reveals *all* the truth cannot be shown by science. (The best argument for scientism is an inductive argument that science has explained more and more; so, eventually, science will explain everything there is. My two chapters here cast doubt on this argument by indicating areas that fall outside the purview of science.) Nevertheless, scientism is just assumed in much of the educated world today.

Without realizing it, perhaps, even those who feel threatened by science bend to scientism. For example, sophisticated Creationists now support a science of Intelligent Design that they claim to be superior, *as science*, to Darwinian natural selection.[2] I think that the Creationists are on the wrong track. The methodology of science clearly rules out any appeal to supernatural forces in a scientific explanation. Such methodological naturalism is partly constitutive of science. There is no point in complaining that science should not have the methodology that it has, the methodology that has produced an amazing explosion of knowledge in the past 300 years.

Theists ought rather to distinguish between *methodological* naturalism (the thesis that scientific explanations do not appeal to supernatural forces) and *metaphysical* naturalism (the thesis that there are no supernatural forces). Methodological naturalism is internal to science, but metaphysical naturalism is not. It is reasonable for theists to accept methodological naturalism while rejecting metaphysical naturalism. The inference from methodological naturalism to metaphysical naturalism is an inference from what is excluded from scientific explanation to what is excluded from reality. This inference is

---

2　See Johnson 1993, 1995. A different way to use science to bolster theism comes from Denton (1998). Denton argues that science provides evidence that 'the cosmos is uniquely fit for human existence' (xii). One difference between Johnson and Denton (in addition to the fact that Denton is a scientist and Johnson is a lawyer) seems to be this: what Johnson draws on as fact is disputed within the scientific community; whereas Denton appeals, I think, to undisputed facts, but gives them a disputed interpretation.

invalid – unless scientism is true. But I have argued that scientism is false. So, atheism does not follow from the godless character of scientific explanations. The fact that many – even Creationists – assume that anything that is left out of scientific explanation is left out of reality just shows how far scientism has insinuated itself into our thinking. Respect for science should not beguile us into endorsement of scientism.

Conclusion

The commonsense conception has its home in the life-world. Let me enumerate reasons why I am dubious that the life-world itself can be fully assimilated into a domain of science:

First, the life-world is negotiated by skills, practices, and know-how. The commonsense conception yields knowledge-that about the world of know-how, but not in any systematic way. There is nothing so systematized as a domain for the commonsense conception to be a theory *of*. In the world as we encounter it, as Gibert Ryle saw, 'Intelligent practice is not the step-child of theory' (Ryle 1949: 26).

Second, scientific knowledge, with its organized, articulable laws and theories, I take it, is the fruit of scientific practice. But scientific practice presupposes the commonsense conception just as any other practice does. The background of scientific practice cannot be understood in terms of organized, articulable laws and theories. The commonsense conception is prior to theory, both temporally and conceptually. Presupposed by theorizing, it cannot be absorbed into theory.

Indeed, if the commonsense conception is a presupposition of science, then the success of science gives further reason to hold that the commonsense conception is cognitively legitimate: Whatever vindicates science, indirectly vindicates what scientific practice presupposes. The enormous success of science vindicates science; scientific practice presupposes the commonsense conception. Therefore, the enormous success of science indirectly vindicates the commonsense conception.

Third, in terms of making sense of the world that we encounter, commonsense explanations cannot be matched by systematic scientific explanations. For example, if you want to know why Jane's car insurance went up, discovering that she had been arrested for speeding is all the explanation that you need. Like any explanation, this one is defeasible; but even if it were defeated, it would be replaced by another commonsensical explanation, not by a 'deeper' explanation from a mature science. It is difficult to know what a 'deeper' explanation of the higher insurance premium would even be.

To conclude: Scientific knowledge does not encompass all knowledge. Science is the source of a great deal of knowledge, but is not the arbiter of knowable reality. The commonsense conception provides the terms for making sense of the world that we encounter – that is, for our third-person understanding. It is also cognitively legitimate, and its legitimacy does not rest on the deliverances of any science. Therefore, third-person understanding, along with first-person knowledge, points to aspects of reality beyond what science reveals.[3]

3   Many thanks to Katherine Sonderegger and to Gareth Matthews for help on this paper.

References

Baker, L. R. (1981) 'Why computers can't act', *American Philosophical Quarterly*, 18: 157–63.

— (1987) *Saving Belief: A Critique of Physicalism*. Princeton: Princeton University Press.

— (1995) *Explaining Attitudes: A Practical Approach to the Mind*. Cambridge: Cambridge University Press.

— (1998) 'The first-person perspective: A test for naturalism', *American Philosophical Quarterly*, 35: 327–48.

— (2000) *Persons and Bodies: A Constitution View*. Cambridge: Cambridge University Press.

— (2002) 'The ontological significance of persons', *Philosophy and Phenomenological Research*.

Burge, T. (1996) 'Our entitlement to self-knowledge', *Proceedings of the Aristotelian Society*, 46: 91–116.

Castañeda, H.-N. (1966) 'He: A study in the logic of self-consciousness', *Ratio*, 8: 130–57.

— (1967). 'Indicators and quasi-indicators', *American Philosophical Quarterly*, 4: 85–100.

Chalmers, D. (1996) *The Conscious Mind*. New York: Oxford University Press.

Chisholm, R. (1981) *The First Person: An Essay on Reference and Intentionality*. Minneapolis: University of Minnesota Press.

Churchland, P. M. (1979) *Scientific Realism and the Plasticity of Mind.* Cambridge: Cambridge University Press.

Dennett, D. C. (1987) 'Instrumentalism reconsidered', in *The Intentional Stance.* Cambridge, MA: MIT/Bradford Press: 69–81.

— (1991a) *Consciousness Explained.* Boston: Little, Brown and Co.

— (1991b) 'Real patterns', *Journal of Philosophy,* 88: 27–51.

— (1993) '*Back from the drawing board*', in Dahrom, Bo (ed.) *Dennett and His Critics.* Oxford: Basil Blackwell.

— (1998) 'Self-portrait', in *Brainchildren: Essays on Designing Minds.* Cambridge, MA: MIT/Bradford Press: 355–66.

— (2001) *The fantasy of a first-person science.* Electronic ms. http://ase.tufts.edu/cogstud/papers/chalmersdeb3dft.htm

Denton, M. J. (1998) *Nature's Destiny: How the Laws of Biology Reveal Purpose in the Universe.* New York: The Free Press.

Gallup, G., Jr (1977) 'Self-recognition in primates: A comparative approach to bidirectional properties of consciousness', *American Psychologist,* 32: 329–38.

Gettier, E. (1963) 'Is justified true belief knowledge?', *Analysis,* 23: 121–3.

Goldman, A. (1992) 'Reliabilism', in Dancy, J. and Sosa, E. (Eds), *A Companion to Epistemology.* Oxford: Blackwell.

Hill, C. S. (1997) 'Critical study of *explaining attitudes*: A practical approach to the mind' *Noûs* 31: 132–42.

Hume, D. (1977) *An Enquiry Concerning Human Understanding.* Indianapolis: Hackett. [1748]

Johnson, P. (1993) *Darwin on Trial.* Downer's Grove, IL: Intervarsity Press.

— (1995) *Reason in the Balance: The Case Against Naturalism in Science, Law, and Education.* Downer's Grove, IL: Intervarsity Press.

Kaplan, D. (1989) 'Demonstratives', in Almog, J., Perry, J., and Wettstein, H. (eds), *Themes from Kaplan.* New York: Oxford University Press: 481–614.

Kornblith, H. (ed) (1985) *Naturalizing Epistemology.* Cambridge, MA: MIT/Bradford Press.

Lewis, D. (1979) 'Attitudes *De Dicto* and *De Se*', *Philosophical Review,* 88: 513–43.

Matthews, G. B. (1992) *Thought's Ego in Augustine and Descartes.* Ithaca, NY: Cornell University Press.

Needham, R. (1972) *Belief, Language, and Experience.* Oxford: Blackwell.

Perry, J. (1979) 'The problem of the essential indexical', *Noûs,* 13: 3–21.

Quine, W. V. O. (1960) *Word and Object.* Cambridge, MA: MIT Press.

Ryle, G. (1949) *The Concept of Mind.* London: Hutchinson.

Sellars, W. (1963) 'Empiricism and the philosophy of mind', in *Science, Perception and Reality.* London: Routledge & Kegan Paul: 127–96.

Wittgenstein, L. (1953) *Philosophical Investigations.* New York: Macmillan.

Wright, C., Smith, B. C., and MacDonald, C. (eds) (1998) *Knowing Our Own Minds.* Oxford: Clarendon Press.

Part V
Metaphysics and Theology

Brian Hebblethwaite

9
The Nature and Limits of Metaphysical Understanding

Brian Hebblethwaite

It will doubtless seem rash to many of our contemporaries if I speak of metaphysical *understanding*. For more than two centuries, metaphysics has been consigned to the flames, dismissed as nonsense, or held to have come to an end. Even Kant, who insisted, at least, on some kind of future for metaphysics, resolutely banned it from the scope of human *understanding*.

Against all this, my intention in this chapter is to defend not only the possibility but the necessity of metaphysical thinking, and then, to argue that such thinking, despite its limits – those limits arising in part from its difficulty, even more from its diversity – nevertheless contributes greatly to human understanding.

But what is meant by metaphysics? I suggest that the two main considerations leading to the domain of metaphysical thinking are, first, recognition of aspects of our world left unexplained by the natural and the human sciences, and, second, and perhaps more crucially, the human mind's insistent drive to think holistically, to try to make sense of and to relate to each other all the main aspects of our world and our experience. In fact, one could define metaphysics as such holistic thinking.

It needs to be pointed out at once that those who reject the view that there are aspects of our world left unexplained – at least in principle – by the natural and the human sciences are themselves thinking metaphysically. Materialists – physicalists –

are metaphysicians, attempting to think holistically, making large claims about everything. I shall shortly be giving reasons for thinking them not very good metaphysicians. But materialism is certainly metaphysics, not science.

P. F. Strawson has familiarized us with the distinction between revisionary metaphysics and descriptive metaphysics (Strawson 1959: Introduction). The former – revisionary metaphysics – are large-scale 'constructive' world views (although the term 'constructive' needs qualification, since human constructions can lead to discoveries), examples being the philosophies of Plato, Leibniz, Hegel and Whitehead. The latter – descriptive metaphysics – restrict themselves to laying bare the conceptual scheme presupposed or displayed in our actual practices, whether of science or everyday life, examples here being Aristotle (some of the time, at any rate), Kant, Strawson himself, and Michael Dummett. That Dummett can be so classified is clear from his book *The Logical Basis of Metaphysics* (1991), where he shows how a realist metaphysic is implied by the logic of our ordinary language. (The view that Dummett is a constructivist in all areas of philosophy is surely mistaken.) Indeed, the older ordinary language philosophy, so anti-metaphysical in temper, is in fact full of metaphysical implications. J. L. Austin's famous paper 'Ifs and Cans' (Austin 1961: ch. 7), for example, with its powerful refutation of conditional analyses of our uses of the word 'can' and its correlative demonstration of the categorical nature of such uses, is highly pertinent to the metaphysics of freedom – a topic I shall come to anon.

The plan of this chapter is as follows: I begin by drawing out the limitations of scientific thinking – here using the word 'science' in its English sense of the natural and the human sciences. I argue that the 'theories of everything' proposed from these sources – especially from physics and cosmology – have little hope of really accounting for everything. I then explore five areas where this seems especially so: first, the phenomenon of consciousness. Here I draw on John Searle's work, but, I hope, go beyond it. Secondly, I discuss morality and freedom, probing the implications of our living in a moral universe. Thirdly, I move on to art, asking what it means for metaphysical understanding that our universe has it in it, not only to evolve consciousness, but to come up with Dante, Shakespeare, and Goethe. Fourthly, I say something about philosophy, concentrating here on revisionary metaphysics, including metaphysical theism – Eastern as well as Western – and its contribution to human understanding. And fifthly, I consider the phenomenon of religion, bracketing off for now the contribution of theology to human understanding, but exploring not only what John Bowker called 'the sense of God' but also theistic world views as phenomena in human history, and what all this means for holistic understanding.

What I am undertaking in these two chapters could be thought of as a reversal of Auguste Comte's three stages of human thought. Comte suggested that humanity had proceeded from a theological stage typified by St Thomas Aquinas in the middle ages, through a metaphysical stage, typified by the great rationalist philosophers of the seventeenth century, to a positive stage, made possible by the rise of modern science. I suggest, by contrast, that the perceived inadequacies and limitations of positivism lead us back to metaphysics, and that the unavoidable problems which I discuss in this chapter are best tackled by rational theology – the topic of Chapter 10, where, up to a point, I shall be defending the old idea of theology as 'the queen of the sciences', there using the word 'science' in its German sense, including the *Geisteswissenschaften* as well as the *Naturwissenschaften*.

Of course, I must in both chapters say something about the diversity problem – the problem that agreement in metaphysics and theology is much harder to secure than in, at least, the natural sciences.

But first some, very brief, reflections on the limitations of scientific thinking. Here I simply stand on the shoulders of previous Gifford Lecturers, such as Ian Barbour (1990) and John Barrow (1990), who have shown that neither in fact nor in logic could a Grand Unified Theory such as Einstein sought, or a Theory of Everything such as Hawking proposes, predict or explain the capacity of the world stuff – if I may crudely call it that – to come up with life and consciousness, let alone mind, freedom, and morality, and all the products of intelligence, insight, and creativity in philosophy and culture generally. It would, no doubt, be a remarkable scientific achievement – well worthy of a Nobel Prize – to come up with a theory of everything. Its expressibility in a single mathematical equation would be highly impressive. But it would not enable us to explain any of the features of the world I have just listed.

Reductionism in biology and sociobiology fares no better than reductionism in physics. Here again I refer to previous Gifford Lectures by John Eccles (1979), Arthur Peacocke (1990), and John Polkinghorne (1994). One does not have to be an expert to see that Dawkins' account of altruism or Wilson's account of culture, or Churchland's account of what he calls 'folk psychology' does not begin to account for or do justice to human love, human knowledge, including scientific knowledge, or human creativity as exemplified by Dante, Shakespeare, and Goethe.

Cognitive science has been held to pose the greatest threat to the autonomy of these domains, which, I am claiming, resist reductionism and demand metaphysical explanation. But again one does not have to be an expert to see that 'information' in information technology is being used in a purely metaphorical sense, or to agree with Peter Geach that 'machines manifestly have no life, no sense, no feeling, no purposes except their makers'...'. 'It is a suitable nemesis of human pride', Geach goes on, 'that men should be getting ready to perform acts of brutish idolatry – to humble themselves before the superior minds that they, like the heathen before them, believe they can get to inhabit inanimate artefacts' (1969: 41).

Consciousness and Mind

This brings me to the topic of consciousness and the metaphysical questions raised by this phenomenon. The implausibility of scientific reductionism at this point is particularly striking. This goes for Hume's give-away reference to 'this little agitation of the brain which we call thought', for Darwin's equally give-away reference to thought as 'a secretion of the brain', and for the contemporary attempts of such scholars as Crick, Dennett, Chalmers, and even Edelman to give a purely physicalist or biological account of consciousness. The irreducibility of consciousness – and *a fortiori* of mind – as facts of nature have been well brought out by John Searle in his *The Mystery of Consciousness* and earlier works (1997, 1984, 1992), and, from a more Wittgensteinian perspective, by Anthony Kenny in *The Metaphysics of Mind* (1989). I will concentrate here on Searle's position. For Searle, it is a fact of nature that evolution has produced developed organisms with brains that, somehow, cause consciousness. This experienced fact rules out pure physicalism. The fact that the stuff of the world has the capacity to evolve consciousness shows that there is more to matter or energy than the aspects of nature studied in physics. But Searle rejects any resort to mind–body dualism. 'We can accept irreducibility ... without accepting dualism', he says (1997: 214). In this he would be supported not only by Kenny, but also by Polkinghorne, who insists that we are talking about one world, with all its amazing capacities and powers to evolve consciousness, mind, and all the products of mind.

In the end I want to stay with this one world view, if I can, but I have to say that the case for dualism is stronger than Searle allows. The arguments of H. D. Lewis (1969), Richard Swinburne (1986), Karl Popper and John Eccles (1977) are strong arguments and they take into account features of our experience as agents and thinkers that get less than adequate attention in Searle's extended naturalism, as I shall spell out in a moment. Searle refers at one point to Eccles' religious commitment to the existence of a soul, but this does not do justice to the arguments actually used for dualism. Popper, of course, has no such religious commitment, and I have found no discussion of Popper's view in Searle's writings. Swinburne's arguments in his Gifford Lectures are purely philosophical arguments and, while Swinburne's mind–body dualism plays a pivotal role in his overall defence of theism, it is not itself a product of his theistic metaphysics. Polkinghorne's theistic world view, as I have already noted, is resolutely anti-dualistic, as is that of many contemporary Christian theologians. Clearly there is no necessary link between religious commitment and mind–body dualism.

This matter of religious or indeed non-religious presuppositions deserves some reflection. Philosophers tend to be coy about this, except when writing off views coming from an explicitly religious source. (Recall Bertrand Russell's totally inadequate treatment of Thomas Aquinas in his *History of Western Philosophy* [1946: ch. 13].) Alvin Plantinga, of course, is anything but coy. His 'Advice to Christian Philosophers' was precisely that they should have confidence in the import of their theistic world view on the central problems of philosophy (1984: 253–71). I shall myself be urging that a theistic metaphysic makes most sense of the world as we know it to be. On the other side, Derek Parfit is one of the few secular philosophers who urge a comparable confidence in bringing out the implications of atheism. At the end of his *Reasons and Persons* (1986), he points out that, since disbelief in God is relatively recent, non-religious ethics is at a very early stage. Not surprisingly he acknowledges a similarity between his own atheistic view of persons and that of early – non-theistic – Buddhism.

Certainly one should be alert to the question of the bearing of one's theistic – or non-theistic – perspective on the whole mind–body problem. And no assumptions should be made, without scrutiny, about the benignity or malignity of such influences either way. But since, as I say, there is no necessary connection between theism and dualism, nor between anti-dualism and atheism, I propose to concentrate here on the factors themselves that require to be reckoned with in any plausible metaphysics of consciousness and the mind.

Searle's non-reductive view of consciousness as a basic datum of experience and his hypothesis that consciousness is somehow *caused* by the brain may be taken as starting points for our discussion. But the *sui generis* nature of consciousness is not brought out by comparison with supervenient properties such as liquidity, which cannot be reduced simply to the movement of water molecules. Moreover, *qualia* – the experienced states of awareness on the part of conscious beings such as ourselves – while they are indeed, in some unknown manner, the product of brains in receipt of external and internal data, are nevertheless themselves causally efficacious, not only in respect of behaviour, as Searle acknowledges, but also in respect of the neural firings which accompany behaviour. The case for mind–body interac-tionism is very strong. If, for example, I say that I will demonstrate the power of mind over matter by raising my arm after a count of five, it is my conscious intention to prove the point that brings about the movement of my arm, and, presumably, the complex neural firings in my brain and what occurs between my brain and my arm to make it go up. This example brings out the further point that we are not just talking about different types of properties – physical and mental – that the natural world contains. It is not just a question of mental states with their causal powers (using 'cause' here in a wide sense to include reasons and intentions) supervening upon brain states with their causal powers (in a more limited sense of 'cause'). What we are talking about is human subjectivity – the conscious and self-conscious ownership of one's mental states, one's sensations, one's thoughts, one's intentions and one's actions. The self or person, far from being just a bundle of perceptions as Hume famously called it (1739: IV. IV) (to his own very proper dissatisfaction) possesses what Kant called a transcendental unity of apperception (Kemp Smith 1929: 152–5/B132ff.) – and not just apperception. I am not only this animal organism, still less this brain. As a human subject, a self, an agent, a person in relation to other persons – I am deliberately echoing the language of John Macmurray's Gifford Lectures here (1957, 1961) – I transcend my physical and biological base; and metaphysics has to do justice to this transcendence. I repeat, it is not simply a matter of my mental states initiating changes in my physical states – as in raising my arm to prove a point – it is I, *qua* subject, who bring about these changes.

Our ignorance about how all this works is very great. One is all too conscious of the limits of human understanding at this point. In Chapter 10 I shall say something about apophaticism in theology. But the secular mind has no business mocking the doctrine of divine incomprehensibility, for which, as I shall indicate, there are very good reasons, when so much ignorance about earthly matters has to be acknowledged. Apophaticism is as rampant in science and philosophy as it is in theology. John Searle admits that we do not know how the brain causes consciousness A fortiori, we do not know how consciousness causes physical movement, including neural firing. We do not know how a higher animal organism with a developed brain becomes a conscious thinking subject and a free agent.

But just as apophaticism in theology need not and should not prevent us from saying something about God and God's relation to the world, so our ignorance about the mind–brain relation need not and should not prevent us from exploring that relation and coming up with – admittedly highly tentative – hypotheses concerning the nature of a universe that has it in it to evolve consciousness and to evolve persons. This will inevitably take us beyond science into metaphysics.

In no way am I ignoring the progress made by neurophysiologists in locating the correlations between brain states on the one hand and thoughts and intentions – and language capacities – on the other. But the scope for misinterpreting these results is very great. In a recent television programme on these matters a certain philosopher seemed to be suggesting that the discovery that her decision to press a certain key was *preceded* by, not just correlated with, a set of neural firings showed that the decision was *caused* by physical processes in the brain. But this conclusion is quite unwarranted. Any actual decision is going to be preceded not only by reflection but also by largely unconscious ranging over the possibilities. All of this will of course be accompanied by and correlated with, but surely not just caused by, the appropriate neural firings.

I should perhaps give some reasons why I do not embrace mind–body dualism, despite my conviction of the *sui generis* nature not only of consciousness, but also of the mind, the self, persons in relation, and the cultural products of human intelligence and creativity. There are three main reasons why I prefer to stick to a one world metaphysics, provided full justice is done to all aspects of this one world. In the first place, we have to reckon with the lower forms of consciousness. I do not know at what point consciousness appears, either in evolution or in the hierarchy of living beings. But clearly plants are not conscious, animals are. There is a threshold here, which undoubtedly gets crossed, just as there is a threshold between inanimate and living beings. But the fact of lowly degrees of consciousness, say in insects or fish, makes it implausible to suppose that we are talking of a separate mental substance when we enter the realm of consciousness.

This brings me to my second reason for avoiding dualism. We now know so much about the dependency of consciousness upon brain activity – I have agreed with Searle that, as far as products of evolution are concerned, and that includes ourselves, brains cause consciousness – that the idea of mind as a separate substance is difficult to sustain. The reality of consciousness is part of the world's reality. We need an ontology of nature comprehensive enough to include its capacity to evolve life, consciousness, intelligence, and selfhood. Not that the idea of pure mind or pure spirit, unconnected with a material base in an evolved nervous system, is a complete nonsense. No theist could hold that. A more basic dualism between God and the world is still defensible. And God is incorporeal Spirit. I argue below that an infinite creative mind makes better sense of the created world's capacity to evolve minds and selves. But created minds and selves are best thought of as built up from below in and through nature.

My third reason for avoiding dualism is in fact a theological reason – and here I anticipate Chapter 10. One of the oddities of Swinburne's Gifford Lectures is that, while he believes that the soul is correlated with a certain complex organism, on whose operation it depends, at least for the time being, for its conscious functioning, Swinburne nevertheless postulates its special creation as a separate substance at a certain stage of physical and biological development, both in the course of evolution and in the course of each animal and human embryo's growth. Surely creation is better thought of as the calling into being of a universe of energies endowed from the beginning with the capacity and power to come up with the conditions of life and to evolve consciousness, minds, and persons.

From this one world perspective, I have to put a question mark against Karl Popper's talk of three worlds. It will be recalled that Popper speaks of 'World 1' as the world of physical reality, 'World

2' as the world of mental states and acts, and 'World 3' as the world of the linguistic, intellectual, and cultural products of 'World 2' activity (1972: ch. 3). Without denying the reality of what Popper is classifying, I would prefer to see these as three aspects or elements in the one world, all of them requiring attention and explanation in any plausible metaphysics. As for Roger Penrose's three worlds, the physical, the mental and the mathematical (1994: II.8.7), a view which Searle ascribes to Penrose's Platonist metaphysics, I shall have to reinterpret this, as I do towards the end of this chapter and in the next, in terms of the rational structure of the one created world reflecting the rationality and mind of the maker – God.

One further point about the capacity of this one world to evolve minds: it is a point often made, but it is worth repeating. The sheer size of the universe is no reason to depreciate the significance of the evolution of mind in one tiny corner of one solar system in one galaxy among myriads. The quantitative dimensions to the physical base of the evolution of life, consciousness, and intelligence are totally irrelevant to the question of the significance of these qualitative developments. And it seems to be the case anyway, as cosmologists driven to posit some anthropic principle point out (Barrow & Tipler 1986: ch. 6), that such a vast mass of energy is a necessary condition for the cosmic evolution of conditions stable and fruitful enough for the thresholds into life, consciousness, and mind to be able to be crossed anywhere. Of course, there is much debate as to whether this is likely to have happened many times – in our own galaxy or in distant galaxies – or only once here on Earth. I am inclined to think belief in extraterrestrial intelligent life reflects secular prejudice. The arguments in its favour are purely statistical, and the empirical evidence points to uniqueness. Not only is there no evidence for extraterrestrial intelligent life (Barrow & Tipler 1986: ch. 9), purely statistical probabilities are outweighed by the extraordinary number of *im*probable coincidences that have to obtain before the thresholds in question can be crossed. One cannot argue simply from the evident capacity of the world stuff to evolve minds that it must have done so in many places and at many times.

But my present point is that, whether the universe has in fact evolved minds many times or only once, the appearance of the noosphere – to use Teilhard de Chardin's term – is a qualitative leap of vast significance, given its nature and its results, quite irrespective of the sheer size of the mindless universe out of which it has appeared.

Freedom and Morality

I now turn to freedom and morality, two major and, of course, linked elements in this new significant dimension – the noosphere – of this one evolving world. What we have to try to make sense of, in our holistic metaphysical thinking, is the capacity of the world stuff to evolve not only consciousness and mind, but free beings and moral persons and communities.

Again with Searle, I take it as a basic datum of our experience as human beings that we are free. Our freedom of thought and action is far more certain than the alleged results of any piece of rational argument or scientific research. The very processes of rational argument and scientific research themselves presuppose our freedom. Arguments in defence of the freedom of the will, insofar as they are needed, have been set out by Austin Farrer in his Gifford Lectures (1958) and by John Lucas in his book, *The Freedom of the Will* (1970). Lucas's use of Gödel's theorem to show the impossibility of formalizing an account of our thinking in such a way as formally to include recognition of its own validity has been widely discussed, but never, to my knowledge, refuted. Recent obituaries of Elizabeth Anscombe have referred to her alleged demolition of C. S. Lewis's presentation of an informal version of this argument. But, as Michael Dummett pointed out (in his obituary of Anscombe, *The Tablet,* 13 January 2001), Lewis was far from decisively refuted. He returned with a refined version of the argument (1960: ch. 3), and Anscombe herself subscribed to a version of it in her own inaugural lecture (see Anscombe 1981). It has recently received a powerful restatement by Stephen Clark in his book, *God, Religion and Reality* (1998: 96–101). Briefly, the argument goes like this: if a belief of mine is the determined outcome of chemical processes in my brain, then there is no way of telling whether or not it is true.

The point of such arguments, formal or informal, is to bring out the fact of our freedom of thought, our ability to range freely, in thought, over relevant considerations, to weigh evidence and arguments, and to reach responsible conclusions as to where the truth lies or probably lies. Lewis was accused of confusing reasons and causes, but, as I have already mentioned, reasons are a species of cause in a wide sense of cause, though of course they effect things in a very different way from, say, chemical processes operating willy-nilly. In particular they are not determining causes. They do not compel their effects. They provide sufficient conditions, not in the sense of that, given which, the effect is bound to occur, but rather, that, given which, the effect – whether a belief or an action – makes most sense and is seen to be justified and thus likely to be held or to be done.

All this, as I say, applies to both thought and action. Where action is concerned, our freedom and responsibility are presupposed by our whole form of life as individuals and as members of society. While this is most evident in the moral sphere – all our language of praise and blame, the whole institution of reward and punishment, presupposing freedom and responsibility – it is also true of more humdrum choices, such as which book to read or which friend to visit. And I stress again that the activities of scientific research themselves cannot be explained deterministically.

Clearly there are degrees of freedom, and it is interesting to enquire at what point in evolution or in the life history of a child rudimentary freedom becomes a reality. Not even animal behaviour, I suggest – at least that of the higher animals – can be accounted for wholly in terms of stimulus and response.

Metaphysical questions arise over how it is that organisms can evolve these capacities and powers. Again I refer to Anscombe's recognition that, while indeterminacy is not the same as freedom, it may well be 'the physical correlate of human freedom of action, and perhaps also of the voluntariness and intentionalness of the conduct of other animals ...' (1981: 146). Certainly the indeterminacy of quantum physics and chaos theory has made it much easier to see that the physical universe does possess the flexibility and openness required for the emergence of autonomous beings, able to take control of things and shape the future for themselves in the spheres of both thought and action.

That freedom and morality are linked needs little argument. 'Ought' implies 'can'. Kant's second postulate of practical reason is seldom questioned even by those who do question his first and third postulates: immortality and God (see Kant 1996; 246–7). But equally 'can' implies 'ought'. It is our freedom that opens up to us the moral dimensions of responsibility and choice between good and evil. But how are we to understand this moral sphere? Is it just a matter of subjective and intersubjective preference? Or do we find ourselves subject to moral constraints and demands from the very nature of things? Kant's conviction of the categorical nature of the moral law was the lynchpin of his whole philosophy. As Allen Wood has shown (1970), the critical philosophy cannot be understood if we fail to take seriously Kant's conviction that a strict delimitation of theoretical understanding was necessary in order to make room for moral faith.

Moral faith, for Kant, involved not only recognition of the demands of the moral law. It also involved drawing out the implications of the fact that we exist under its constraints. This is where all three postulates of practical reason come in. The postulates of immortality and God are required not simply to explain the realizability of the highest good. They are required as conditions of this universe in which we find ourselves being, despite appearances, a moral universe.

Kant made discussion of this matter very difficult for himself by his insistence on the inaccessibility of the noumenal world to theoretical understanding. His immediate successors in German idealism soon breached these boundaries. And, in our own day, as I have already indicated, moralists have less to fear from post-Newtonian science, which lacks rigid deterministic implications. Also I do not think we have to restrict ourselves to Kant's own rigid epistemology. Our conceptual framework is a much more flexible product of continual interaction with a real-world environment, and our reflection on experience is capable of much greater analogical extension in speculative metaphysics than Kant allowed. Kant's own practice, in moral philosophy, in teleology, and in philosophical theology, in fact went much further in spelling out the necessary conditions of this being a moral universe than his strict epistemology would allow.

Be that as it may. I now want to introduce the names of two more recent philosophers who have explored the implications of the objectivity of morals in the interest of a wider metaphysics, Iris Murdoch and Donald MacKinnon.

Murdoch's Gifford Lectures, *Metaphysics as a Guide to Morals* (1992), could equally well have been entitled *Morals as a Guide to Metaphysics*. Not that she actually develops a metaphysical world view that tries to make sense of the Good and the Beautiful as objective realities, basic to the nature of things. But her Platonic insistence on the Good as a transcendent object of attention and of love is very striking. 'We *experience*', she writes, 'both the reality of perfection and its distance away, and this leads us to place our idea of it outside the world of existent being as something of a different unique and special sort. Such experience of the reality of good is not like an arbitrary and assertive resort to our own will; it is a discovery of something independent of us, where that independence is essential' (1992: 508).

Murdoch herself would not accept a theistic interpretation of the objectivity of the Good, since, for her, a god could only be an existent object among other objects, and she shared the modern demythologizing attitude to such supernatural entities. She endorsed Don Cupitt's 'taking leave' of God in this sense, but not his extreme anti-realism. That simply failed to do justice, she thought, to our moral experience of the objectivity and transcendence of the Good.

It has to be said that Murdoch's position is deeply obscure. No one, I think, has succeeded in explaining the ontological status of her – any more than Plato's – objective Good as the transcendent object of attention. As I shall be arguing, Neoplatonism's theistic reinterpretation of Plato was a necessary development, if sense was to be made of the objectivity of goodness and beauty. But that involved a theism that precisely did not see God as one – the supreme – object among others in the inventory of the furniture of the world. All the same, I take Murdoch's insistence on the objectivity of value as a pointer in the direction of a metaphysic broad enough to make sense of a universe that has not only evolved consciousness and minds and free persons in relation, but beings capable of discerning goodness, beauty, and truth. And what they discern at this high point of evolutionary development are dimensions of reality way beyond the physical, chemical, and biological base from which such discernments have evolved. Unlike Murdoch, I shall be arguing that a theistic metaphysic makes best sense of all this.

I might insert at this point a note on my friend and colleague Don Cupitt's inability to sustain a purely subjectivist, expressivist, anti-realist approach. Having previously endorsed postmodernism's deconstruction of every kind of metaphysical realism, he now, in a recent book (Cupitt 1998), finds himself driven to admit that language cannot be the whole story. There must be something given, which language forms up into our human world. He calls this something 'being', with reference to Heidegger, though in a sense remote from that thinker's highly obscure existential ontology. Often he writes 'be-ing' with a hyphen, to indicate its dynamic, wholly unformed nature, till language clothes it with ever-changing forms. How strange that Cupitt's return to metaphysics should come about this way! He now finds himself postulating something not unlike the Presocratic Anaximander's 'unlimited' or 'indefinite' – the formless matter of a world yet to be shaped up, in Anaximander's case by separating out of opposites, in Cupitt's case by human language. We are right back, then, at the very beginnings of Western metaphysics with an obscure, primitive, theory that explains absolutely nothing. Indeed Cupitt's new-found metaphysic is even more opaque than Anaximander's; for why on earth suppose that it is human language that gives form to the basic stuff of the world and to the natural kinds that we discover in the universe and here on Earth?

Returning to the theme of how moral philosophy implies a metaphysic of transcendence, I now cite the work of my teacher, Donald MacKinnon and in particular his Gifford Lectures, *The Problem of Metaphysics* (1974). The burden of those lectures, worked out with typical earnestness and agonizing over the import of tragedy and parable, was that 'in moral experience transcendence is present to us all along' (1974: 147). MacKinnon saw in Kant's doctrine of the primacy of practical reason the classical expression of the approach that sees the metaphysical as 'something that presses on us with a directness and immediacy which requires no argument to convince us of its reality'. And he adds here, in a footnote, 'It is the analysis of this pressure that constitutes the crux of this whole book', his Gifford Lectures. The parables of Jesus are analysed by MacKinnon as paradigm examples of the way in which we have to do with perception of the way things are. And similarly the tragedies of Sophocles and Shakespeare are called upon to demonstrate our discontent with any kind of naturalism. 'It is', MacKinnon writes, 'as if we are constrained in pondering the extremities of human life to acknowledge the transcendent as the only alternative to the kind of trivialisation which would empty of significance the sort of experience with which we have been concerned' – that is, in exploring the significance of Antigone and Lear (1974: 145).

Let me try to put the argument a little more straightforwardly. What I am talking about is the way in which moral facts point ineluctably to transcendence. When confronted with the moral law or with the moral significance of human life in situations of tragedy or of supreme goodness or radical evil, we find ourselves unable to subscribe to a naturalistic philosophy of value as just intersubjective preference. And we have to try to make metaphysical sense of an evolving world, which has come to manifest such values. Obviously, one has to admit that moral facts are hard to comprehend. One of J. L. Mackie's main arguments for the subjectivity of morals in his book, *Ethics: Inventing Right and Wrong* (1977), was 'the argument from queerness'. Objective values are very queer entities. So they are – from a naturalistic perspective. But given the pressures to admit them, pressures we have seen articulated by Kant, Murdoch, and MacKinnon, we are driven to question the naturalistic perspective. As I shall argue, a theistic metaphysic makes most sense of these otherwise queer facts. Ironically, Mackie admits this, hypothetically – if we could embrace theism, which Mackie himself could not. But the unacceptability of naturalism, its trivialization of moral experience, should make us look again at the question of the coherence of theism, too easily dismissed by Mackie.

As an aside, I might point out that this argument is structurally similar to the argument from truth which I have used elsewhere (1988: ch. 7). In brief: Nietzsche's aphorism that, with the death of God, truth becomes fiction, falls foul of our obstinate conviction that truth is a matter of discovery not invention. This is best accounted for on the supposition of a creator God who has given the world its discoverable reality and sustains it.

Art and Culture

I now turn to the indubitable fact that this evolving universe has come up, not only with consciousness, mind, freedom, and moral value, but with great art and culture – yet more profound and objective values in the sphere of beauty. Our question now is, how are we to make sense of a universe capable of manifesting the beautiful and the sublime, as well as evolving beings capable of sublime artistic creativity, of coming up, that is, with Dante, Shakespeare, and Goethe?

The spheres of morality and aesthetics are clearly linked, as MacKinnon's wrestling with Antigone and Lear shows. But beauty is a dimension of the real that includes many more facets than those seen in surpassing goodness or confronted in the depths of tragedy. Natural beauty, comedy (I think of play as one of the sociologist Peter Berger's 'signals of transcendence' [1971: 76–9]) the heights and depths of musical composition, the serenity of a Claude landscape, or the teasing ambiguities of Poussin's *A Dance to the Music of Time*, the exquisite cadences of poetic expression – George Steiner cites Shakespeare's 'There sleeps Tytania sometime of the night' from *A Midsummer Night's Dream* – all these wonders resist the subjectivist proverb about beauty being in the eye of the beholder and give substance to Keats's conclusion to his 'Ode on a Grecian Urn': 'Beauty is truth, truth beauty – that is all Ye know on earth and all ye need to know'. I recall the journalist Bernard Levin writing of the ultimate pleasure of Shakespeare in the *Listener*: 'the deep, sustaining realisation that his work is not only beautiful, thrilling, profound and funny, but, above all, true'. But it is not just a question of pleasure. As Levin's own words make clear, it is a question of 'realisation', perception, recognition of truth. But what kind of truth? The whole burden of objectivism in aesthetic theory – an objectivism which, like ethical objectivism, will not go away – is that what we perceive in the beauty of nature and the sublimities of artistic creation is something of the true nature of things.

Such reflections have informed major strands in the history of philosophy – Platonism, German Idealism, Romanticism – to which we turn below. Schopenhauer, Schelling, and Hegel all saw music and art as representations of the infinite. For Hegel, artistic beauty reveals absolute truth through perception (Knox [trans.] 1975). Of course, the fact that art yields metaphysical knowledge in sensual form does, for Hegel, mean that art must be transcended by religion, just as religion must be transcended by philosophy, if conceptual knowledge of the Absolute is to be attained. This progress from art, through religion, to philosophy will be questioned shortly; but clearly, Hegel had a higher view of the cognitive significance of art than, say, R. G. Collingwood, for whom the figments of the imagination that constitute art only hint at the realities discovered and experienced in religion (1924: ch. 3).

For much of modernity and postmodernity all this has been lost sight of. Few secular philosophers now will be disposed to affirm the metaphysical significance of great art. And yet, as I say, the objective value of beauty, like cheerfulness, keeps breaking in. This has seldom been better expressed in the context of our current cultural situation than by George Steiner, who, in his book, *Real Presences*, asks us to reconsider the assumption 'that all serious art and literature, and not only music to which Nietzsche applies the term, is an *opus metaphysicum*' (1989: 134). Steiner gives many examples, including examples from Dante and Shakespeare, where this assumption is virtually forced upon us. But his prime examples still come from music. Music, he says, 'has long been ... the unwritten theology of those who lack or reject any formal creed'. And he asks us just to listen to the slow movement of Schubert's C Major Quintet. I shall return to this kind of insight in a moment. But, in summary, Steiner extends his argument to cover all great art. I quote him at some length:

> It is, I believe, poetry, art and music which relate us most directly to that in being which is not ours. Science is no less animate in its making of models and images. But these are not, finally, disinterested. They aim at

mastery, at ownership. It is counter-creation and counter-love, as these are embodied in the aesthetic and in our reception of formed meaning, which puts us in sane touch with that which transcends, with matters 'undreamt of' in our materiality . . . The arts are most wonderfully rooted in substance, in the human body, in stone, in pigment, in the twanging of gut or the weight of wind on reeds. All good art and literature begin in immanence. But they do not stop there. Which is to say, very plainly, that it is the enterprise and privilege of the aesthetic to quicken into lit presence the continuum between temporality and eternity, between matter and spirit, between man and 'the other'. It is in this common and exact sense that *poiesis* opens on to, is underwritten by, the religious and the metaphysical.' (1989: 226–7)

To return to music; it is sometimes suggested that the deep aesthetic experience of a Promenade Concert audience listening to a Mahler Symphony in the Albert Hall, or of a Wagner audience in Bayreuth, or of a solitary individual – Inspector Morse, perhaps – listening to the Schubert C Major Quintet, is a kind of religion substitute, providing solace and depth to the human spirit in ways religion used to do. But this fails totally to do justice to the nature and significance of what is experienced in great music – or in the poetry of Dante, Shakespeare, and Goethe, to cite those giants of European culture once again. As I have written elsewhere, 'art and culture can and should be seen not just as products of human sensibility but as clues to the meaning and worth of the whole cosmic process out of which we have evolved. It is the very nature of aesthetic, as of moral, value that belies materialism as a total world view, and provides one of the many starting-points for a cumulative argument for the existence of God' (1996: 26).

Literary critics have long inclined towards such intimations of transcendence. In an essay on 'Goethe as the Sage' (1957: 207–27), T. S. Eliot writes first of the permanence and universality of figures such as Dante, Shakespeare, and Goethe – their ability to speak to successive generations and, albeit from a specific cultural background, to readers worldwide. He then writes of the abundance, amplitude and unity of their work – its range and diversity, and the way it illuminates life and the world. He writes of the wisdom of these authors, a wisdom discernible and acceptable whether or not we agree with their own particular philosophical or religious views. The point is made with specific reference to Goethe; but in a much earlier essay on Dante (1932: 237–77), Eliot made a similar point with reference to the Tuscan poet. We do not have to share Dante's mediaeval Catholicism in order to understand and appreciate the depths and heights and the sheer range of human sensibility that the *Divine Comedy* manifests. But the question that concerns us here – and again it is George Steiner who asks it most explicitly – is whether the wisdom and understanding found in and conveyed by poets such as Dante, Shakespeare, and Goethe is just a matter of human sensibility, however profound, or whether we do not find in such work insight into the very meaning of life and the very meaning of the world in a more transcendental sense. As Steiner puts it in his own essay on Dante, while adverting to the particularities of time and place in Dante's, as in Proust's, design: 'The text is timeless, universal, because utterly dated and placed. Dante and Proust, like no others, give us the gossip of eternity' (1978: ch. 7). But, of course, Shakespeare and Goethe do the same.

The relation between art, metaphysics, and religion must now be considered explicitly. It can hardly be, as Hegel thought, a matter of progression from art to religion and thence to philosophy. That gives an exaggerated significance to the conceptual. Indeed I shall be discussing philosophy *before* I explore religion. But I do not wish to replace Hegel's progression with a revised progression – from art, through metaphysics to religion. For art, like morals, has itself, as Steiner shows, both metaphysical and religious significance. And if theistic metaphysics yields the best explanation for the capacities of the universe to evolve both goodness and beauty, then the best metaphysics will turn out to be an aspect of religion. But only an aspect; for the very nature of the universe – the values it has come up with in the realms of morality and of art – demand practical and affective responses as well as cognitive and conceptual ones. And these are key elements in religion, which concerns itself not only with knowledge but with love, with wonder, and with joy.

Philosophy

However, I do first turn to philosophy, in particular to revisionary metaphysics, to use Strawson's phrase once more. I am not only concerned to ask which strands in the history of philosophy make most sense of the phenomena of consciousness, mind, freedom, morality and art, and of a world productive of such things. I am also concerned to ask the more Hegelian question of how best we are to understand a cosmos capable of coming up with just such philosophies – themselves, on any reckoning, remarkable constituents of Popper's 'World 3' or, better, of Polkinghorne's 'One World'.

I have already referred to Platonism and Neoplatonism as one of the most fertile strands in philosophy in respect of its ability to fashion a comprehensive account of the place of mind in nature, and of the beautiful and the good as not only requiring metaphysical explanation but affording the key ideas for metaphysical explanation. The Cambridge Platonists, and in particular Cudworth in his *True Intellectual System of the Universe* (1678), still retain great visionary power. My colleague Douglas Hedley has recently shown the striking congruence between Coleridge's Christian Platonism and certain strands in German Idealism (Hedley 2000). As Hedley observes, 'Coleridge's metaphysics attempts to explain the "lower" (nature) in terms of that which is higher (spirit) whereas the naturalist explains the higher in terms of the lower, the spiritual realm in purely natural terms' (2000: 23). We have already seen how Platonism recurs again and again in the philosophy of mathematics, as in Roger Penrose's work (1994) or in Gödel's response to the later Bertrand Russell (see Monk 2000: 267–70). And the strength of Neoplatonism as a continuing tradition of holistic explanation may be seen in the aforementioned work of Stephen Clark (1998).

It may well be that Platonism fails to get the relation between nature and spirit quite right. I have already criticized its weakness vis-à-vis the doctrine of creation. But recognition of the ultimate dependence of nature on spirit and a preference for 'top-down' rather than 'bottom-up' explanation are features of lasting import in this tradition as they are in seventeenth-century rationalism and in nineteenth-century German Idealism.

It is easy to criticize the great seventeenth-century rationalists for their exaggerated view on the power and scope of human reason. And it is easy to point to specific implausibilities in the systems of individual thinkers – Descartes' extreme mind–matter dualism, Malebranche's 'occasionalist' denial of causal efficacy in nature, Spinoza's pantheistic determinism, Leibniz's 'pre-established harmony' between mind and body. But, as recent interest in and work on these philosophers has shown (see Cottingham 1992; Nadler 2000; Garrett 1996; Jolley 1995), we are dealing here with minds that have seen the problems, ranged over the possibilities, debated with the ancients and the moderns, and exemplified the kind of holistic metaphysical thinking that enlarges our understanding even when we disagree. Above all, they have taken seriously the phenomena of mind and reason, their place in nature, and their transcendence of nature.

The same is true of German Idealism. I have already mentioned its breaking out from the self-imposed limitations of Kant's critical philosophy. There is much to admire in Fichte's attempt at a transcendental explanation of consciousness and experience, and his (Kantian) conviction of the fundamental nature of freedom and the moral law. But his philosophy of nature leaves much to be desired, and, certainly for the theist, the biggest problem with Fichte is his inability to recognize the explanatory force of infinite Spirit vis-à-vis the contingencies of nature and finite spirit. On these grounds both Hegel and Schelling have been found more fruitful for the kind of metaphysics called for if sense is to be made of the whole history of the world, including the spheres of mind, morals, art, philosophy, and religion under special consideration here. Recent Hegel studies by Charles Taylor (1975), Peter Hodgson (1985), and Raymond Plant (1997) – to name but a few – have shown the continuing fertility and power of Hegel's all-embracing philosophy. But it is not surprising, given Hegel's (admittedly dynamic) monism, that it was Schelling's later philosophy that proved the greater influence, both on Coleridge's Christian Platonism and on Paul Tillich's theistic ontology.

Similarly, the monistic Absolute of the British Idealists gave way to the much more plausible Personal Idealism of J. R. Illingworth (1894), Hastings Rashdall (1924), and C. C. J. Webb (1919), whose theistic metaphysics still repays close study, as does that of A. E. Taylor (1921) and William Temple (1934), both brought up in the idealist tradition, but moving away from it in a more realist direction. Temple's insistence, in his Gifford Lectures, that the process that has led to the emergence of mind and spirit here on Earth should be evaluated in terms of its highest product exemplifies perfectly the line of thought I recommend here.

Space prevents more than a mention of process thought. But the considerations that led A. N. Whitehead away from mathematical logic to an all-embracing metaphysic of becoming are precisely those informing our present concerns (1929).

Existentialism, too, gets little more than a mention here. For all the profundity and insight of its characterization of authentic – and inauthentic – human existence, it fails to satisfy unless, as with Heidegger, it seeks to unfold a more general ontology, relating human being to being as such. Not that Heidegger really satisfies, given his obscurity and his wholly implausible generalizations concerning Western metaphysics as leading inexorably to the apotheosis of technology. Very little of the revisionary metaphysics cited here would fit that description. Nevertheless the later Heidegger's depiction of poetry as the 'shepherd of Being' can be taken as an obscure hint in the direction of a metaphysics of art, towards which George Steiner points, and which I endorsed as one strand in the overall world view being sought. (On the later Heidegger, see Pattison [2000].)

As we move more and more into one world of global communication in many different spheres, economic, technological, political, communicational, and ethical (I think of Hans Küng's global ethics project at this point) we become increasingly aware of the common heritage of world philosophies – their great diversity, but also their recurring commonalities. To read Ninian Smart's book, *World Philosophies* (1999), or to browse through Blackwell's *A Companion to World Philosophies* (Deutsche & Bontekoe 1997), is to see how again and again, out of different cultural backgrounds, the same metaphysical and epistemological questions have been addressed, often with strikingly similar results. This is especially true of the theistic world views that have been developed out of centres in the Middle East, the Indian subcontinent, parts of Africa, and to a certain degree, in other parts of the globe. Comparative studies by scholars such as my colleague, Julius Lipner with regard to the eleventh/twelfth-century Hindu theologian Ramanuja (1986), by R. C. Zaehner with regard to the twentieth-century Hindu thinker, Sri Aurobindo (1971), and by Keith Ward(1994, 1996, 1998, 2000), whose comparative theology I discuss in Chapter 10, are among the many which show the fertility and power of theistic metaphysics to make sense of a universe capable of coming up with mind, morality, art, philosophy, and religion. Of course, world philosophy includes many examples of non-theistic, sceptical, and anti-metaphysical philosophies. But the question has to be pressed: can these provide any explanation, let alone more adequate explanation, for the data which experience of being in the world – and world history – thrusts upon us?

Theistic metaphysics, in a number of different ways, suggests that a nature productive of finite spirit and of the values of goodness, beauty, and truth is best understood as the creation of infinite Spirit, itself supremely good, beautiful, and true – the creative act endowing the universe with its given nature, its given powers and its ultimate meaning and destiny. Also, as I mentioned above, theistic metaphysics offers the best explanation for all the necessary features of the contingent world – its mathematical expressibility, for example, its conformity to the laws of logic, the properties and abstract ideas it instantiates – all the features discerned but not explained by pure Platonism. For theistic metaphysics, mathematics and logic reflect the consistency and rationality of God's necessary being, abstract ideas and properties are God's creative ideas. So all the necessities in the created world – and indeed in any possible world – depend on either the nature or the will of God (see Menzel 1987).

The two principal difficulties with such theistic metaphysics are, of course, the question of the coherence of theism and the problem of evil. These difficulties cannot be addressed here, but, clearly, the plausibility of theistic metaphysics in providing the best explanation of the world process and of the possibilities it realizes depends on at least some success in defending theism's coherence and offering a theodicy.

Religion

In singling out theistic metaphysics from the plethora of world philosophies I am already entering the field of religion. The phenomenology of religion as practised by Rudolf Otto (e.g., 1923), Gerardus van der Leeuw (e.g., 1938), and Ninian Smart (e.g., 1996), and the history of religions as practised by Ernst Troeltsch (e.g., 1991) and Mircea Eliade (e.g., 1978–85), yield data, including theistic metaphysics and including the theologies to be discussed in Chapter 10, which themselves provide clues to the meaning of the whole world process that has come up with such things. But I conclude this chapter by drawing attention to the other central aspects of religion that offer, perhaps, more all-embracing clues to the meaning of the whole world process than the theoretical, explanatory, aspects characteristic of metaphysical theism.

I have already adverted to these more central aspects in referring to love, wonder, and joy. What I have in mind, too, are the dimensions of spirituality and the sacred, which are found, as the phenomenologists and the historians of religion show us, throughout history and all over the globe. Both the mystical and the numinous are pervasive features of human experience in both its subjective and its objective sense. Again I stress the objective sense. I am interested in *what* is experienced: dimensions, modalities of the real, which themselves call for metaphysical explanation. What does it tell us about the cosmos that it evolves mystics and opens itself up to mystical penetration and becomes the vehicle of the sacred?

Religion has its dark side, of course. The problem of evil is found as much here as elsewhere. But so is the problem of good. What does it tell us about the cosmos that it evolves saints and the communion of saints – in every developed culture and in every developed religion?

I can do no more than touch on these issues at the close of this survey. The limitations of such holistic metaphysical understanding are obvious and great. In particular the huge variety of world views and world philosophies, not least those stemming from the world religions, contrast most strikingly with the relative uniformity of the scientific world view. Yet how much this uniform scientific *Weltanschauung* leaves out of account! For all its diversity – and I have drawn attention also to its commonalities – the kind of metaphysical thinking that attends to the heights and depths of reason, morality, art, and religion has a fair claim to enlarge our understanding, if only by asking pertinent questions.

References

Anscombe, E. (1981) 'Causality and determination', in Anscombe, E., *Metaphysics and the Philosophy of Mind. Collected Philosophical Papers Volume II*. Oxford: Basil Blackwell: 133–47.

Austin, J. L. (1961) *Philosophical Papers*. Oxford: Clarendon Press.

Barbour, I. G. (1990) *Religion in an Age of Science*. London: SCM Press.

Barrow, J. D. (1990) *Theories of Everything. The Quest for Ultimate Explanation*. Oxford: Oxford University Press.

Barrow, J. D. and Tipler, F. J. (1986) *The Anthropic Cosmological Principle*. Oxford: Oxford University Press.

Berger, P. L. (1971) *A Rumour of Angels. Modern Society and the Rediscovery of the Supernatural*. Harmondsworth: Penguin Books.

Clarke, S. (1998) *God, Religion and Reality*. London: SPCK.

Collingwood, R. G. (1924) *Speculum Mentis*. Oxford: Clarendon Press.

Cottingham, J. (ed.) (1992) *The Cambridge Companion To Descartes*. Cambridge: Cambridge University Press.

Cudworth, R. (1678) *The True Intellectual System of the Universe*. London: Printed for R. Royston.

Cupitt, D. (1998) *The Religion of Being*. London: SCM Press.

Deutsch, E. and Bontekoe, R. (eds) (1997) *A Companion to World Philosophies.* Oxford: Blackwell.

Dummett, M. (1991) *The Logical Basis of Metaphysics.* London: Duckworth.

Eccles, J. C. (1979) *The Human Mystery.* New York: Springer International.

Eliade, M. (1978–1985) *A History of Religious Ideas,* 3 Vols. Chicago: University of Chicago Press.

Eliot, T. S. (1932) *Selected Essays.* London: Faber and Faber.

— (1957) *On Poetry and Poets.* London: Faber and Faber.

Farrer, A. (1958) *The Freedom of the Will.* London: Adam & Charles Black.

Garrett, D. (ed.) (1996) *The Cambridge Companion to Spinoza.* Cambridge: Cambridge University Press.

Hebblethwaite, B. (1988) *The Ocean of Truth.* Cambridge: Cambridge University Press.

— (1996) *The Essence of Christianity. A Fresh Look at the Nicene Creed.* London: SPCK.

Hedley, D. (2000) *Coleridge, Philosophy and Religion.* Cambridge: Cambridge University Press.

Hodgson, P. C. (1985) 'Georg Wilhelm Friedrich Hegel', in Smart, N. *et al.,* (eds), *Nineteenth Century Thought in the West, Vol. I.* Cambridge: Cambridge University Press.

Hume, D. (1739) *A Treatise of Human Nature. Book 1: Of the Understanding.* London: John Noon.

Illingworth, J. R. (1894) *Personality, Human and Divine.* London: Macmillan.

Jolley, N. (ed.) (1995) *The Cambridge Companion to Leibniz.* Cambridge: Cambridge University Press.

Kant, I. (1996) *Practical Philosophy.* Cambridge: Cambridge University Press.

Kemp Smith, N. (1929) *Immanuel Kant's Critique of Pure Reason.* London: Macmillan.

Kenny, A. (1989) *The Metaphysics of Mind.* Oxford: Clarendon Press.

Knox, T. M. (1975) *Hegel's Aesthetics.* Oxford: Clarendon Press.

Lewis, C. S. (1960) *Miracles.* Revised edition. London: Collins.

Lewis, H. D. (1969) *The Elusive Mind.* London: George Allen & Unwin.

Lipner, J. (1986) *The Face of Truth. A Study of Meaning and Metaphysics in the Vedantic Theology or Ramanuja.* London: Macmillan.

Lucas, J. R. (1970) *The Freedom of the Will.* Oxford: Clarendon Press.

Mackie, J. L. (1977) *Ethics. Inventing Right and Wrong.* Harmondsworth: Penguin Books.

MacKinnon, D. M. (1974) *The Problem of Metaphysics.* Cambridge: Cambridge University Press.

Macmurray, J. (1957) *The Self as Agent.* London: Faber and Faber.

— (1961) *Persons in Relation.* London: Faber and Faber.

Menzel, C. (1987) 'Theism, Platonism and the metaphysics of mathematics', *Faith and Philosophy* 4: 365–82.

Monk, R. (2000) *Bertrand Russell 1921–70. The Ghost of Madness.* London: Jonathan Cape.

Murdoch, I. (1992) *Metaphysics as a Guide to Morals.* London: Chatto & Windus.

Nadler, S. (ed.) (2000) *The Cambridge Companion to Malebranche.* Cambridge: Cambridge University Press.

Otto, R. (1923) *The Idea of the Holy.* Oxford: Oxford University Press.

Parfit, D. (1986) *Reasons and Persons.* Oxford: Oxford University Press.

Pattison, G. (2000) *The Later Heidegger.* London: Routledge.

Peacocke, A. (1990) *Theology for a Scientific Age.* Oxford: Basil Blackwell.

Penrose, R. (1994) *Shadows of the Mind.* Oxford: Oxford University Press.

Plant, R. (1997) *Hegel.* London: Phoenix.

Plantinga, A. (1984) 'Advice to Christian philosophers', *Faith and Philosophy* 1: 253–71.

Polkinghorne, J. (1994) *Science and Christian Belief.* London: SPCK.

Popper, K. (1972) *Objective Knowledge. An Evolutionary Approach.* Oxford: The Clarendon Press.

Popper, K. R., and Eccles, J. C. (1977) *The Self and its Brain. An Argument for Interactionism.* New York: Springer International.

Rashdall, H. (1924) *Philosophy and Religion.* London: Duckworth.

Russell, B. (1946) *History of Western Philosophy.* London: George Allen & Unwin.

Searle, J. R. (1984) *Minds, Brains and Science.* London: BBC.

— (1992) *The Rediscovery of Mind.* Cambridge, Mass.: MIT Press.

— (1997) *The Mystery of Consciousness.* London: Granta Publications.

Smart, N. (1996) *Dimensions of the Sacred. An Anatomy of the World's Beliefs.* London: Harper Collins.

— (1999) *World Philosophies.* London: Routledge.

Smith, W. C. (1967) *Questions of Religious Truth.* London: Victor Gollancz.

Steiner, G. (1978) *On Difficulty and Other Essays.* New York: Oxford University Press.

— (1989) *Real Presences. Is There Anything In What We Say?.* London: Faber and Faber.

Strawson, P. F. (1959) *Individuals. An Essay in Descriptive Metaphysics.* London: Methuen & Co Ltd.

Swinburne, R. (1986) *The Evolution of the Soul.* Oxford: Clarendon Press.

Taylor, A. E. (1921), 'Theism', in *Hastings Encyclopaedia of Religion and Ethics*, Vol. XII. Edinburgh: T. & T. Clark. 261–87.

Taylor, C. (1975) *Hegel.* Cambridge: Cambridge University Press.

Teilhard de Chardin, P. (1959) *The Phenomenon of Man.* London: Collins.

Temple, W. (1934) *Nature, Man and God.* London: Macmillan.

Troeltsch, E. (1991) *Religion in History. Essays Translated by James Luther Adams.* Edinburgh: T. & T. Clark.

Van der Leeuw, G. (1938) *Religion in Essence and Manifestation. A Study in Phenomenology.* London: George Allen & Unwin.

Ward, K. (1994) *Religion and Revelation.* Oxford: Clarendon Press.

— (1996) *Religion and Creation.* Oxford: Clarendon Press.

— (1998) *Religion and Human Nature.* Oxford: Clarendon Press.

— (2000) *Religion and Community.* Oxford: Clarendon Press.

Webb, C. C. J. (1919) *God and Personality.* London: George Allen & Unwin.

Whitehead, A. N. (1929) *Process and Reality.* New York: Macmillan.

Wood, A. (1970) *Kant's Moral Religion.* Ithaca: Cornell University Press.

Zaehner, R. C. (1971) *Evolution in Religion. A Study in Sri Aurobindo and Pierre Teilhard de Chardin.* Oxford: Clarendon Press.

10
The Nature and Limits of Theological Understanding

Brian Hebblethwaite

In speaking of the contribution of theology to human understanding I may appear to be sticking my neck out even further than in speaking of the contribution of metaphysics to human understanding. In journalistic – even political – parlance today, the word 'theology' is often used derogatorily for any kind of doctrinaire gobbledegook. That such talk stems from ignorance or prejudice is evident to anyone who has actually studied the subject and its master practitioners such as Augustine, Aquinas, Calvin and Hooker, in the past, or Barth, Rahner, Pannenberg and Küng, in our own time. But a defence of theology as a subject of genuine interest and real importance for human understanding rests not so much on the impressive contribution of its leading practitioners as on the nature and significance of what theology is all about.

Let us begin then with a definition of theology. I take this one, somewhat arbitrarily, from the *Times English Dictionary*: 'The systematic study of the existence and nature of the divine and its relationship to and influence upon other beings.' The use of the impersonal 'its' begs a number of questions of course, but the gist of this definition is fair enough. And indeed the impersonal 'its' may serve as an initial indication that the metaphysical case for taking transcendence seriously that I sketched in Chapter 9 is not confined to the case for theism. Early Buddhism, the philosophy of Schopenhauer and Iris Murdoch's non-theistic Platonism are clear examples of philosophies postulating a transcendent realm, without giving it cash-value, so to speak, in terms of personal theism. Nevertheless, many of the factors to which I drew attention in my chapter on metaphysics did point to objective theism as offering the best explanation of a world that can evolve consciousness, mind, personal and interpersonal life, and all the creative products of culture, including, of course, the many forms of theistic religion. Agent causality, purpose, and choice can only be ascribed to a personal source or ground for the whole world process, namely to the Mind of the Maker.

In this chapter I shall be restricting myself to theism. *The*ology, strictly speaking, has its place only within *the*ism; and so the impersonal 'its' in the dictionary's definition of theology is inappropriate. What I explore here is belief in God and the contribution to human understanding made by belief in God. I shall concentrate on the theoretical side of this, since under-standing is our subject matter, but, unlike metaphysics, theology is full of spiritual and practical import, simply because of the nature of its primary object. Theism is not just a matter of 'best explanation' metaphysics. I shall certainly have to touch on the spiritual and practical aspects of theology, but my main concern is the way in which theology contributes to the enlargement of our understanding of everything.

For as the dictionary definition rightly says, theology is concerned not only with the divine but also with the relationship of the divine to and its influence upon other beings. And by this it means all other beings. Theology, like metaphysics, is a species of holistic understanding. It is because, as this chapter shows, theology goes beyond metaphysical understanding of everything that I wish to defend its claim to be 'the queen of the sciences'. From theology you get a real theory of everything!

Revelation

In a nutshell, what enables theology to go beyond metaphysics is revelation. Here we seem to be opening a can of worms indeed. For appeal to revelation is likely to strike the philosopher as an abandonment of rationality. (One thinks of Brand Blanshard in this connection [Blanshard 1974].) And are there not many claimed revelations, spawning many rival and incompatible theologies? The diversity problem, which was bad enough where metaphysics was concerned, appears even more intractable with revelation-claims. But let us look at this question of diverse theologies based on diverse revelation-claims more closely.

The notion of revelation does not in itself presuppose a revealer. We speak of many different types of insight and experience as 'revelations'. 'Travelling cross country to the Far East was a revelation to me', one might say. In the Hindu tradition, *sruti*, translated 'revelation', is more the result of mystical penetration into the mysteries of non-duality than a message from on high. But in theistic religion, revelation does entail a revealer. And it is not unreasonable to suppose that, if there is an infinite mind and will behind the whole world process, that mind will be likely to make itself known to God's personal, rational, creatures one way or another. In the first instance that may well take the form of general revelation, the disclosure of God's reality and something of God's nature in and through the things that God has made. General revelation may be correlated with the kind of theistic metaphysics which I was considering before. This is the sphere of natural theology, the prime subject matter of Lord Gifford's Foundation. Natural theology is the result of the human mind's rational reflection on the world about us – its existence and beauty and its capacity to evolve persons in relation, human cultures, and moral communities. I said something in my previous lecture about the commonalities discernible across cultures and traditions where theistic metaphysics – or natural theology – is concerned.

But the history of revelation-claims in theistic religion is not restricted to such indirect communication, mediated generally through factors accessible to the human mind at any time or place. And theology is very far from being restricted to natural theology. For the most part theologies – and here one has to use the plural – are built up, transmitted, and developed within particular historical communities and traditions, allegedly responding to much more specific, less indirect, *special* revelations. In this sense one cannot speak of theology in general. One is considering Jewish theology, Christian theology, Muslim theology, Hindu theology, Sikh theology, Bahai theology, and so on. Here, as I said, is the diversity problem writ large.

But a number of factors may serve to mitigate the apparent arbitrariness of appeals to special revelation. The first point to be made is an extension of the point made in respect of natural theology. It is not unreasonable to suppose that if there is a God, he will be likely to have made himself known much more specifically than just through general revelation. For it is likely that there are much more specific purposes, salvific purposes, for instance, that suggest or require more specific revelation and action vis-à-vis the intended consummation of the whole creative process. The second point to be made is that such purported special revelations, if they are going to enhance holistic understanding of the kind we are interested in here, are unlikely to be matters just of esoteric information, inaccessible elsewhere, imparted to isolated individuals. Only a claimed revelation that has actually led to a sustained tradition of interpretation capable of yielding such enhanced understanding will be worth taking seriously here. The third point to be made is that the alleged locus of divine special revelation may well be a specific developing tradition of faith and understanding rather than a once-off impartation of information, and there may well be good reasons for the choice of such an extended vehicle of special revelation. Alternatively, the locus of special revelation may be a personal presence of the divine which, in the nature of the case, requires a particular historical context to be formed and developed for its realization. We shall explore the logic of Christian incarnational belief in this connection below. The fourth point to be made is that, contrary to first impressions, there may be commonalities between alleged special revelations, just as we saw there to be between different theistic metaphysics or natural theologies. There may be a number of common disclosures, or complementary disclosures, discernible through the disciplines of comparative theology, to which we shall turn in a moment.

The Rationality of Appeals to Revelation

Let me now offer some reflections on the rationality of appeals to revelation. I do not wish to disparage all appeals to authority. Anyone who has answered a child's questions by reference to the *Encyclopaedia Britannica* knows their importance and necessity in everyday life. But that encyclopaedia is a generally acknowledged authority and we have good reasons for trusting it, by and large. In religion, at least where special revelation is concerned, we do not have generally acknowledged authorities across the borders of faith communities. The Christian Scriptures and traditions, including the Magisterium, are acknowledged as authorities only within the Christian Church, and, as my reference to the Magisterium indicates, there are many internal disputes about their authority as well as about their interpretation. So there is no escape from the necessity of reasoning about revelation and its authority – certainly when we are talking to others, religious or secular, outside our own faith tradition, but even internally, when, for example, Christians argue with each other about the meaning and scope of the world view in which their faith and experience are embedded.

I quote Bishop Butler – a notable authority! – at this point. 'Reason ... is indeed the only faculty we have wherewith to judge concerning anything, even revelation itself' (1736: II.3). Note that I am not just appealing to Butler as an authority. I am trying to explain, defend, and argue for what he is saying here.

Internally, the use of reason to articulate what we may call the inner theological rationale of developed Christian faith can be clearly seen even in Karl Barth and in the so-called 'Reformed Epistemologists' such as Alvin Plantinga. Plantinga's negative apologetics, defending against charges of incoherence a Christian world view assumed as basic, is rational through and through (1998). But why should we restrict such argumentation to negative apologetics? Not only is there a case for natural theology, if not as a foundation, then as a support for, say, a Christian world view, but also the internal explication of that world view's rationale can serve as a positive case for taking it seriously as, among other things, the best explanation of our experience of being in the world and the best prognostication of the world's and our ultimate future. In other words, given the negative apologetic, given, for instance, a plausible theodicy, the whole Christian story, spelled out in systematic and philosophical theology, can be claimed to make better sense of everything. That, at any rate, sketches the overall structure of the line I wish to pursue.

If special revelation can be argued for in this way, if its content is open to rational scrutiny and reflective judgement, so that we are invited not simply to accept it on authority, but rather to recognize its scope and power to make sense of everything, then the traditional contrast between natural theology and revealed theology is open to challenge. Of course the phrase 'revealed theology' is a misnomer. No one is suggesting that any *theology* is revealed from on high. What the traditional contrast supposed was that some divine truths could be discerned by human reason anywhere and at all times – that is the sphere of natural theology – and some divine truths could be known through inspired Scriptures or through the words and works of Jesus, God incarnate, or some other authoritative source – that is the sphere of revealed theology. The contrast, traditionally, was between reason and revelation. But if revelation is open to rational scrutiny, the contrast is not so sharp. Rational scrutiny is possible across the board, as the Butler quotation suggests. The difference between natural and revealed theology is simply the difference between rational reflection on data universally available and rational reflection on data that only become available through particular people, particular events, particular histories, and particular traditions. Of course, all these specificities become generally available to rational scrutiny in the course of universal history.

This softening of the contrast between natural theology and revealed theology has become something of a commonplace. Prefigured in Joseph Butler, it was explicitly argued for by H. H. Farmer in his unjustly neglected book, *Revelation and Religion* (1954). Indeed Farmer went so far as to suggest that a specifically Christian world view, including both an interpretation of the whole history of religions and what he called 'a theism of incarnation and reconciliation' could be brought under the rubric of natural theology, providing 'nothing is introduced in a merely authoritarian and overriding way and regarded as outside the scope of critical examination' (1954: 19). I myself, in *The Problems of Theology*, remarked that the distinction 'between what reason can achieve and what requires revelation breaks down ... reason and revelation cannot be treated as different sources of knowledge. On the contrary revelation-claims, despite being channelled through particular historical traditions, are part of the data upon which reason has to operate' (1980: 79). In saying this I was endorsing the view of Wolfhart Pannenberg who, in opposing the combination of subjectivism and authority which he finds in Bernard Lonergan, urges us 'to let theology be discussed without reservation in the context of critical rationality' (Pannenberg 1975: 78). I also note that this view finds support from James Barr in his Gifford Lectures on *Biblical Faith and Natural Theology* (1993).

I know that to quote Butler and Pannenberg on reason and revelation is to invite Alasdair MacIntyre's question, 'Which Rationality?'(1988). In recent decades the notion that 'critical rationality' is a common possession of humanity across cultures and across the ages has been strongly challenged in philosophy and cultural studies alike. The denial of universal standards of rationality, the assertion of incommensurability between world views, and the consequent relativism have been pushed to undiscussable extremes in the writings of certain French deconstructionists; but MacIntyre's work on 'tradition-constituted enquiry' is clear and eminently discussable, and must be reckoned with if the ideas of natural theology and the rational scrutiny of revelation-claims are to be defended and sustained.

There is no denying the fact that all rational debate is contextualized and takes place within particular horizons, indeed on the basis of certain absolute presuppositions, as Collingwood showed (1940: ch. 5). But we may well question *how* absolute such presuppositions are. The scientific community itself is the product of a long history. Its achieved standards of conjecture and experimental proof – and refutation – may have become global in extent, at least in practice. (*Philosophers* of science tend to disagree with each other as much as in any sphere of human interest.) But the achievement of universal standards of rationality where the practice of the natural sciences is concerned was possible only because of the limitations of scientific understanding to which I drew attention in Chapter 9, namely its restriction to the empirically verifiable. World-views that do justice to morality, art, philosophy and religion are open to rational scrutiny in a much broader and looser sense of verification, including what I called 'best explanation metaphysics', and including practical success and spiritual penetration, as we shall see. And all these matters can be and are being discussed and probed cross-culturally, not only in cultural studies, but in comparative theology, to which I turn in the next section.

MacIntyre himself has moved in the direction of acknowledging some criteria whereby preferences can be defended in respect of his 'tradition-constituted' versions of enquiry (1990). He now holds that the Aristotelian–Thomist tradition of moral enquiry succeeds better in making sense of and coping with certain key features of life and experience than does the Nietzschean 'genealogical' version, or post-Enlightenment scientism. MacIntyre, I know, is primarily interested in moral philosophy, but, as I hope Chapter 9 showed, recognition of this as a moral universe is only one key element in a holistic world view. Practice is and has to be imbedded in theory. My own defence of theistic metaphysics can be thought of as analogous to MacIntyre's version of moral enquiry. Indeed, MacIntyre's positive evaluation of Thomism is an indication of the need for theological enhancement of both moral and metaphysical vision.

Certainly there are some totally incommensurable world-views. It would be difficult to have envisaged a fruitful discussion between Ian Paisley and the late Ayatollah Khomeini, and we have only to read the discussion – if it can be called that – between John Searle and Jacques Derrida to appreciate the possibility of getting nowhere, even in philosophical debate; although I am bound to say that, unlike the former hypothetical case, this latter actual one is evidently only one-sided in respect of its irrationality (see Derrida 1977, 1978; Searle 1977).

Be that as it may, my present point is that, given reflective self-criticism and a broad enough concern for universal history and holistic understanding, theologies developed on the basis of putative divine revelation are susceptible of rational scrutiny and debate concerning their relative success in providing a vision of the world and its future that makes sense of everything.

Without denying these general points concerning the accessibility of specific faith traditions to rational scrutiny, we may further point out that some world views positively require a specific, historically formed, context of interpretation for their inner rationale to become discernible. What Farmer called 'a theism of incarnation and reconciliation' only became available – so Christians claim – in response to the actual Incarnation of God the Son in Jesus of Nazareth and his salvific work and fate. That Incarnation, as Farmer points out, did not come out of the blue (1954: 195–6). It required the long providential preparation of the people and faith of Israel for the conditions to obtain in which Incarnation could take place. All this is part of the logic of God incarnate, as we shall see.

Comparative Theology

First, however, let us consider the more general topic of comparative theology. Despite the fact that theologies are developed within particular faith traditions on the basis of specific revelation claims, it has proved perfectly possible to embark on interfaith dialogue at this theoretical level, to compare theistic world views, to look for both commonalities and irreconcilable differences, and to argue for particular theological systems. Included in such comparative theology must, of course, be comparative theology of religion. We have to compare and evaluate the ways in which the different theologies from the different faith traditions endeavour to make sense of the whole history of religions and of each other. I will look briefly at four examples of such work, stemming from the Christian tradition, namely the contributions of John Hick, Wilfred Cantwell Smith, Hans Küng, and Keith Ward.

These remarks should, perhaps, be prefaced by recognition of the fact that not all theistic religions are equally productive of, or interested in, theology, let alone comparative theology. This undoubtedly constitutes a limit to theological understanding. It may be a temporary phenomenon – different religions being at different stages of development, and the pressures of the modern world, including the necessity to relate religion and science and the exponential growth of global intercommunication, requiring more and more theological reflection from every religion. Or the downplaying of theology may be an integral aspect of some theistic religions, in which case this very fact has to be weighed and evaluated in comparative theology.

John Hick's Gifford Lectures, *An Interpretation of Religion*, significantly sub-titled 'Human Responses to the Transcendent' (Hick 1989), represent one end of the spectrum of views on comparative theology. In fact, Hick's position is a philosophical rather than a theological position; for the key to his theory of religious pluralism lies in the suggestion that all theologies, and indeed all non-theistic religious world views, are symbolic, metaphorical, representations of an ultimate reality beyond all human conceptualization. These culturally and historically shaped human responses provide a variety of life-transforming channels whereby people in every generation and across the globe are enabled to make the transition from ego-centredness to 'reality-centredness' and to form liberated and sanctified communities of faith. It is the power of the ultimate that enables this transition – Hick is certainly not an anti-realist like Don Cupitt – but in itself that power remains inaccessible. It can only be represented mythically, at the human 'phenomenal' level, by the various theistic and non-theistic, personal and impersonal, religious systems. Just because these systems are not, ultimately speaking, reality depicting, they do not conflict. This philosophy of religious pluralism, one might paradoxically say, achieves universal, holistic, understanding, only by locating the ultimate beyond all understanding. And there, I fear, lies its incoherence. For, quite apart from the fact that no actual theologian would accept the reduction of theology's analogical God-talk to non-depicting metaphor, it is incoherent to suggest that the active power, not ourselves, that makes for righteousness (I deliberately assimilate Hick and Matthew Arnold) is, in reality, wholly beyond the personal and the moral.

Wilfred Cantwell Smith, whose pluralism looks at first sight very close to Hick's, in fact remains much more of a theologian (Smith 1981). Despite the common emphasis on practice and authenticity, Smith continues to write in theistic terms. His emphasis on 'personal truth' (1967) still presupposes, and finds expression in, talk of the love of God. Smith is able to sit lightly to the present differences and incompatibilities between the theologies of the theistic religions because he sees the history of religions as very much in process and orientated towards future developments and growth together, which will yield a world theology only in the end. But I have to say that Smith's future-oriented theology lacks rigour. When challenged on specifics, he retreats to talk of personal truth and authenticity, and simply postpones theological verification to the eschaton.

Hans Küng has made a significant contribution in recent decades to all the areas relating to the nature and scope of theological understanding. Despite a surprising diffidence where natural theology is concerned, his work in negative apologetic (1980), responding to the sceptical critiques of Nietzsche, Marx, and Freud, is exemplary, as is his self-critical exposition of the content and context of Christian faith (1977), even if his Christology and Trinitarian theology fail to satisfy at every level. But most significant for our present purposes is the work Küng has produced on comparative religion and on global ethics. Examples of interfaith dialogue (1987) and in-depth studies of the world religions (1992, 1995) have now been complemented by a book entitled *Theology for the Third Millennium* (1991), in which Küng spells out the norms for a genuinely critical and ecumenical Christian theology in the context of a theology of the world religions. For Küng, there are three main criteria of a rationally responsible faith-decision for Christians, and, *mutatis mutandis*, for members of other religions: a general ethical criterion, invoking our common humanity, a general religious criterion, invoking authenticity in practice and spirituality, and, for Küng *qua* Christian, a specifically Christian criterion, invoking the revelation of the Absolute in the life and work and destiny of Jesus Christ. He allows that other religions will appeal to other specifics at this point, but goes on to urge what Vatican II called 'fraternal emulation' over where true humanity is to be found. The way in which the general religious criterion and the specific criterion are rooted in the general ethical criterion is illustrated by Küng's most recent work on global ethics (1998). Küng stresses the importance of peace and cooperation between the religions in the fostering of global standards of justice, solidarity, and the common good, and refers appreciatively to the 'First Conference on a Global Ethic and Traditional Indian Ethics' held in New Delhi in 1997, where the participants observed that 'ethical principles which refer to and arise from the ethical domain alone may not be sufficient to ensure discharge of ethical responsibilities. It is spirituality, the dynamism of faith, which has through the ages empowered and spurred individuals and groups to live up to ethical standards' (Küng and Schmidt 1998: 132). If, despite all the negative aspects of religion, this is in fact the case, then the importance of religious – and theological – frameworks that sustain such spiritual dynamism is surely vindicated.

Keith Ward's four recent books were mentioned in Chapter 9 (1994, 1996, 1998, 2000). They constitute an impressive foray into comparative theology by a skilled philosopher and theologian. The first book, *Religion and Revelation*, explores four scriptural traditions – Judaism, Vedanta, Buddhism, and Islam – and Christianity not as a fifth scriptural tradition so much as the focus of revelation through historical self-manifestation. This allows Ward to develop a non-exclusive view of the Incarnation as the climactic revelation of the divine love. He concludes with a chapter on the way in which revelation-based faith traditions transcend the scientific world view and enlarge human understanding as well as enabling growth towards union with Supreme Value. Ward's second book, *Religion and Creation*, shows how four major theologians in the Jewish, Christian, Muslim, and Hindu traditions have each modified classical, absolutist, theism in the direction of a more dynamic, interactionist, conception of the divine. Admittedly, Ward is more persuasive on the relation between such a dynamic theology of God and the world as seen in modern science than he is on the specifics of Christian Trinitarian theology. Here his doubts over social Trinitarianism lead him to suggest that some creation or other is necessary to God, a view which, as we shall see, is alien to most Christian theologians. But there is no denying the power of Ward's sustained philosophical analysis of mainstream theological topics. His third book, *Religion and Human Nature*, compares the anthropologies, soteriologies, and eschatologies of the major world religions, bringing out differences as well as common motifs. He admits the difficulty of securing any unified view of truth in these areas, but, just because of their importance for fundamental issues of meaning and destiny, he defends the task of pursuing truth as fairly and comprehensively as possible from within one's

own tradition but in conversation with others and with readiness
to learn from other traditions (1998: 327). The fourth book,
Religion and Community, surveys the social teachings of five world
religions, stressing the importance of religion for social formation
and envisaging a global community of many faiths and cultures,
in which each makes its distinctive contribution. In discussing the
Christian contribution, Ward echoes Paul Tillich in seeing every
age of history as the sphere of the Spirit's enabling and trans-
forming work, but goes beyond Tillich in seeing the ultimate
meaning and fulfilment of history in the eschatological kingdom
of God (2000: 325–6).

Theology: The Queen of the Sciences?

It is clear from this brief survey of comparative theology that we
are not, *pace* Cantwell Smith, going to see the development of a
single world theology. The pursuit of holistic understanding in
the light of critically sifted revelation-claims is bound to be
pluriform, each world religion's theology offering an all-
embracing and developing interpretation of the world, life,
history, and the future from its own developing perspective, but
now in dialogue with what the other religions and their
theologies have to offer. How then can I possibly defend the
notion of theology as the 'queen of the sciences'? How indeed
can I possibly defend Christian theology, the theology of my own
tradition, as 'queen of the sciences'?

Well, despite the diversity of theologies coming out of the
different faith traditions, despite the diversity of theologies
produced within any one faith tradition – in Christianity's case,
the theologies of Aquinas, Calvin, Schleiermacher, Barth,
Rahner, Moltmann, Pannenberg, and Jensen, to name but a few
– and despite the limits, in any and all of these theologies, to their
ability and success in articulating holistic understanding, I still
maintain that theology goes beyond the natural sciences and the
other human sciences, including revisionary metaphysics, in two
key respects. In the first place, it draws on and reflects critically on
sources not otherwise available, namely those of revelation and
religious experience. And in the second place, it is concerned
with, and opens up perspectives on, *all* the dimensions and
modalities of the real, not just some of them.

What is at stake here is, in a phrase, the nature of things. In
books of that title, the Roman Epicurean, Lucretius (1951), and

the Oxford Epicurean, Anthony Quinton (1973), offered materialistic versions of holistic metaphysics, whose inadequacy in accounting for the phenomena of consciousness and mind, let alone the good, the beautiful and the true, I endeavoured to demonstrate in Chapter 9. I argued there that theistic metaphysics offered better explanations for the capacity of the world stuff to evolve mind, personhood, ethics, culture, philosophy itself, and religion. I am now suggesting that closer rational scrutiny of the dimensions of reality opened up in religious experience, both numinous and mystical (see Smart 1968), and closer rational scrutiny of those understandings of reality that emerge from participation in the faith (and worship) of the world religions which have developed as responses to divine revelation, yield even greater insight into the nature of things.

From now on I restrict myself to what I know best, namely Christian theology, and its claim to be 'the queen of the sciences'. Christian theologies, as I say, are various, but they all attempt to grapple with the same problems and the same subject matter. They have to meet the challenges to Christian belief, most notably the problem of evil and the alleged incoherence, not only of God-talk generally, but of incarnational and Trinitarian theology in particular. And they have to show the power of Trinitarian theology, Christology, Christian soteriology and eschatology to make sense of the world, its products and its destiny, when seen as the triune God's creative enterprise.

There is not space here to examine the fruitfulness and rational force of the systematic theologies produced by the figures I named a few moments ago. I have myself found the work of Wolfhart Pannenberg particularly illuminating, not least because of his commitment, already mentioned, to the discussion of all these issues in the context of critical rationality (see Pannenberg 1991–8). But I would like to include some remarks on the work done in *philosophical* theology in recent decades, by Anglo-Saxon analytical philosophers of religion. This has been one of the most interesting developments in the philosophy of religion. Without abandoning the standard philosophy of religion topics – arguments for the existence of God, the epistemology of faith, religious language, and the problem of evil – philosophers of religion such as Richard Swinburne, Alvin Plantinga, Thomas V. Morris, and many other members of the Society of Christian Philosophers in America (whose journal, *Faith and Philosophy*, has become the leading journal in this subject area) have made very significant contributions to the clarification and defence of specifically Christian doctrine. Sadly, their work has found little favour with professional theologians, and an unfortunate rift has opened up between the Christian philosophers and the Christian theologians. The latter accuse the former of insensitivity to the special problems involved in talk of God – the otherness of God, the inability of human language to express the transcendent, the errors, even the idolatry, involved in treating God as one object among others, or God's action as one causal factor among others – the former accusing the latter of looseness, lack of rigour, inability to recognize the logical issues at stake in everything we say, even when talking about God, and failure to appreciate the help which philosophical analysis can give to the articulation and elucidation not only of a theistic, but of a Christian world view.

The reception of Swinburne's work – both in its earlier and later phases – illustrates this problem. Swinburne's early book, *The Coherence of Theism* (1977), was a resolute attempt, by a skilled philosopher, to meet one of the two main objections to theistic metaphysics, namely, its alleged incoherence. As such, it should have been welcomed by systematic theologians, as at least providing negative apologetic for their whole enterprise. But one has to admit that Swinburne did tend to give a hostage to fortune by devoting the second part of his book (the first was devoted to religious language) to a defence of the coherence of the notion of a contingent God, before proceeding in the third and much shorter part of the book to a defence of the notion of a necessary God. Such a procedure can be defended – the logic of contingent God-talk providing a more manageable analogy for the logic of necessary God-talk. But it would surely have been wiser to address the latter topic throughout, since, for any developed theism, the idea of a contingent God is at best part of its prehistory and at worst idolatry. The contrast between necessary and contingent, infinite and finite, absolute and limited, belongs to the heart of theism and, of course, to the question of its coherence. Nonetheless, there is much in Swinburne's treatment of the coherence of theism that deserves respect and scrutiny. Swinburne's latest book, *Providence and the Problem of Evil* (1998), addressses the other main challenge to theism in ways that have also evoked considerable hostility. Swinburne attempts to provide a theodicy by showing the goods which the permission of evils, even horrendous evils, alone make possible. While it is true that a viable theodicy can only take some such form as this (a 'greater good defence', as it has been called) it is surely wiser to restrict the argument to the more general level – showing that such an evolving world as this, with its concomitant risks, is the necessary condition of the creation of finite personal lives and communities (see Hebblethwaite 1988) – rather than to attempt to pinpoint the supervenient goods that can emerge from specific horrors such as the Holocaust. Be that as it may, theologians who reject the whole enterprise of theodicy (e.g., Surin 1986; Lash 1986: 214) are surely cutting off the branch on which they sit. The question why God permits so much evil and suffering in the world cannot be bypassed by concentrating on the resources of Christianity for the overcoming of evil.

These matters cannot be pursued here. Here I consider the contributions of analytic philosophers to the explication and defence of the main Christian doctrines and the way in which these doctrines form together a total Christian world view. One of the most significant developments in recent Christian theology, both systematic and philosophical, has been the recovery of incarnational and Trinitarian theology. Among the philosophers who have contributed to this recovery are David Brown, Thomas V. Morris and, again, Richard Swinburne. Brown's book, *The Divine Trinity* (1985), was a landmark in philosophical investigation of the doctrines of the Incarnation and the Trinity. First, Brown argues for a theistic, rather than a deistic, conception of the divine, that is, for a concept of God as active in revelation, seen as a divine–human dialogue culminating in the Incarnation. The coherence of the Incarnation is explored in detail with two models – the kenotic model and the two natures model – held to be equally coherent alternatives. Finally, Brown considers the logic of Trinitarian belief, with distinct preference for the social rather than the psychological analogy.

Morris, in *The Logic of God Incarnate* (1986) and in a subsequent essay (1989), advanced a 'two-consciousness' view of the Incarnation, whereby the divine mind of God the Son is held not only to contain, without being contained by, the human mind of Jesus, but also to be the ultimate subject of his personal cognitive and causal powers. Swinburne, too, in *The Christian God* (1994), defends the coherence of incarnational belief, but is particularly interesting in the way in which he argues for a social model of the Trinity. Clearly, as a matter of historical fact, it was belief in the divinity of Christ and the gift of the Spirit that led to the development of a Trinitarian understanding of God, and it can be argued that only a social model of the Trinity can account for the interpersonal relations, and especially the love, between the Father and the Son. But Swinburne recovers and re-presents an independent argument, found in Richard of St Victor in the twelfth century (see Fortman 1972: 191–4), whereby reflection on the nature of love requires its prime analogate, the divine love, to be spelled out in terms of love given, love received, and love shared still more. The inadequacy of a concept of God modelled on the isolated individual is only too apparent. As we have already seen in the case of Keith Ward, to reject the social analogy is to make creation necessary to God; for only by creation can such a God have an object of his love. But Christian Trinitarianism sees relationality – mutual love – as basic in the divine. It does not, of course, postulate three separate gods. In the logic of the infinite, the one God is internally differentiated and interrelated; but, as Brown and Swinburne show, that must mean three centres of consciousness and will in the divine.

There is much to be debated and argued about, where the work of these authors is concerned. It is far from clear whether Brown was wise to make so sharp a contrast between the kenotic model and the two natures model of the Incarnation. Morris has been rightly criticized for focusing on the mind of God incarnate rather than on the whole person and life of Jesus of Nazareth as that of the incarnate Son. Swinburne's use of the Freudian analogy of a divided self – an analogy also deployed by Brown – is of dubious use in clarifying the two natures doctrine. But none of these objections seriously devalues the contribution of these philosophers to the demonstration and articulation of the scope and power of Christian incarnational and Trinitarian doctrine.

I have myself attempted to enlarge the scope of Christian incarnational theology by showing what would be lost to a total Christian world view if the doctrine of the Incarnation were to be demythologized (1987). In explicating the rationale of incarnational theology, one has not only to show its logic and metaphysics, as Morris attempts to do, but also to show its fruitfulness in terms of at least five major aspects of holistic understanding: namely our encounter with the love of God in person; the consequent revelation that the mind of the maker is a mind and heart of love, and indeed a mutuality of love given and received; the revelation of the true nature of humanity as made in the image of God; the demonstration, indeed the achievement, of divine forgiveness and reconciliation; and the opening up, through Christ's resurrection, of the promise of a future consummation of the creative process when God will be all in all. I will add a few remarks about the last two of these five aspects of incarnational – and Trinitarian – theology, that is, about Christian soteriology and Christian eschatology.

Christian soteriology, too, has received perceptive attention and analysis from philosophers of religion. I think particularly of two essays by Eleonore Stump (1988, 1989) and another of Swinburne's books, *Responsibility and Atonement* (1989). In my own discussion of these and other authors, I have praised the former for her stress on God's own self-sacrificial love in action as the means whereby we are opened up to transformation by divine grace within, and I have criticized the latter for a somewhat artificial insistence on reparation as an essential element in atonement. In agreement with Vernon White's *Atonement and Incarnation* (1991), I have urged that it is the Incarnation that creates the conditions under which humanity is enabled to be renewed and taken into the triune life of God through incorporation into Christ's risen body. I cannot go into all this theology here. I mention it simply to show how in a Christian world view, the nature of things includes not simply the present reality of the world with all its potentialities as God's creation, but also the renewal and transformation of a sinful human world into conformity with the creator's intention for the ultimate future of creation. I admit that this scenario can be seen as falling under Hick's characterization of all religion as being concerned with the change from ego-centredness to reality-centredness, but I fear that, in Hick's philosophy of religious pluralism, both the resources for and the goal of this change are lost in the utter vagueness of his conception – or non-conception – of the Ultimate.

Mention of the ultimate future of creation brings me to the topic of Christian eschatology. Here is another dimension of the real which is inaccessible to the natural and the human sciences. The curious discipline known as 'futurology' can only make tentative predictions based on extrapolation from empirically known variables. Many of the relevant factors are unknown, and themselves unpredictable – not least the scientific discoveries that made, for example, information technology possible. The predictions of economists are notoriously fallible, like weather forecasts. The only sure prediction, long-term, from a scientific point of view, is the heat-death of the universe. (I do not think we can take seriously Frank Tipler's extravagant speculations about information technology creating a future cosmic 'mind'; see Polkinghorne 1994: 165–6.) Philosophy alone cannot get us any further. It is notorious how even a thoroughly historicized metaphysic such as Hegel's culminates not in some eschatological future consummation but in the present with the appearance of Hegel's own philosophy. Christian eschatology, by contrast, in its many different forms, is based on revelation: the teaching of Jesus about the kingdom of God, the Easter story, the Church's developing doctrine concerning the Four Last Things, and those existential moments of mystical or numinous experience that give a foretaste of eternity. Examples include, most notably, the theology of Teilhard de Chardin (1959), Jürgen Moltmann (1996) and the Process theologians (see Cobb 1972); but eschatology plays a key, if more sober, role in the theology of Wolfhart Pannenberg (1991–8: III. ch. 15) and all the mainstream figures mentioned earlier. I have surveyed and discussed all this in my book, *The Christian Hope* (1984). No one denies the limitations of our understanding of these matters. The Christian tradition is quite clear that we see in a glass darkly and that it is simply not given to us to know the precise nature of the eschaton. But this dimension is opened up, and there are intimations and analogies that make the expression of the Christian hope a real possibility for participants in the experience, faith, and worship of the Church, and this takes us beyond anything the natural or the human sciences can provide. Moreover Christian theology can and does reflect rationally upon these otherwise unobtainable data and build the results into an overall, however tentative, world view.

So I deem theology the queen of the sciences just because it explores – and yields albeit partial insight into – aspects of reality to which the natural and the human sciences, including metaphysics, are blind. These include not only something of the nature of the mind and heart of love behind the whole world story, but also something of the nature and final destiny of that story. And as far as our own part in that story is concerned, theology reflects on what has gone wrong and what enables transformation and renewal, as well as what the transformed human world is heading for. Its sources are revelation and experience, but its tools are those of critical rationality.

Experience, Practice, and Reflection

Mention of experience, salvation, practice and worship leads me to include a short section on these dimensions of religion and how they relate to our overall theme of theological understanding. I have concentrated on the theoretical side of theology, its contribution to human understanding. But clearly the nature of theology's primary object – the divine and its relationship to everything else – requires us to consider religious experience, spirituality and worship, personal renewal, social ethics, and much else of a highly evaluative nature. Indeed there can be no fact–value division where the world view of Christianity is concerned. If God is love, value is basic to the nature of things, and the whole universe is designed to evolve the good, the beautiful, and the true, and to culminate in a perfected fellowship mirroring the divine.

Now, all these dimensions of reality are open to rational scrutiny by the reflective theologian. All I can do here is point to one or two examples. On the cognitive force of religious experience, I am happy to recall the opening chapters of Austin Farrer's *Faith and Speculation* (1967), where he writes of the experiential verification of a rationally articulated and defended faith. But now we have a full-scale study of religious experience by the doyen of Christian philosophers, William Alston. His *Perceiving God* (1991) is required reading for the student of religious epistemology. Alston's case for taking religious experience – he calls it 'mystical experience' – as seriously as sense experience and treating it as appropriate material for the formation (the social formation) of beliefs is extremely persuasive, as is Alvin Plantinga's case, in *Warranted Christian Belief* (2000), for including the internal operation of the Holy Spirit among the belief producing factors in a person whose cognitive faculties are functioning properly according to God's design plan. (I confess to some doubts, however, about the way in which Plantinga treats the Holy Spirit as an extra factor over and above the belief-producing powers with which we were originally created. I would rather see the divine Spirit as working in and through our God-given powers, including our reason. But I cannot pursue this debate here.) Where spirituality and worship are concerned, I will simply mention two books, Patrick Sherry's *Spirit and Beauty* (1992) and Ninian Smart's *The Concept of Worship* (1972), as examples of the way in which one might philosophize about these dimensions, which are undoubtedly just as central to a Christian world view as those of belief and practice.

I have already said something about practice in speaking of the personal and social transformations enabled and required by the subject matter of Christian soteriology. It is obvious that theological understanding cannot be restricted to discernment of the nature of things as they are. It is as much concerned with

Lenin's question, What is to be done?, and with the resources available to humankind for at least the partial realization of God's kingdom here on Earth. Inspiration to energize such practical commitment comes, as I say, not least from Christian eschatology, as Jürgen Moltmann's theological endeavours have shown.

I know I have said little in this chapter about faith, although I think what I have said could well fall under the rubric of faith seeking understanding. But I am suspicious of an appeal to faith as an argument-stopping device. In my opinion, faith is what one has when one finds the Christian world view convincing and participates in the community of faith that lives within the framework of belief and practice fostered by that tradition of holistic understanding. Nothing in this form of life lies outside the scope of critical reflection.

The Limits of Theological Understanding

But there are limits to how far one can go in this domain. And I must end by stressing the limits of theological understanding. Not that theology has a monopoly in apophaticism. There is much in the sphere of science that we do not know. I quoted Searle's categorical statement that we do not know how the brain causes consciousness. For all the scope and power of quantum theory, we do not fully comprehend the quanta of energy that constitute the basic stuff of the universe. In philosophy, confessions of ignorance are common. Kant, for example, claimed that things in themselves are quite beyond the scope of our theoretical under-standing. In theology, there is a long tradition of apophaticism, and the doctrine of divine incomprehensibility has a central place in Jewish, Christian, and Islamic tradition. But, at least in Christian theology, the negative way has generally been recog-nized as being parasitic upon a positive theology of the love of God, the image of God, and the gospel of salvation. Aquinas criti-cized Maimonides for excessive use of the negative way, and defended the way of analogy, whereby we do get some knowledge of God through the things that God has made, insofar as they represent or mirror, to some degree, the perfections of the maker (Thomas Aquinas 1964). Everything I have said in this chapter about the power and rationality of Christian theology stands under this rubric. Any enhancement of our understanding that comes from natural theology, from revelation, from religious experience, from practice and from liturgical participation, is

partial and, in the nature of the case, veiled and incomplete. But
I hope that I have given some reasons for thinking that human
understanding is, nevertheless, enhanced by theology.

References

Alston, W. (1991) *Perceiving God. The Epistemology of Religious Experience.* Ithaca; Cornell University Press.

Barr, J. (1993) *Biblical Faith and Natural Theology.* Oxford: Clarendon Press.

Berger, P. L. (1971) *A Rumour of Angels. Modern Society and the Rediscovery of the Supernatural.* Harmondsworth: Penguin Books.

Blanshard, B. (1974) *Reason and Belief.* London: George Allen & Unwin.

Brown, D. (1985) *The Divine Trinity.* London: Duckworth.

Butler, J. (1736) *The Analogy of Religion Natural and Revealed to the Constitution and Course of Nature.* London.

Cobb, J. B. (1972) 'What is the Future?', in Cousins, E. H. (ed.), *Hope and the Future of Man.* Philadelphia: Fortress Press.

Collingwood, R. G. (1940) *An Essay on Metaphysics.* Oxford: Clarendon Press.

Derrida, J. (1977) 'Signature Event Context', *Glyph* I: 172–97.

— (1978) 'Limited Inc abc', *Glyph* II: 162–254.

Farmer, H. H. (1954) *Revelation and Religion.* London: Nisbet & Co.

Farrer, A. (1967) *Faith and Speculation. An Essay in Philosophical Theology.* London: Adam & Charles Black.

Fortman, E. J. (1972) *The Triune God. A Historical Study of the Doctrine of the Trinity.* London: Hutchinson.

Hebblethwaite, B. (1980) *The Problems of Theology.* Cambridge: Cambridge University Press.

— (1984) *The Christian Hope.* Basingstoke: Marshall, Morgan & Scott.

— (1987) *The Incarnation. Collected Essays on Christology.* Cambridge: Cambridge University Press.

— (1988) 'The problem of evil', in Wainwright, G. (ed.), *Keeping the Faith. Essays to Mark the Centenary of Lux Mundi.* Philadelphia: Fortress Press.

— (1996) *The Essence of Christianity. A Fresh Look at the Nicene Creed.* London: SPCK.

Hick, J. (1989) *An Interpretation of Religion. Human Responses to the Transcendent.* New Haven: Yale University Press.

Küng, H. (1977) *On Being a Christian.* London: Collins.

— (1980) *Does God Exist?* London: Collins.

— (1987) *Christianity and the World Religions. Paths of Dialogue with Islam, Hinduism and Buddhism.* London: Collins.

— (1992) *Judaism.* London: SCM Press.

— (1995) *Christianity. Its Essence and History.* London: SCM Press.

— (1991) *Theology for the Third Millennium.* London: Harper Collins.

— (1997) *A Global Ethic for Global Politics and Economics.* London: SCM Press.

Küng, H. and Schmidt, H. (eds.) (1998) *A Global Ethic and Global Responsibilities. Two Declarations.* London: SCM Press.

Lash, N. (1986) *Theology on the Way to Emmaus.* London: SCM Press.

Lucretius (1951) *The Nature of Things.* Harmondsworth: Penguin Books.

MacIntyre, A. (1988) *Whose Justice, Which Rationality.* London: Duckworth.

— (1990) *Three Rival Versions of Moral Enquiry.* London: Duckworth.

Moltmann, J. (1996) *The Coming of God. Christian Eschatology.* London: SCM Press.

Morris, T. V. (1986) *The Logic of God Incarnate.* Ithaca: Cornell University Press.

— (1989) 'The Metaphysics of God Incarnate', in Feenstra, R. J. and Plantinga, C. (eds.), *Trinity, Incarnation, and Atonement. Philosophical and Theological Essays.* Notre Dame: University of Notre Dame Press.

Pannenberg, W. (1975) 'History and meaning in Bernard Lonergan's approach to theological method', in Corcoran, P. (ed.), *Looking at Lonergan's Method.* Dublin: The Talbot Press: 88–100.

Pannenberg, W. (1991–1998) *Systematic Theology.* 3 Vols. Edinburgh: T. & T. Clark.

Plantinga, A. (1998) 'Christian philosophy at the end of the twentieth century', in Sennett, J. F. (ed.), *The Analytic Theist. An Alvin Plantinga Reader.* Grand Rapids, Michigan: William B. Eerdmans: 328–58.

— (2000) *Warranted Christian Belief.* New York: Oxford University Press.

Polkinghorne, J. (1994) *Science and Christian Belief.* London: SPCK.

Quinton, A. (1973) *The Nature of Things.* London: Routledge & Kegan Paul.

Rashdall, H. (1924) *Philosophy and Religion.* London: Duckworth.

Searle, J. R. (1977) 'Re-iterating the Differences: A Reply to Derrida', *Glyph* I: 198–208.

Sherry, P. (1992) *Spirit and Beauty. An Introduction to Theological Aesthetics.* Oxford: Clarendon Press.

Smart, N. (1968) *The Yogi and the Devotee.* London: George Allen & Unwin.

Smith, W. C. (1967) *Questions of Religious Truth.* London: Victor Gollancz.

— (1981) *Towards a World Theology.* London: Macmillan.

Stump, E. (1988) 'Atonement according to Aquinas', in Morris, T. V. (ed.), *Philosophy and the Christian Faith.* Notre Dame: University of Notre Dame Press.

— (1989) 'Atonement and Justification', in Feenstra, R. J. and Plantinga, C. (eds), *Trinity, Incarnation, and Atonement. Philosophical and Theological Essays.* Notre Dame: University of Notre Dame Press.

Surin, K. (1986) *Theology and the Problem of Evil.* Oxford: Basil Blackwell.

Swinburne, R. (1977) *The Coherence of Theism.* Oxford: Clarendon Press.

— (1989) *Responsibility and Atonement.* Oxford: Clarendon Press.

— (1994) *The Christian God.* Oxford: Clarendon Press.

— (1998) *Providence and the Problem of Evil.* Oxford: Clarendon Press.

Teilhard de Chardin, P. (1959) *The Phenomenon of Man.* London: Collins.

Thomas Aquinas (1964) *Summa Theologiae.* Blackfriars Edition, Vol. III. London: Eyre & Spottiswoode.

Troeltsch, E. (1991) *Religion in History. Essays Translated by James Luther Adams.* Edinburgh: T. & T. Clark.

Van der Leeuw, G. (1938) *Religion in Essence and Manifestation. A Study in Phenomenology.* London: George Allen & Unwin.

Ward, K. (1994) *Religion and Revelation.* Oxford: Clarendon Press.

— (1996) *Religion and Creation.* Oxford: Clarendon Press.

— (1998) *Religion and Human Nature.* Oxford: Clarendon Press.

— (2000) *Religion and Community.* Oxford: Clarendon Press.

White, V. (1991) *Atonement and Incarnation. An Essay in Universalism and Particularity.* Cambridge: Cambridge University Press.

Zaehner, R. C. (1971) *Evolution in Religion. A Study in Sri Aurobindo and Pierre Teilhard de Chardin.* Oxford: Clarendon Press.